Conversations Behind the Kitchen Door

Praise for

CONVERSATIONS BEHIND THE KITCHEN DOOR

"I was struck by how well Emmanuel captured the exploratory nature of a chef's life and experience. He does a fantastic job of portraying some of the "blind faith" that seems to be a prerequisite for pursuing a career in cooking. This book vividly captures the inherent curiosity of the cooks who became chefs and offers a guide for both the younger generation of chefs as well as the 'curious' home cooks."

— Chef and restaurateur **Jose Garces**,
James Beard Award-winning Iron Chef

"Emmanuel has interviewed dozens of acclaimed chefs on his podcast *flavors unknown* and gives you a front-row seat to their intriguing life experiences. You learn what motivates them to create incredible dishes that trigger new memories. By reading this book, the culmination of all his conversations, you are given the essence into the common denominators at the heart of so many seemingly disparate flavors."

—**Gabriel Kreuther**, Chef/Owner from the two-Michelin star
Gabriel Kreuther restaurant in New York City

"*Conversations Behind the Kitchen Door* brings the author, Emmanuel Laroche, and the evolution of the culinary world together. I enjoyed getting to know Emmanuel through his retelling of personal stories, and I loved the way he brought the ideas and passions of fifty chefs into this book."

—Chef and restaurateur **Jamie Bissonnette** in Boston

"*Conversation Behind the Kitchen Door* is a modern-day gastronomic travelogue across America bringing to light everything that drives today's culinarians. The book artfully and whimsically weaves a tale about some of the chefs and their food in America that is reminiscent of Twain's writings about the foods he loved most. With wonderfully visual portrayals of his own personal culinary adventures as a foundation for exploration, Emmanuel brings us something way more valuable and eye- opening than any cookbook that I've read. An absolute must read for any curious culinarian looking for inspiration told via an epic story."

—Chef **Jeremy Umansky**, owner of Larder Deli & Bakery
in Cleveland and author of Koji Alchemy

"I've witnessed Emmanuel's appreciation for food firsthand and his rich culinary background stirs engaging conversation. His book provides a refreshingly intimate perspective of how chefs and like minds navigate the food world and maintain inspiration. It's a way to vicariously experience food culture through the eyes of many remarkable and highly revered personalities."

—Pastry Chef **Sam Mason**, the wizard behind
all of Odd Fellows' ice cream creations

"Emmanuel Laroche's passion and curiosity are evident on every page of this book. From his experience as a youth in France to his dining as an adult around the globe, he has a unique way of approaching conversations about food and technique that bring out the inner foodie in everyone, from amateur chefs to seasoned culinary professionals. Truly a book for everyone."

—Chef and Restaurateur **Kelly English** in Memphis

"Emmanuel has a curiosity for food, culture, and understanding that captivates listeners on his podcast, *flavors unknown*. In this book, we get an opportunity to come along for the ride in his discovery of how chefs think and create. In the dialogue between Emmanuel and the chefs you get to watch the creative process unfold and see his understanding of food grow in real time as mine did as well. If you are interested, curious, and seeking insight, this book is a must-read."

—**Andre Natera**, Former Executive Chef from
Fairmont Hotel in Austin, Texas

"As a Marketing professional in the food business, Emmanuel Laroche takes us on a fascinating ride behind the scenes from American restaurants and bars. He knows what questions to ask chefs so they will reveal more of the secrets about their food and the restaurant business. This book is full of culinary insights for both the amateur and professional foodie."

—**Jeremy Gutsche**, CEO of Trend Hunter and
New York Times Bestselling Author

"Emmanuel's passion for the culinary world is infectious. Packed with colorful personal anecdotes from his extensive food travels and chock full of insights from some of the world's most thoughtful chefs, *Conversations Behind the Kitchen Door* is an essential guide for how to appreciate food and cooking through the lens of a chef."

—**Will Blunt**, Managing Director at StarChefs

"Emmanuel Laroche has the access, curiosity, and insight that anyone interested in professional cooking would love to have. His conversations and gustatory adventures with leading chefs are fascinating and inspire envy."

—**Matt Starwell**, Managing Partner at Kitchen Arts & Letters

"*Conversations Behind the Kitchen Door* offers Emmanuel's personal and revealing insights into the minds of top creative chefs, their motivations, and their approach to exploring and experimenting with flavors. Anyone interested in cooking and trying new flavors will be inspired. Readers will learn how kitchens can be a metaphor for life. This "must-read" book shows how using top chefs' methods will change your outlook and passion for life."

—**Peter Krainik**, Founder, The CMO Club

"From nacho cheeseburgers and burnt onion ice cream to candied amaranth and malted maitake mushrooms, Emmanuel Laroche provides an insightful look at the inspiration and innovation behind modern cuisine."

—**Matt Siegel**, author of *The Secret History of Food: Strange but True Stories About the Origins of Everything We Eat*

Conversations
BEHIND THE
KITCHEN DOOR

50 American Chefs Chart Today's Food Culture

Emmanuel Laroche

NEW YORK

LONDON • NASHVILLE • MELBOURNE • VANCOUVER

Conversations BEHIND THE KITCHEN DOOR

50 American Chefs Chart Today's Food Culture

Published in New York, New York, by Morgan James Publishing. Morgan James is a trademark of Morgan James, LLC. www.MorganJamesPublishing.com

Proudly distributed by Ingram Publisher Services.

Morgan James BOGO™

A **FREE** ebook edition is available for you or a friend with the purchase of this print book.

CLEARLY SIGN YOUR NAME ABOVE

Instructions to claim your free ebook edition:
1. Visit MorganJamesBOGO.com
2. Sign your name CLEARLY in the space above
3. Complete the form and submit a photo of this entire page
4. You or your friend can download the ebook to your preferred device

ISBN 9781631959172 paperback
ISBN 9781631959189 ebook
Library of Congress Control Number:
2022933903

Cover Design by:
Rachel Lopez
www.r2cdesign.com

Interior Design by:
Chris Treccani
www.3dogcreative.net

Morgan James is a proud partner of Habitat for Humanity Peninsula and Greater Williamsburg. Partners in building since 2006.

Get involved today! Visit MorganJamesPublishing.com/giving-back

To my children Frederic, Laura, and Alexandre:

"You can do anything you set your mind to."
—Benjamin Franklin

"Think before you speak. Read before you think."
—Fran Lebowitz

*"Let me tell you the secret that has led to my goal.
My strength lies solely in my tenacity."*
—Louis Pasteur

*"If I'm an advocate for anything, it's to move. As far as you can,
as much as you can. Across the ocean, or simply across the river. The
extent to which you can walk in someone else's shoes or at
least eat their food, it's a plus for everybody.
Open your mind, get up off the couch, move."*
—Anthony Bourdain

And to all the chefs, pastry chefs, and mixologists who take
us on a journey filled with unexpected flavors.

Author's Note

Interviews with the chefs and others featured in this book were conducted over the past three years on my podcast, *flavors unknown*. Some of these people may have changed positions since I spoke with them and some of the restaurants mentioned in the book may no longer be open.

Why the deli plastic containers on the book cover?

There are three reasons:
- Countless kitchens and bars run on deli containers. They are the gold standard when it comes to organizing ingredients and leftover storage.
- Various elements of a recipe (sauces, pickles, toppings, stocks) can be prepared in advance, stored in these containers, and then assembled right before serving.
- On my podcast *flavors unknown*, I end the recording with a series of rapid-fire questions. I always ask, "What is your biggest pet peeve in the kitchen?" Very often my guests answer, "Not taking the tape off the deli containers when they are empty!"

Table of Contents

Foreword by Chef Elizabeth Falkner   xiii

Introduction   xvii

Chapter 1   The Making of a Chef   1

Chapter 2   The Flavor-Memory Database   41

Chapter 3   Farmers, Foraging, and Roadside Riches   83

Chapter 4   A Mosaic of Cultures   121

Chapter 5   Creative Decisions   157

Chapter 6   Beyond French Techniques   197

Chapter 7   The Kitchen as a Metaphor for Life   227

Acknowledgments   265

Download The *flavors unknown* Digital Recipe Book. It is Free!   269

About the Author   273

Bibliography   275

List of all podcast episodes (with QR codes)   277

Foreword

BY CHEF ELIZABETH FALKNER

Over the years, I have often felt that interviews with chefs include the same mundane questions that never reveal the inner world of this profession. Fortunately, Emmanuel's podcast *flavors unknown* offers an insightful and entertaining look into this intense, demanding, and rewarding profession. Emmanuel is clearly a food enthusiast and a good interviewer because he's a great listener.

When I met Emmanuel several years back during one of the International Chef Congress from StarChefs at the Armory on Park Avenue in Manhattan, I already noticed his passion and curiosity for food and the industry. Later, as I have been one of the culinary individuals interviewed on his podcast, I didn't feel it was the "same as it ever was" kind of questioning or conversation. Emmanuel genuinely seems like he was trying to solve a puzzle, which is why this book is an important piece of writing.

In *Conversations Behind the Kitchen Door,* he interviews fifty chefs who talk about their early food memories, in what Emmanuel calls the "Flavor-Memory Database"; their collective philosophies in the kitchen and around quality ingredients; the connection of the many cultures; and how American food is truly a food of immigrants. He also describes his travels and dining experiences with non-stop detailed descriptions of the many dishes he has sampled from around the world. It is fascinating to hear about some of the dishes Emmanuel has tasted; you feel as if you have been traveling along with him.

Emmanuel has featured many chefs from different parts of the country. Many questions come up: Where do our perceptions about certain cuisines come from? What does it take to change our ideas about what's "good and bad"? Throughout the interviews in this book, you will gain a collective consciousness of how and why people are committed to the food business.

The restaurant industry was already in crisis before the pandemic. There were many fragilities in the business that still exist today, and most chefs over the last few decades have gotten into this business for different reasons, usually not because they wanted to run a business. The restaurant world has been a rapidly transformative industry over the last twenty to thirty years. Technologies and legislation have evolved quite a bit since the '80s, and after 2000, I have seen this industry attempt to keep up with these changes while still holding onto a management system developed more than a century ago.

In the last chapter, *The Kitchen as a Metaphor for Life*, several of the chefs describe the will, passion, and stamina it takes to survive in the business. While this is true, I do hope that part of this sentiment will continue, as cooking and hospitality are an ongoing education, and several of these chefs have helped evolve and shape a more equitable future for the food business and everyone who is involved in and around it.

While the pandemic has forever changed the food business, what I love the most is seeing many chefs coming back to the basic realization that cooking simply, with the seasons, using truly local organic farmed produce, is more flavorful and more nutrient-packed, and that this is the future of food.

We spend all of our time with this near-obsessive desire to perfect our craft, create perfect dishes and share with guests just to see the expression on their faces. Chefs will persist to invent new ways to continue to cook for others and make people happy because they are innately creative and aware that businesses need to adapt and change in order to survive.

After reading Emmanuel's book, the following quote from chef Levon Wallace stayed with me: "All the food scenes are all so different and beautiful to me, but what I love about them is that they tell a story. That's what food does, food tells the truth. A dish can be used as a tool for cultural understanding." This is one of my favorite excerpts and I can relate so many stories told by the chefs interviewed by Emmanuel in his book and on his podcast, *flavors unknown*. Food does tell the truth about a society, and we have entered a new era of understanding what our truth is with food.

—Chef and Author **Elizabeth Falkner**, ChEF Production

https://www.elizabethfalkner.com
@cheffalkner
#thefalkster

Introduction

I was born in Versailles, in 1963, just across from the famous Chateau of King Louis XIV. Though my parents moved away when I was only three months old, I like to say that this is probably why I love luxury food and ingredients like truffle, foie gras, caviar, and champagne! My former manager in the United States even gave me the nickname "Champagne Charlie!"

I am the youngest of four children and there is quite an age difference between my siblings and me: twenty years with my older brother, eighteen years with my sister, and thirteen years with my closest brother. They had essentially left the house by the time I was old enough to recall memories. But one thing I can clearly remember is that food was truly ubiquitous. I remember Sunday lunches carefully prepared by my mother and shared with the family, and solo train rides to Paris eating croissants, croque monsieurs, or ham and butter on a crispy baguette sitting outside of cafés. Sadly, I lost my father when I was eleven years old, but I still vividly remember our trip together to the boulangerie Sunday mornings after church. He always bought fresh, well-cooked baguettes and either got croissants, chocolate croissants, or "pain aux raisins" that we ate together on the way home. That was our ritual. I looked forward to that moment all weeks! Clearly, I established an emotional bound with food at an early age.

My father was a high school French teacher and we always traveled during the holidays and summer vacations. I remember how excited I was to leave our house in the suburbs of Paris and drive south to our family vacation house on the French Riviera or drive northeast to my parents' families in Lorraine, near the Alsace region. I caught the travel bug during these trips. They meant reconnecting with my siblings or other family members spread out in various regions of France all well-known for their food specialties and wines (Lorraine, Touraine, Burgundy, and Provence). At that time my excitement was probably also related to being with people other than my parents, but looking back, food and wine were the other common factors. I was always impatient to discover what was being prepared in the different pots and pans of these kitchens.

I would have loved to have known more about my uncle, my mother's brother, who owned a hotel-restaurant. Though he died when I was still a child, I remember being fascinated by what was happening in the kitchen at his restaurant. It was not a fancy establishment, but it was where I learned how to bartend. As a kid, I had the opportunity to bring drinks to clients and learn how to make a series of cocktails based on Pastis that used to be very popular: "La Mauresque," "Le Perroquet," and "La Tomate"! I can still hear my uncle shouting at me, "It's not complicated. For a Mauresque add orgeat syrup (a sweet syrup made from almonds, sugar, and rose water or orange flower water) to the Pastis; for a Perroquet add mint syrup to it; and for a Tomate add grenadine syrup!" Great drinks for the summer if you like the taste of anis!

I loved spending time in these kitchens, and my mother started teaching me how to cook when I was young. The first thing she taught me to make was an easy yogurt cake when I was about six or seven. It was an easy recipe, and all the ingredients were measured with a yogurt container. The second dish I learned to cook was the "Lorraine Quiche." My mother was from the Lorraine region, so she knew it well, and she was always very particular about the ingredients. She would not accept that other "tarts" using a mixture of crème fraiche and eggs and any other ingredients were called "quiche." I can still hear her saying, "A quiche only uses crème fraiche, eggs, smoked stripped bacon, salt, and pepper. That's it!"

My mother instilled a passion for cooking in me. When I was newly married, my wife and I spent every Sunday evening flipping through cookbooks and creating weekly grocery and farmers' market shopping lists based on selected recipes. Each day of the week, we followed these recipes and re-created dishes for dinner. For four years, we never cooked the same recipe twice!

I have been fortunate to travel all over Western Europe for my job as marketing manager for a global flavor manufacturer. I have spent years on the roads of Spain, the United Kingdom, Scandinavia, Germany, and France. I had the opportunity to taste the delicacies from the Boqueria market in Barcelona, tapas in small restaurants across Spain, the wines from the regions of Rioja and Ribera del Duero, and the seafood specialties in Galicia. I took part in many ferias (Spanish fairs) in Valencia, the most iconic celebrations in Andalusia featuring an extravaganza of colorful flamenco, horses, and sherry, and visited the private sherry cellars near the city of Jerez de la Frontera in Andalusia. I loved Copenhagen, my favorite city in Europe after Barcelona. The smørrebrød (Danish open-face sandwiches) held no more secrets for me. One time I tasted fourteen different aquavits in Denmark. I had no idea that this spirit could be so complex in taste. I ate at a Russian restaurant in Helsinki, and for the first and only time in my life, I tasted bear meat as part of a soup recipe. I can also remember eating this impossible name to pronounce, the Karjalanpiirakka (rice pies) and fresh cheese traditionally made from cow's beestings (the first milk drawn from a cow after it has given birth) served alongside coffee or cloudberry jam. I always returned from my Scandinavian trips with various jars of herrings and bags of Salmiakki (salty licorice).

In 2002, I moved with my family to the US. Like many Europeans, I had misconceptions about this country, thinking that every city looked like New York or there was only fast food available. Gradually, I started to get acquainted with American chefs and bartenders around the country. I knew that this country could offer delicious food for those who were curious, spent a bit of time doing research, and were willing to get past the brightly colored, over-air-conditioned fast-food outlets that line the highways, selling meals wrapped in paper and cardboard on plastic trays, as described in *Fast Food Nation* by Eric Schlosser. Over the past twenty years, I have been to nearly all fifty states for either business or personal travels. I always enjoyed unique food specialties: regional sandwich types, local craft breweries, fine dining restaurants, third wave coffee shops (a movement in coffee marketing emphasizing high quality), regional pizzas (Detroit style being my favorite!), ice cream shops, craft cocktail bars, tiny saloons, and taco trucks.

In 2008, a former colleague of mine introduced me to StarChefs, an organization based in Brooklyn, N.Y. Once a year, this organization holds a three-day convention, the International Chef Congress, bringing together industry leaders, best chefs, mixologists, and pastry chefs from around the world showcasing their skills and sharing their culinary knowledge. I have attended the event year after year and discovered the world of hospitality in the US. I was lucky to cross paths with many famous chefs including Anthony Bourdain, Emeril Lagasse, Marco Pierre White, Pierre Hermé, Pierre Ganière, Heston Blumenthal, and Albert Adria. In 2015, Antoinette Bruno, CEO of StarChefs, and I established an exclusive partnership with my employer, Symrise, the global flavor company, and since then she and her business partner, Will Blunt, have introduced me to many chefs, pastry chefs, and bartenders around the country.

In 2018, I decided to launch my podcast, *flavors unknown*. In episode #27, I explained how I came up with the name: "There are two main reasons. The first one: people don't really understand too much about flavors, and balance of flavors is one key element that chefs, pastry chefs, and mixologists experiment with every day to make customers happy. I wanted to go behind the scenes, understand, and share what new ingredients and flavors chefs were exploring and creating. 'Unknown' is the part of the name that really resonates with me most as I am always the one to discover and experience new things. It was also very important for me to pay homage to Anthony Bourdain as I launched the podcast not too long after he passed away. He was an important figure in the U.S. culinary scene. He showed people new ways to look at food and around the world. It was, for me, a new way as well to think about street food. The unknown part of the name comes from his TV show, *Parts Unknown*."

The book *Conversations Behind the Kitchen Door* is based on the several seasons of my podcast. I have realized (through Instagram comments) that most people listen to a couple of episodes based on the guests I have on the show. There was an opportunity to gather the most important moments and to give a second life to these episodes by introducing my guests to a wider audience through a book. This book is based on what I have learned by speaking with trending chefs, pastry chefs, and mixologists across America during the past four years. I wanted to paint a realistic image of what goes on behind the scenes of a restaurant kitchen or a bar. The people I interviewed work incredibly hard, and I hope that by sharing their candid conversations, readers will gain an appreciation for the varied food and the talented chefs working across the country.

This is not a typical cookbook. *Conversations Behind the Kitchen Door* is the result of fifty-plus dialogues with awarded culinary leaders from various backgrounds and cultures who have kindly shared their personal stories. They are humble human beings who have offered insights into their strengths and shortcomings, revealing their passion, worries, and concerns in a simple, honest, and transparent manner.

This book has seven chapters, focused on the most common themes that came up during my conversations with the guests on my podcast.

The countless interviews I've had with chefs has helped me realize how charmed I am by the stories related to their motivations: why and how they do what they do and getting to the epiphany that caused them to acknowledge what they needed to become who they are now.

There are countless ways for someone to become a culinary expert today and, surprisingly, even more ways to turn a passion for cooking into a business. Being a chef at a restaurant is only one of numerous options.

Whatever the path someone decides to express a passion for cooking, recognize that it requires hard work. There are no natural prodigies. It takes skills and repetition for somebody to bring something new into the world. It requires time to taste, to learn, to harness the memory, and takes art to bridge the gap between what someone has in mind for the rest of the world to see and taste.

The book starts with why and how chefs understood early on that their vocation was to make people happy by celebrating what Mother Nature has to offer. If some of them were "born in the kitchen," others found it in the hierarchy of the kitchen that gave a sense to their life. Many were born in the US, while others came from Australia, Europe, Asia, or Latin America. These immigrants or second-generation American chefs revealed how much early exposure to cooking influenced their interest in the kitchen, and how much their family influenced their way of cooking. It is fascinating how immigration played a critical part in the story of food in this country. Despite these very heterogeneous backgrounds, readers will find that these chefs have a lot in common.

While some of them bet on their own originality, most choose to anchor their craft in the history of the region where they are established, the local culture, and the flavors that have shaped the palate of those who come to sit at their restaurant's table. Even if it initially means choosing to create dishes that will connect with their local customers and then lead them, step by step, to discover and love new flavors and new ingredients.

They also have in common a quest for quality ingredients. From farmers to breeders and fishermen, chefs meet the produce at the source. These purveyors become more than just suppliers; they are long-term partners in selecting the best produce. Chefs demonstrate the greatest respect for those who supply them with the ingredients that their artistic fingers will enhance and sublimate. Rooted in the "terroir" (a French term used to describe the complete natural environment in which a particular crop is produced), the cuisine becomes seasonal, and the dishes adapt to the calendar.

Beyond these common points, each chef draws their inspiration from a multiplicity of sources. Let children be active with their parents and grandparents in the kitchen, as it is from the alchemy of this family time from which some of our great chefs draw to reinvent the dishes that educated their palates before delighting ours.

Gradually, chefs will add their savoir faire to their early life experience and their interest in other arts like music, painting, ceramics, and many others to influence their creative process. Let's also not forget the flavors, ingredients, or spices brought back from their travels. Wild honey from the Middle East, curries and madras from India, sauces from Asia, modernized fermentation processes from Scandinavia, and chili peppers from South America add to the creation of unique dishes. Chefs will combine the treasures from their travels with their personal and family culture, often with the sole objective in mind to discover, memorize, and build their taste and olfactive database.

In the kitchen and behind the bar, chefs and mixologists challenge their imagination with the ones from their team members, and their already complex inspiration becomes many. Even if the temptation is great to give free rein to their originality, chefs are not only artists, they also must develop a business sense and create appealing and convincing dishes that will resonate with their customers.

To transform the artistic work into a great dish, culinary leaders use all their experience and techniques learned in culinary school and on the job. Without a strong technique, there is no dish. And without creativity, there is no innovation. The people I spoke with do not seem to favor creativity or technique as both are indispensable and inseparable. With the correct technique, quality produce can be transformed into a dream dish. Many chefs consider French techniques to be an essential entry point; however, today there's more at their disposal than French culinary skills. Instead, they suggest that people go beyond the French tradition and broaden their culinary horizons to the richness that the rest of the world can offer.

Chefs also believe that the traditional way of operating in French kitchens is no longer suitable in today's culinary environment. The demand for quality and efficiency can no longer be associated with an authoritarianism of barking orders and verbal abuse. The young generation of cooks who are attracted to the profession crave a managerial style comprised of accepted rigor, discreet and respectful reminders to order, and creative discipline to reach one main objective: consistency! Chefs are not only creative artists, technical experts, or business leaders; they must also be mentors and learn how to motivate their teams.

Now, chefs are seen as people and their authority naturally imposes itself through the virtue of example. They can transmit that it takes more than technique and creativity to become a successful chef. They teach future chefs to be ready to face all difficulties as a team, to never give up, to turn mistakes into learnings, and to always pursue their goals. Many of the chefs I interviewed pivoted their business during the pandemic and demonstrated that "each day is a new day. Today's problems are what we deal with today and tomorrow's problems are what we don't worry about today!"

Conversations Behind the Kitchen Door shows how to be more creative and draw inspiration from a variety of things. The objective of this book is to demonstrate that people shouldn't be afraid of experimenting in the kitchen. Recipes should be viewed as guidelines but your imagination is really what matters in the kitchen.

Readers will learn where and how to select the best ingredients and understand some of the shortcuts used by talented chefs. They will begin to seek inspiration during travels and collect ideas and ingredients that will surprise their guests.

My podcast, *flavors unknown*, as well as my worldwide search for new foods and flavors, are at the core of *Conversations Behind the Kitchen Door*. Scores of chefs offer essential insights and entertaining observations about the food scene today—information that will be of interest to new and aspiring chefs, as well as foodies and home cooks who follow trends in restaurants and recipes. Readers will walk away from this book with a deeper understanding of the minds and creative practices of famous chefs, as well as a map to begin to create sensational dishes of their own.

Chapter 1

THE MAKING OF A CHEF

"Think differently and be the exception to the rule."
—ANDRÉ NATERA

List of culinary individuals featured in this chapter:

Chef/Co-Owner **Brad Miller** of The Inn at the Seventh Ray in Topanga Canyon, California

Chef/Owner **Gabriel Kreuther** from two-Michelin star Gabriel Kreuther restaurant in New York City

Chef **Hari Cameron** former chef/owner at a(MUSE.) in Rehoboth, Delaware

Chef/Owner **Brian Ahern** of Boeufhaus in Chicago

Chef **Johnny Spero** from Reverie in Washington, D.C.

Chef/Co-Owner **Drew Adams** of Meloria in Sarasota (was at Bourbon Steak in Washington, D.C.)

Chef and Author **Chris Shepherd**, operating Underbelly Hospitality Group in Houston

Chef **Trigg Brown** from Win Son in Brooklyn

Chef/Owner **Ehren Ryan** from Common Lot in Millburn, New Jersey

Chef/Owner **Michael Gulotta** of MoPho and MayPop in New Orleans

Chef **Shamil Velazquez** from Delaney Oyster House in Charleston, South Carolina

Chef/Owner **Brother Luck** from Four by Luck at Colorado Springs, Colorado

Chef/Co-Owner **Fiore Tedesco** from L'Oca d'Oro in Austin, Texas

Executive Chef **Alex Harrell** of Virgin Hotels in New Orleans (was at the Elysian Bar in New Orleans)

Executive Chef **Rikku O'Donnchü** at London House Private Club in Orlando (was at Amorette in Lancaster, Pennsylvania)

Former Executive Chef **Andre Natera** from Fairmont Hotel in Austin, Texas

Iron Chef, author, entrepreneur, and food innovator **Jose Garces** from Philadelphia

Chef/Owner **Michael Fojtasek** of Olamaie and Little Ola's Biscuits in Austin, Texas

In-home personal chef and culinary instructor chef **Chris Spear** of Perfect Little Bites in Frederick

Chef, author, and restaurateur **Chris Cosentino** in San Francisco

Chef/Owner **Brett Sawyer** of Good Company in Cleveland (was at the Plum Café in Cleveland)

Chef **Andrew McLeod** from Avenue M in Asheville

Chef/Owner **Kim Alter** of Nightbird and Linden Room in San Francisco

Consulting Chef **Elizabeth Falkner** based in Los Angeles

Sayat and Laura Ozyilmaz formerly at Noosh in San Francisco

Chef/Owner **Alison Trent** of Alison Trent Events in Los Angeles (was at Ysabel in Los Angeles)

As I drove up the Pacific Coast Highway from Santa Monica where the shoreline curved around the bay and the mountains descend into the sea, I exited the highway at the Getty villa and turned right into Topanga Canyon Road. I rolled down the windows and played the song "Hotel California" on my phone. I knew about Topanga Canyon long before I moved to the US. As a teenager in France in the late '70s, I came upon the music of the Eagles and Neil Young and read everything about them. Some members of these bands lived and played music in local joints in Topanga Canyon, and that name has been engraved in my mind ever since. On this late afternoon of June 2021, I finally realized my one of my teenage dreams: driving through Topanga Canyon.

I had previously made dinner reservations at The Inn of the Seventh Ray to meet with chef Brad Miller, whom I interviewed a year before on the podcast. Six miles after I left the coast, and still singing the Eagles in my head, I reached the restaurant.

The Inn of the Seventh Ray, a terraced creekside restaurant that opened in the early '70s, continues to rate as the most romantic destination near Los Angeles. The place is surrounded by grand old sycamores and waterfalls. I followed the hostess to my table down a curvy red brick pathway, around fountains and private dining areas protected by vegetation.

While waiting for chef Brad Miller, I began my dinner with the charred leek and potato soup which has since been in my top list of favorite dishes I tasted around the country. Once, somebody asked me what was my one favorite dish I ever tasted since I began the podcast and talking with culinary experts. It was an unfair question to me, as well as for my podcast guests.

How could I pick one single dish among all the amazing tasting moments I've experienced?

Recently, though, I decided to look through my phone for pictures of all the dishes I have tasted since 2018. I settled for twenty memorable dishes from chefs I had on the show. I organized this list by cities, going from East Coast to West Coast:

- The Uni Bocadillo with White Miso and Pickled Mustard Seeds from chef Jamie Bissonnette at Toro in Boston.
- The Onion Tart with Gruyere Cheese, Pine Nuts, Frisée, and Sherry Vinaigrette from chef Sam Freund at White Birch in Flanders, New Jersey.
- The Twelve-hour Braised Lamb Shoulder from chef Ehren Ryan at Common Lot in Millburn, New Jersey.
- The Sturgeon and Sauerkraut Tarte (and the Tarte Flambée) from chef Gabriel Kreuther at Gabriel Kreuther in New York City.
- Baked ricotta kabocha squash, chilies, mint, grilled sourdough, grilled sourdough by chef Dan Kluger at Loring Place in New York City.
- The Fried Eggplants with Labneh and Spiced Cashews from chef Trigg Brown at Win Son in Brooklyn, New York.
- The Quinoa, Banana Mayonnaise, Avocado, Bacon, and Cashew from chef Erik Ramirez at Llama Inn in Brooklyn, New York.
- The Eggplant Braciole with Smoked Eggplant Rice, Salsa Verde, Black Olive, and Piquillo Pepper from chef Richard Landau from Vedge in Philadelphia.
- The Faro Dish with Morels, Poached Egg Yolk, Wild Garlic, and Wild Onion Foam from chef Drew Adams at Four Seasons in Washington, D.C.
- The Smoked Chicken Wings with White BBQ Sauce from chef Edward Lee at Succotash in Washington, D.C.
- The Pastrami Rueben Sandwich from chef Jeremy Umansky at Larder in Ohio City, Ohio.
- The Short Rib Beignets from chef Brian Ahern at Boeufhaus in Chicago.

- The Slow Roasted Lamb Neck, Green Curry, and Creole Cream Cheese Roti from chef Michael Gulotta at MoPho in New Orleans.
- The Sour Cherry Dumplings from chef Bonnie Morales at Kachka in Portland, Oregon.
- The Tea Braised Pig Tails, Sarson Ka Sagg, Pickled Collards, Texturized Yolk, and Peanut Chili Crunch from chef Misti Norris at Petra and the Beast in Dallas.
- The Boiled Peanut Dish and the Biscuits from chef Michel Fojtasek at Olamaie in Austin, Texas.
- The Grilled Octopus with Salsa Verde from chef Andre Natera at Garrison in Austin, Texas.
- The Potato Gnocchi with Pancetta, Parmesan, Sage, and Black Truffle from chef Tim Hollingsworth at Otium in Los Angeles.
- The Green dish (Halibut in Shio Koji marinade) from the Pride menu by chef Kim Alter at Nightbird in San Francisco.
- And the Charred Leek and Potato Soup from chef Brad Miller at The Inn of the Seventh Ray in Topanga Canyon, California.

To follow this exquisite soup on that day, chef Miller sent me the yellowfin tuna crudo with white ponzu, pickled mustard seeds, herbs, cucumber, and olive. Then, I continued with grilled Spanish octopus served with olive oil, lemon poached tomato, olives, garlic, and rosemary polenta. My pasta dish was house-made gnocchetti with sunflower pesto, asparagus, snap peas, parmesan, and watercress. A side dish intrigued me on the menu, so I ordered the crispy Brussel sprouts with charred pineapple aioli, pumpkin seed, garlic dukkah, and Parmesan.

At the end of the meal, chef Miller joined me at the table with a huge smile on his face. "Welcome to The Inn of the Seventh Ray! It is nice to finally to meet you in person. How was the food?" he asked.

"The food was stunning," I replied, looking back at the menu. "I particularly loved the charred leek and potato soup, and the charred pineapple aioli in the Brussel sprouts was positively surprising."

While we were chatting, millions of little lights began twinkling around us as the evening progressed.

"How did you know you wanted to become a chef?" I asked Miller.

"My father had a butcher shop outside of Chicago and that led me to be naturally interested in food. He and my grandmother always cooked. I just had a knack for wanting to cook, but first, I was not good at it. I took part of a food class in high school, and I suddenly saw it as a possible goal. When I started liking cooking, my father and I always cooked together. I could have ended up as a butcher, but instead I went to culinary school. Then I worked at a bunch of great resorts and restaurants in Arizona. I had the path of most chefs: I worked under amazing chefs and some Michelin chefs too. I just kept working and learning."

I commented that famous chefs came from families with a food business, or had grown up on a farm that naturally led them to be interested in cooking. Three famous names came to mind. Chef Dan Barber grew up on the Upper East Side of Manhattan and spent a lot of time on his grandmother's farm in Massachusetts, where he developed a passion for sustainable agriculture. Similarly, chef Daniel Boulud's family had a farm in the suburbs of Lyon in France, and he always said that he learned the true taste of food there. And chef Rick Bayless (chef and restaurateur who specializes in traditional Mexican cuisine with modern interpretations) mentioned in past interviews that his family was in food businesses. He is the fourth generation to be working in the field.

I asked Miller if he knew Gabriel Kreuther, chef of the eponymous two-Michelin star restaurant on Manhattan's Bryant Park. At eleven years old, he spent time with his uncle in the summertime during school vacations.

This is what Kreuther had told me: He had one uncle who owned a hotel restaurant, a second uncle who had a pastry shop, and a third uncle who was a butcher. The family, on his mother's side, had a duck and a goose farm.

Kreuther was deeply involved in food. He spent most of the time with his uncle at the hotel restaurant. His uncle gave him a hard time to make sure it was what he wanted to do, and he became first Meilleur Apprenti Cuisinier de France in 1987, at the age of eighteen, then moved to America and started working for Jean-Georges Vongerichten (a French chef and restaurateur with restaurants in Miami Beach, Las Vegas, London, Paris, Shanghai, and Tokyo, and New York).

Like Miller and Kreuther, other chefs had the chance to get an early education in foods and exposure to unusual flavors. For example, I did an interview with chef Bryce Shuman and was intrigued to learn that he lived a year with the Innuits in the Arctic as a young child. His mother was an anthropologist conducting research in the North Pole region.

I told Miller I was fascinated by Shuman's story, about his opportunity to taste raw seal and caribou when he was a kid! "Interestingly enough," I continued, "Shuman's close friend, chef Hari Cameron from Rehoboth, Delaware, who introduced me to Shuman, was himself conscious of a variety of food from a very young age."

As a child, Cameron was made aware of different cultures and of the significance their food had on people. Some of his earliest childhood flavor memories were vegetarian Indian curries. He remembered meditating on ashrams in front of gurus with his father. Cameron could also remember the first time that he ate sushi, when he was six or seven years old. Sushi is pretty much mainstream today, but that was not the case when Cameron was a kid. He told me that he could distinctly remember the Tobiko Caviar popping in his mouth! And he recalled how foreign the flavor and texture of raw fish were to him.

He could also remember the first time he ate an Ethiopian meal, where he had to sit down on the floor with his parents. They ate injera (a sour fermented flatbread). He still could visualize the chicken bone, the egg, and the raisins that gave a sweet and savory profile to the dish.

Miller and I agreed how essential it is to let children be active with their parents or grandparents in the kitchen, and for parents to expose their children to all different kinds of food. It is from the alchemy of family time that some great chefs drew, in order to reinvent the ingredients and dishes that educated their palates before delighting ours.

I thought of chef Brian Ahern from Boeufhaus in Chicago who studied fine arts at the College of Charleston and in my mind will always be connected to delicious short rib beignets. He worked his way through school in a kitchen. But thinking back, Ahern realized that his father had an influence on him way before that. Ahern's father wasn't particularly interested in fine dining, but he always took his children to eat at places off the beaten track. When he was ten or so, his father took him for ice cream after soccer practice. Today, it's not a big thing to get cookie dough ice cream or any other ice cream with inclusions, but in 1990, there was only one small place near where Ahern lived that was mixing it to order with paddles on cold marble. That little old Italian place has always sort of stuck with Ahern. His father taking him to these little-known places had an impact on him.

Miller and I agreed that clear career paths and established educations, or training programs, exist if someone wants to become a doctor or a lawyer; however, if an individual is passionate about cooking and wants to become a chef, there are currently an array of options that will take you there.

Among the chefs I interviewed, many took classic training and went to culinary school, but others started as dishwashers during summer jobs in high school or college and fell in love with cooking along the way. Some went into the industry to survive and make ends meet. Most "staged" (took internships to expose them to new techniques) at multiple restaurants before experiencing the "aha" moment that made them decide to turn to cooking as a profession.

For chef Johnny Spero, from Reverie in Washington, D.C., it happened while watching a famous television show. "I was seventeen, and I was looking at going to culinary school, and I had just recently stumbled upon Anthony Bourdain's *No Reservations* TV show. I didn't really know too much about the outside culinary world, and there was an episode where he basically dedicated the entire hour to El Bulli in Spain. That episode completely blew my mind. It changed everything." Spero explained that that show was what probably started him on the path that he is now, and, stylistically, to the food that he has always been attracted to.

model. For me, cooking started at a very young age out of necessity, but then it became the supplement of the male role model from the street to now, the chef and the toques. That was where my transition really started. After getting into a culinary program in high school, I was awarded multiple scholarships. I ended up graduating with $30,000 in scholarships to go to culinary school."

"It was an opportunity to eat a steak sandwich at the end of the night. It was a few dollars in my pocket for washing dishes and working at a restaurant was a feeling of family."
—CHEF BROTHER LUCK

When chef Hari Cameron finished high school, he studied business and communications for a semester and quickly realized that wasn't the right path for him. He was going to rave clubs and headed for trouble.

As he recalls, "I got caught with one hundred pills of ecstasy and was set up. I had more ambition at that time than I had intelligence. I did six months in jail. I was seventeen, turning eighteen. When I got done with that, I thought that I was smarter than this. I had more energy than this. I was more talented than this. I needed to do something productive with my life. I didn't know what I wanted to do, and I kept working at outlets.

"At first, I was in the front of the house working as a server, and one day the pantry person didn't show up. They asked me if I could make salads? I said, 'Yeah. Of course, I can make salads. I've cooked in restaurants my whole life!' So, I started on salads. I was the kind of kid who played with his Skittles growing up, making beautiful patterns with them. I've always been good with my hands, and with my mind, in figuring out puzzles. I started plating salads. They said, 'Hurry up. You're plating them too slowly. Stop making love to food.' I said, 'All I want to do is make love to food for the rest of my life!'

"At the end of the day, it was like I didn't find cooking, it found me! I discovered that I was naturally good at it, and I enjoyed doing it. I came up through kitchens very quickly. By the time I was twenty-four I was a chef, and I was managing lots of money. I'd learned all I could on my own from teachers, mentors, and books. Then I decided to go to culinary school. I went to Walnut Hill College in Philadelphia, where I graduated amongst the top of my class while working "eight days a week" living in Delaware, opening a restaurant in D.C., traveling for two years straight. The teachers stopped calling on me because I knew all the answers. I became a teacher's aide. Culinary school did not expose me to new techniques—I already knew them from working at restaurants. It taught me discipline. It helped me set the discipline that is needed as a chef. Culinary school was great for that, and it helped me setting goals for myself. I started staging at a lot of places around the world. I was making money, started eating at lots of Michelin star restaurants, and traveling."

In working in a kitchen and learning culinary techniques, others found connections with other disciplines in which they were enrolled. Some established a link with the creative dimension in cooking, others identified a connection with science, and others recognized the same team spirit in sports.

Chef Fiore Tedesco from L'Oca d'Oro in Austin, Texas was a drummer and played in a band before he switched to the culinary industry. Tedesco is a great storyteller and his tale on how he suddenly got into cooking is one of a kind.

"I played a show in Felino, Italy, in the foothills of Umbria. We had gotten into town that day and had gone through the soundcheck at a club that we were playing at. The owner of the club was friends with our Italian tour manager, and he offered to take us to dinner at a friend's restaurant. After the soundcheck, we drove straight up the side of a mountain and got to this wonderful restaurant. We were there for several hours, tasting wines and food that I'd never had before. That experience reminded me of my childhood. The chef's mother was grilling a wild boar flank on a charcoal grill outside the restaurant. She reminded me so much of my mother. She came and gave me a kiss on the head. I was so moved that I started sobbing openly at the dinner table.

"We were having a wonderful time and drinking too much. I looked down on my watch and realized it was one in the morning. We had been there since seven o'clock! We got back to the club and played an amazing show.

"That night, I had a dream about that magic meal. In the dream I was eating that meal again, except the food did not look the same. Every dish looked like slightly tinted white clouds. I would put my face into the clouds and eat them. They tasted all the same flavor of this beautiful wild boar flank with the pistachio lavender cream under it. It was mind-blowing. This dream changed my life. I woke up in the morning and I could remember every bit of it. What came to me was I wanted to learn how to re-create what just happened in that dream, being able to transform that into some other shapes, some other forms, be able to put that in front of someone and have them experience the way I did in the dream. This is what I want to do now. And I decided to quit the band and switch to cooking!"

For many chefs, culinary education was an obvious choice, whereas a few others, like chef Alex Harrell, from New Orleans, never intended to cook for a living and had chosen an entirely different path.

"I actually was in school studying biology," said Harrell. "My focus was environmental science, ecology, and freshwater systems. I really wanted to go into resort research and restoration of habitat from an environmental science standpoint. We always cooked in my family though. I grew up going to my grandparents' farm, which was thirty minutes away from my hometown. I spent as much time as I possibly could down there fishing in the pines, digging around in the garden, planting, and cooking with my grandmother.

"I was aware that people cooked for a living. I knew it was a career, but I never considered it. I was doing postgraduate studies at the University of Alabama, but quite frankly, I got tired of academic life, and just wanted to take a break. I thought I was going to take a summer off, and then go to find a job. Coincidently, a family friend was opening a small seafood restaurant in northwest Florida. He invited me to come down to help open and work at the restaurant. I thought it was a great idea. I could have a summer paid for. I wouldn't have any overhead or any bills, and all I had to do was work in a restaurant. I couldn't pass this up. I had no idea what the work entailed. I got in there and it was something that connected with me.

"Once I was in the kitchen, I really enjoyed the work. I still didn't really consider it as a full-time job, and after the summer ended, I decided to move back to Alabama. I found another restaurant job, and one thing led to another, and I ended up about a year later in New Orleans. At that point, I was really starting to focus on the fact that I could do this."

Like chef Robert Del Grande, who continued the scientific mindset of experimenting with flavors in the kitchen after receiving a PhD in biochemistry, Harrell realized that he had a connection to food through science.

"Cooking helped fulfill my interests in science. I began to relate to food that way. I continued working in restaurants. I never went to culinary school. I considered it a couple of times, but then I didn't want to go back to an academic lifestyle. I read a lot of the textbooks and curriculum-based books from the Culinary Institute of America. I read anything I could get my hands on, and I would formulate questions as they related to the work I was doing. Whatever station I was working at I would ask questions to the chefs. I used to drive the other cooks crazy. I would sit there and try to gather as much information from them as I possibly could while we were working. There were times they told me to shut up and leave them alone. I learned a lot through that process. I also learned a lot through the multiple failures and missed attempts that I would make known, the times that I would mess up."

There are some surprising similarities in the approaches involved in being a chef and a scientist. Being a chemist myself (before switching to marketing), I see parallels, as both science and cooking start with known ingredients and use common sets of techniques to produce results. Chef Rikku Ó'Donnchü, from Amorette in Lancaster, Pennsylvania, first studied psychology, music, and chemistry. He graduated as a chemist. When he was fifteen years old and looking for a job, he found one at a two-Michelin-star-restaurant down the road where he lived. Not bad as an introduction to the culinary world! His biggest "aha" moment was when he worked later at the Fat Duck with chef Heston Blumenthal. He could connect the dots between chemistry and culinary. For him it was all about pulling from his chemistry and science background, and wanting to taste and understand what flavor really is.

The comparison to sports is obvious too. Working in a kitchen is akin to being on a team. Although the kitchen brigade was based initially on a military model, there is even more in common with a sport team. There is a hierarchy as well as discipline in the kitchen. Many chefs who played sports when they were younger found a similar purpose and structure in restaurant's kitchens. Celebrity chef Charlie Palmer (an American chef, hospitality entrepreneur, hotelier, and author) wanted to be a professional football player. At about the same time he discovered cooking, he realized that only a small percentage of athletes could get to the pro level. He was also part of the wrestling team at school, and he said, "Once you've done high school wrestling, no kitchen seems tough."

Three chefs I spoke with explained the connection between the experience they had in sports with the one in the kitchen.

First, Andre Natera, retired executive chef from the Fairmont hotel in Austin, confessed that he always wanted to be a professional fighter. "It was something that I enjoyed during my youth. I boxed, I wrestled, and did martial arts. What's interesting about gyms is the same thing that's interesting about kitchens—there's a certain social hierarchy inside the locker room or in the training room and that same social hierarchy applies also in the kitchen."

For celebrity chef Jose Garces, from Philadelphia, being a chef was the furthest thing on his mind. "I went to a few years of undergrad, and I still was disillusioned with school and the direction I was going, until I stumbled upon a culinary school in Chicago. I saw the uniforms, the white hats, the crisp aprons, the uniformity, the discipline that I had experienced in high school athletics, and it just spoke to me. In our skills classes, I was looking at ingredients and playing with them, and suddenly, I realized that I had a creative edge over my colleagues. I was making things differently and thinking about food differently. I was preparing things at home on my own in many ways and cooking around the clock. I was just finding a passion for this craft that I didn't even know existed. I felt very fortunate that I found that, because otherwise I didn't know what I would be doing now."

Chef Michael Fojtasek, from Olamaie in Austin, tried several careers before figuring out he wanted to become a chef. "I had always cooked my entire life and I had always enjoyed cooking. As I got older, I was cooking for friends, and I was basing a lot of parties around cooking food for everyone. A close friend was a general manager at a restaurant and invited me in to come 'stage.' I had no idea what that word meant. I had a strong sports background in high school and after spending about two hours in my first kitchen, I recognized the correlation between the team, the coordination that it required, and the leadership that it required like I had seen in sports. On top of that, it was also in line with creating things that were delicious, so it took me about two hours to experience it and realize that it was what I wanted to do. I knew quickly after stepping into a professional kitchen that I wanted to be in that environment for the rest of my career. It was almost like one of those moments where you know the clouds break and you see the sky, and suddenly, you're like, 'Oh, this all makes perfect sense to me.'"

A couple days later, I met chef Brad Miller for coffee at Ten Café in Marina Del Rey.

Ten Café was the new place from Zayde Naquib, a coffee roaster I met a few years back at Bar Nine, his first place that got him a 2017 StarChefs Rising Stars Award.

I sat inside the bright white room waiting for Miller and ordered a Cortado with goat milk, my go-to way of ordering coffee at any coffee shop. For taste exploration, I also requested the orange latte made of house-made orange simple syrups, orange bitters, candied orange peel, oat milk, and their espresso nectar. Espresso Nectar is Bar Nine's proprietary brew process that can deliver the representation of espresso without an espresso machine. An incredible product!

Miller arrived with a huge smile on his face. Since I interviewed Miller, I have been impressed with his energy. Sitting down, he explained to me that he hasn't had a day off in nine days and he has been working sixteen-hour days because of how busy the restaurant was.

"Nobody wants to become a chef at a restaurant nowadays, Emmanuel," he said. "It's a blue-collar job and it is really hard work. Even when I do a show on TV, when I'm done filming, I go right back in the kitchen. The whole filming crew celebrate and wonder what I have to do. I explain to them that I need to fly back to cater a wedding of three hundred people. The crew is always surprised that I do not take time off.

"'Take off? What's that?'" said Miller ironically.

"Nowadays, it seems everybody just wants to have the fame of being a chef and not do the hard work," I added.

"Yeah, and the funny thing is they absolutely can have the fame," he said with a smirk. "Back in the day, you could not become a great chef just by saying you want to become a great chef. Now, you can get that notoriety, that feeling, and that fame from it just by looking stuff up and starting your own YouTube channel!"

Miller paused while sipping his ice-cold brew and added, "You know what? There's nothing wrong with that, because I don't knock anybody's hustle. I believe everybody has a fair chance at life. I don't look back on the old days and say, this is the way it should be."

"But without a proper culinary education and techniques, do you think they are going to last long?" I asked.

"I think there'll be a percentage that will," replied Miller. "But I don't think they're going to open restaurants. I guess we're talking two different conversations. If you are going to open a restaurant, you must know what you're doing. You must be on your feet—and do things like dealing with products, purveyors, ordering, and all the things that are not sexy. But if you want to be a chef on TV, it's absolutely achievable now."

Miller knew what he was talking about as he had just competed on Season 3 of *Hell's Kitchen*. The TV show was not as popular then as it is today, and back in 2007 social media as we know it didn't exist yet—YouTube was only two years old, Twitter was in its infancy, and Instagram not even born. Regardless, a few chefs figured out how to capitalize on their TV time and use it as a launching pad.

Chef Declan Horgan from the DelMarVa area arrived from Ireland and competed in *Hell's Kitchen* Season 19—the same show that Miller was on, but fifteen years later, which makes a huge difference in terms of social media presence!

"I use the show as a platform to advertise myself," affirmed Horgan. "People see how I work in the kitchen and how I work with others, because each service is like a proper restaurant service. All the emotions are here, and the adrenaline is pumping, exactly like during a real restaurant service."

Many chefs I interviewed, such as Elizabeth Falkner, Edward Lee, Brother Luck, Jose Garces, Tiffany Derry, and Lamar Moore, all competed or were judges on cooking shows. They loved the experience, the competitive aspect, and the networking and business opportunities that resulted from it.

Nick DiGiovanni, *MasterChef* finalist on Season 10, is now a social media star and popular food YouTuber with over 4 million subscribers, more than 5 million subscribers on TikTok, and 260 million-plus monthly views (and counting).

In 2018, Miller aired *Food Truck Nation*, a TV show on the Cooking Channel. Miller realized that food trucks were here to stay and almost every major city like Portland, Austin, Los Angeles, Denver, or Charlotte had successful popular food truck scenes.

I asked him what motivated him to do the show.

"The great thing about food trucks is it's a great soundboard to trial your food before you open a brick and mortar," says Miller. "So, I thought that was relevant to show America the quality and creativity of the food served at food trucks."

"And having a food truck is a cheaper path for people to own their own food business if they are passionate about cooking," I added.

"Definitely, and no need to be a classically trained chef to have one."

"There are so many avenues nowadays to be a chef. For introverted individuals and chefs who do not want to interact directly with consumers, they can now work at Ghost Kitchens!" I said ironically.

But, joking aside, ghost kitchens (professional food preparation and cooking facilities set up for the preparation of delivery-only meals) were a $40 billion industry back in 2019, and they are expected to reach $70 billion by 2027, according to Hospitality Technology. A real option for chefs who do not want to work in a traditional restaurant.

Another alternative I know well because of my career in the food industry are research chefs who work in food laboratories at food or food ingredient manufacturers. Many research chefs started in the restaurant industry and decided to look for regular hours, medical benefits, and a 401(k) when they got older and started a family. These chefs are great translating the specifications of the restaurant into the technical language of scientists. They formulate gold standard versions of culinary recipes to test and evaluate food ingredients and prepare recipes for industry production scale-up.

"Another option for them is to become a private chef," I said to Miller. "There are more than 25,000 private chefs in the US and the pandemic expanded an already booming market."

Chef Chris Spear is a private chef based out of Frederick, Maryland. Spear wanted to focus on giving people a restaurant experience in their home. I talked with him about it, and this is what Spear said: "I build customized menus around the preferences of my guests. I send them a questionnaire, find out what they like and don't like, and their diet preferences. I show up with everything. I bring my china, all the cooking pots and pans, and all the food. I make everything for them in their house. I set the table and serve the dishes to my guests. A four- to six-course meal is really like going out to a restaurant."

Spear went to culinary school and got a four-year bachelor's degree. Would he do it again? Probably not, he said.

"I came out with student loan debts that I had to pay for ten years. I graduated in 1998 and the market was $7 an hour for cooking jobs. I couldn't live on that. I found a job working in a retirement community with a decent salary, two weeks paid vacation, medical benefits, and a 401(k). I never really loved the restaurant experience and the kitchen life, working until two in the morning. I applied for jobs out of culinary school and was turned off by the attitude of many of the hiring executive chefs. I just thought these guys sound like jerks, and I didn't really want to work for them."

Also, Spear believes that when people attend culinary school at a young age, they don't necessarily know what they want to do. He suggests, "Get out in the industry and get a taste of things. Once you know what you want to do, you can always go back and take workshops. I'm a big fan of that. For instance, I took meat cutting as a freshman in culinary school at eighteen. Then for the next ten years, I never did any meat fabrication, because every place I worked at was getting precut meat. Five or six years ago, there was the big movement to doing more in-house butchering. I didn't know how to butcher anymore. So, I took a three-day butchering and charcuterie class."

He has only been doing private chef full-time for five years now. He enjoyed being his own boss. "Having the flexibility to do whatever I want, on my own terms has been great. I guess the challenge is not having the support of a team anymore." To balance that, Spear created a Facebook community called Chefs Without Restaurants where he and other private chefs can share best practices, resources, and even gig opportunities.

All culinary specialists will tell you that they followed their passion. Success in the culinary world begins with a passion for food and their craft in the kitchen. Unfortunately, passion is not enough. It doesn't pay the bills, nor does it make young food entrepreneurs successful. That requires the enthusiasm to work hard, and the drive to strive for higher standards. Nothing replaces practical experience and discipline. "There's very little romance in becoming a professional chef," said Anthony Bourdain. "The true god of the restaurant business, of professional cooking, is not brilliance and creativity. It's consistency."

Before the pandemic, most restaurants only became profitable after three to five years, which explains the frightening reality that sixty percent of restaurants don't make it past their first year, and eighty percent go out of business within their first five years. Issues related to bad location, insufficient capital, and lack of food consistency, poor management team, absence of marketing, and menus not resonating with customers were the main reasons for failure. In contrast, a successful restaurant offers a menu that resonates with customers and requires the chef stay in contact with customers and make them care about your passion. A chef, a restaurant owner, or a young entrepreneur needs to understand and appeal to a socially evolving audience.

Chef Fiore Tedesco explained that people need to think twice before turning their passion for food into a business.

"The business of opening a restaurant and how it intersects with creativity is a really difficult relationship. I was talking recently to a friend in New York. She loves food. She's an excellent cook. She was thinking about getting into the food business. She's a mom with two kids. She's also an architect, and a wonderful and super-talented human being. I told her, 'Why? What is the cost of you disrupting everything you have and this beautiful life you have in front of you to make these food products?'

"It has to be more than just making good food. If you want to make people happy making food, have dinner parties. Honestly. It's not enough for business. It's not near enough. If you want to make a living making food, think about it for a long while and really try to come to a very firm understanding of what that means to you, and why you want to do that. Because generally, it's a bad idea. I would say this to 99.9 percent of everyone: don't open a restaurant. There are more important things to do in the world, for most of us. Then for the one-tenth of one percent of you that think that I'm talking to you, understand the language of business and learn about real estate. Once you get past why you want to open that food business—and you're very clear, and you've gotten a lot of other opinions, thinking it's a very good idea for you to do this and that it's a salient idea—then you get to the hard part.

"All the contracts and the commitments and the responsibility, you must really prepare yourself for it. Because, once you get started with that, there's no going back. Then you get to a point of, it's either success or failure. That duality is not fun. That is the least fun part of it to me. I don't thrive in knowing, 'Gosh, we're successful.' It's an empty didactic relationship. I think about it in a more nuanced place, but it's hard to really embrace the joy of success in that paradigm for me. Because you're up against so much all the time, just in doing what it takes to make a business successful."

If you want to make people happy making food, have dinner parties. Honestly. It's not enough for business. It's not near enough. If you want to make a living making food, think about it for a long while and really try to come to a very firm understanding of what that means to you, and why you want to do that. Because generally, it's a bad idea.

—CHEF FIORE TEDESCO

Throughout the seasons of the podcast, I have wondered what motivations gave these culinary leaders their drive. I recall chef Thomas Keller saying, "When you acknowledge that there is no such thing as perfect food, only the idea of it, then the real purpose of striving towards perfection becomes clear—to make people happy."

I circled back with some chefs as I questioned their intention of making people happy. Was it a genuine motivation or a ready-made interview response and a way for chefs to feel good about themselves? All of them said that the satisfaction of their guests was their primary goal, and chef Drew Adams added, "We always talk about being in the 'making people happy' business, but I don't think that is always the driving factor."

My guests named four extra motivations that could come into play. The rule of the business often dictates the need to customize food and drink options to local markets, so it is critical to attracting people from the neighborhood. Then it is about running a business, about making money, being part of an ecosystem, and standing out from the competition. One additional incentive mentioned by the chefs was the element of discovery and curiosity in cooking. Depending on someone's career phase, it could also be about achieving status in the industry and being recognized by peers. Ultimately, seeing the joy on the faces of their customers brought them satisfaction in return and instant gratification.

First Motivation: Make Customers Happy

Chef Erin Ryan from Common Lot in Maplewood, New Jersey, summarized it well: "We are here to create happiness for customers. Both chef and mixologists get into the hospitality industry to create happy memories for guests by expressing themselves through drinks and food."

Fifteen years ago, Flavien Desoblin took advantage of American curiosity and interest in fancy drinks. The wine bar's market in New York was at its prime, doing well, but already saturated. Desoblin took the wine bar concept to the brown spirits side. Since then, the Brandy Library's warm and dark, soothing atmosphere welcomes connoisseurs and amateur drinkers who want to unwind, indulge, and discover rare spirits.

"The very sole purpose of the Brandy Library is to show our customers that those spirits, whether it is Cognac, bourbon, or tequila, are made by real people."

That was how Flavien Desoblin, owner of the Brandy Library greeted me and other guests to an exclusive bourbon vs. rye tasting that took place in his establishment in TriBeCa. He praised the amazing tradition, heritage, and care that the distillers would put into the process of making these spirits: "Wherever they are made from, they deserve our attention."

Every time I visit the Brandy Library, I experience the same care and consideration with the way Desoblin and his staff treat customers. They make each guest feel special. The well-trained servers pay attention to the guests' tastes and help them navigate through the hefty leather-bound menu. The usually out-of-reach spirits become accessible to the average customer. They create happy, lasting memories and loyal customers.

Whether he intended it or not, in my mind celebrity chef Chris Cosentino from San Francisco drew a parallel with medical professions that are duty-bound to care for people.

"We've chosen a career where we ultimately have signed an oath to take care of people," says chef Cosentino. "That's the hospitality business. Think about how amazing it is, that you go to work and you make people happy. It's not like you go to work and say, 'Sit in that chair, I'm going to pull your teeth out,' or, 'Hey, by the way, you owe $30,000 in taxes this year,' or, 'I'm here to tell you that your son is failing algebra.'"

Cosentino recognizes that a chef will never make everyone happy. "Not everybody is going to love my restaurant. There's a time and place for everybody and everything. But if you can remember the reason why we got in this business is to make people happy, to be hospitable and convivial, then you have more of a chance of success than if you try to tell everybody that it's my way or the highway!"

The 18th century French gastronome Jean-Anthelme Brillat-Savarin said, "To invite a person into your house is to take charge of their happiness for as long as they are under your roof."

Since Brillat-Savarin, scientists have discovered that food has both a psychological and physiological effect on people's moods. Two types of neurotransmitters—norepinephrine and serotonin—are responsible for our moods. The first one stimulates people's bodies and minds, and the second one has a calming influence. Serotonin is often called the "happiness" neurotransmitter. Both are created by compounds found in food, and some foods are better at helping the neurotransmitter production than others. For example, beans, legumes, bananas, oatmeal, fish, and meats are known to increase norepinephrine. Other foods like spinach, eggs, cheese, pineapple, soy products, nuts, salmon, and turkey help increase serotonin levels.

While some foods have been proven to contain compounds that impact mood, others make us feel good just by eating them. We call these "comfort foods" and they provide happiness at a psychological level. As an example, eating a quiche makes me happy because it triggers childhood memories and sends me back to a time when I was seven years old, cooking with my mother in France. For other people it could be mac and cheese or freshly baked chocolate chip cookies. Comfort foods are unique to each person and are subconscious reminders of our personal experiences, and this makes comfort foods critical to our emotional balance. We all have our "Madeleine de Proust"—the smells, tastes, and sounds that bring us back to our childhood with a feeling of being taken care of, or a sense of belonging.

Whether it's psychological or physiological, it's clear that foods have a powerful effect on our moods. It can create a sensation of good feelings and positive reinforcement.

The language of food transcends race, ethnicity, sex, sexuality, age, and class. "Food is an international language that people from any part of the word can relate to, and it brings people together," said chef Roy Yamaguchi (a Japanese-American celebrity chef, restaurateur and founder of Roy's Restaurants). "When, people share a bowl of rice or break bread, they're able to relax more, communicate better, and become friends."

For Yamaguchi, the impact that his cooking and dining experience has on his guests is extremely important. "I have only one project right now with the Eating House concept and our humble Market Kitchen on Maui: I want to continue making our dining experience better for our guests, and make people happy. So, I constantly work on that. My concentration has always been on making sure that all our guests get a memorable experience that they deserve when they come to Roy's. This is the main reason I pulled out from the mainland and why everything now is concentrated on Hawaii."

Additionally, chef Brett Sawyer from Ohio City explained to me that making people happy is indeed the enjoyable part of the game. "It is one of the upsides to a difficult business. It is enjoyable to make people happy with your food and beverage, but it is also a necessity. If you aren't making people happy, you won't be in business long!"

And with new technologies and new food business models rising, sustaining the "make people happy" purpose has become even more challenging. Many additional elements are impacting customers' happiness.

"I'm in the restaurant business, so I still want people to come out to eat," says Jose Garces. "At the same time, I embrace the fact that people want to have the same elevated experiences at home and delivered to them. So, how do we get there? How do we keep them happy?"

With the pandemic, chefs had to embrace the fact that new elements contributed to people's happiness; it took more than cooking good food. Suddenly, the aspects of ordering online, preparation, sanitation, packaging, and on time delivery became the priorities to sustain a positive customer experience and make people happy.

Second Motivation: Attract the Neighborhood

If chefs and mixologists' first motivation is to make their customers happy, they shouldn't try to appeal to everyone. In business, one golden rule is "if you try to appeal to everyone, you will appeal to no one," which means that you can't be everything to everyone, and you must find the right audience for your business. One important ingredient for bars, restaurants, or any food business is knowing their customer demographic and their neighborhood.

Mixologist Beau du Bois in San Diego pressed the importance of engaging and listening to the neighborhood when it comes to building and creating menu items. "I think a lot of bartenders and mixologists fall into the trap of trying to win those magazine covers, or constantly pushing boundaries of creativity. That's great, but honestly, a lot of cocktail critics come in and drink for free. They're not really going to help pay bills. The neighborhood will. Make sure that you're not leaving the neighborhood behind."

Chefs start with a concept and an idea of exactly what they want their restaurant to be. Some of them stick to the original idea, but often, over time, guests will define what they want the restaurant to be.

"You don't have to listen to every one of them," says chef Brett Sawyer, from Cleveland, "but you have to listen to some of them. You must be willing to roll with the punches and change a little bit here and there, because you can stick to your ideals and your guns all you want, but if nobody's walking through the door, your ideals aren't going to get you very far.

"We went in first with a certain idea of how we wanted to serve our food and with the way we wanted service to go, and at some point we realized it wasn't working. We addressed the situation, we figured it out, and we changed a little. Our service got better, and people seemed happier."

Sometimes chefs and restaurant owners learn the hard way when they do not communicate with, or listen to, customers. Chef Andrew McLeod from Avenue M in Asheville, North Carolina candidly shared with me what happened when he became the new chef of that place.

He and his partners decided to develop a concept that would resonate with the nostalgic dimension of the location. Originally, the building used to be a restaurant called Usual Suspects and was known as a bar with a late-night menu. "It was a really popular industry hangout, a late-night spot where chefs and cooks would go over for a nightcap and gather after getting off from work," said McLeod. "We were planning on launching a late-night menu, with the idea to get back to the roots of the place. Unfortunately, we did not take into consideration that Usual Suspects transitioned into a restaurant called Avenue M over time and became a neighborhood restaurant and much less of a bar atmosphere. The locals ended up having preferences for certain dishes from the previous menu."

When McLeod took over, he was stunned by the lengthy three-page menu and the system that was currently in place. He did what every good businessperson would do—he went through a lot of sales data to make sense of what people liked about the place. Collaborators told him that they had seen customers ordering off the "specials" menu more than anything else, because they were just getting tired of having the same thing, week after week.

"I didn't really think that there was that much that people were holding onto, and thought that we could change the way that we were purchasing ingredients, as well as the quality of the food, and let it speak for itself. We changed the brunch and the dinner menu in a week. We didn't do the work of getting the message out there."

McLeod explained that a significant portion of customers were just angry the menu changed and that they couldn't get the dishes they had always loved. Other people were really pleased that the place was being refreshed, but the people who were the loudest were the ones who were upset that thing were different.

"We decided to pare down the menu and brought back a lot of the old dishes. I really felt that this was an opportunity to be of service to the community and give people something that they wanted. We decided to source our products differently, and we obviously executed these old dishes in a way that was at a higher level than they had been previously. We received a lot of praise for that."

Even when a restaurant or a chef is praised in the media, that doesn't mean that people will embrace any of the dishes. "Not true!" said chef Michael Gulotta. "The hard part when Maypop first opened in New Orleans is that I thought, because I had won the *Food & Wine* Best Chef award, people would just eat my food whatever I came up with, and that's not true. The customer must crave what you're putting on the plate and has to be excited about it. So, sometimes I base dishes off what I think the customer wants, and then I add my inspiration to it."

Additionally, today there has been a shift in what people are seeking. The public is more informed and knowledgeable about food, ingredients, and how dishes are prepared. And if part of the enjoyment of this industry is being constantly challenged and succeeding, chef Jose Garces says it still comes with new obstacles. Customers' needs are constantly changing with trends.

The millennial generation (people born between 1980 and 1995) started the "foodie lifestyle" with a strong focus on craftsmanship and fresh and local ingredients. Food and drinks were the key topic of millennial conversations. Farmers' markets flourished across the country and neighborhood farms and "pick your own" fruit and vegetables were the new big thing. Food trucks, food carts, and food halls started to be a constant source of innovation, providing simple, good food. Millennials asked for more varied, extreme, and edgy tastes, and food businesses were constantly challenged to produce new items and experiment with new dishes to keep menus appealing to them.

Then the Gen Z generation arrived (people born between the mid-1990s and the mid-2000s), the most ethnically diverse generation in U.S. history. They have been more exposed to health and wellness education than any other generation. A wider spectrum of health and wellness products and services have been available to them throughout their lives. Gen Z are looking for natural and organic ingredients with no additives. They are also prone to select products that have a strong connection to sustainability. Menus now need to reflect healthier choices, allowing more health-oriented substitutions. Young consumers are making note of how food businesses use waste, and are putting pressure on menus to have world flavor options.

Nonetheless, chef Sawyer added, "Customers being more educated and informed is a double-edged sword. It allows chefs to be more creative, but it also makes the guest feel emboldened to act a certain way—a bit snobbier. But the uneducated culinary guest is also more difficult, because they truly don't understand what it is chefs are trying to convey. They just see things they have never heard of."

As a result, a lot of businesses create "customer personas" to help define all the characteristics and important insights related to their customers. A customer persona is a fictitious model of an ideal customer. It generally includes demographics (age, gender, location, and occupation) as well as psychographics (motivations, likes, dislikes). When customer personas are created, business owners can start turning insights into specific actions.

By focusing on what customers are ordering, chefs and mixologists can create dishes and drinks that resonate with them. Understanding the customer persona means speaking their language in material communication, and partnering with people their "personas" love.

Third Motivation: In the Name of Exploration, Curiosity, and Art

Cooking is a way of exploring new territories and bringing people along, both kitchen and bar teams, and consumers.

"Basically, it is taking people outside their box to experience something new and also bringing in new stuff all the time," says chef Sam Freund from restaurant White Birch in New Jersey. "People who work for me have to constantly learn new ingredients. I think it's important to showcase all that you know and also to keep learning. I just want people to really understand the depth of flavor of all food and not just want short ribs every time they come to my restaurant, White Birch. I want them to make that next step, take that leap of confidence, and try something new that they never tried before.

"Chefs around here aren't challenging the consumers enough. I'm all about challenging the consumer by making them want to come back for new dishes, new excitement, and new creations."

Aside from cooking to make people happy, chefs are also cooking for themselves. "We are in a business where we love what we do," says Gabriel Kreuther, "but at the end of the day, we also cook a little bit for ourselves. We cook what we want to eat, and hopefully in doing so, we engage with the customer, and hopefully they have a great moment with us."

Aren't chefs bored cooking the same dishes?

Yes, according to chef Sawyer. "A lot of the places I've worked at repeated dishes in every season and eventually it got boring for the chefs and the cooks. When you've made the same thing a hundred times and it goes away for six or seven months, it comes back, and you must start making it again. It's great for the guests who get to eat the same thing they liked, but for the kitchen it is a little boring.

"At Plum Café, we changed the menu whenever we felt like it. People have embraced the idea that they could come in almost every other week and get something that they didn't have the week before. Well, we did have a couple staples that have stayed on for a little longer than I would have ever liked," added Sawyer with a smile. "But we did understand that you have to please customers sometimes as you can't really run a restaurant without them! I think most chefs get into it for the creativity and love of the game. It is about the practice and the rigor around what it takes to be good."

Whether it is mastering techniques to the extreme of making dishes appear as simple as possible, or learning how to build and balance flavors, for chefs or for mixologists, cooking and mixing cocktails is driven by curiosity and a desire for being unique and discovering unknown, unvalued, or neglected ingredients.

Two simple examples come to mind in terms of chefs challenging the status quo and exploring new territories.

Chef Kim Alter, who came up with an allium (allium vegetables include garlic, onion, leeks, chives, scallions) ice cream at Nightbird in San Francisco, explained, "It's nothing that I think ever went on the menu, but I like to make burnt onion stocks and I've made a burnt onion ice cream and combined it with a really sweet acidic sorbet. I loved the bitterness and sweetness characters from the allium ice cream. I want people to eat something and not be like, 'That's interesting.' I want them to say, 'That's delicious!'"

The second example is from chef Elizabeth Falkner, who added fish sauce to a caramel sauce. "I'm a huge fan of fish sauce. I love putting it randomly on desserts, where people don't know what it is, but they really like it. Especially with caramelized notes, any kind of caramel sauce with a little bit of fish sauce is so tasty. That could be in savory or sweet recipes. One day, I have put it in tiramisu and called it, 'Miso-Funky-Misu!'"

Many of the chefs I talked to refer to themselves as craftsmen and have challenged the artist label. A craftsman is someone who has mastered skills through many hours of study, practice, discipline, focus, and passion. A craftsman excels in what he or she is doing. Consequently, all artists are not craftsmen, and all craftsmen are not artists.

Nonetheless, chef Johnny Spero commented in an interview, "People always say that cooking is not an art, it's a craft. I feel there are different levels of cuisines and different types of restaurants. There are different approaches, but chefs always had an artistic side."

"There are definitely chefs who like to paint on plates and do a little bit more than putting just food on a plate. We're not just cutting a piece of meat and putting a blob of sauce on it and serving it out. It can be an expression of how I see food and how I want it to be perceived. Whether it's the way we garnish it, or the way that something is presented on the plate, or just the plates themselves.

"I make sure the food tastes good; that always has to be the number one priority. After that, we're like, 'OK, how do we want to present this where it's created in our vision, and people can look at it?' We want people to be like, 'That's a dish from Reverie.' Stylistically, we have our own way of doing things. It starts off with what we're plating on. One of my best friends, Amber

Kendrick, has a company called Cloud Terre. She designed most of the plates for Reverie. We talked about it: it's like a canvas. We talk about the colors that I use when I cook, and it's not because I intentionally choose to cook with this; they're usually dark, and there's a lot of berries, and a lot of vibrant herbs. You put that on a black or green plate, it's not going to look the same, but when you have it on this kind of matte white plate that has a little bit of an off-set glaze, and they're all a little bit different, then you have this beautiful, vibrant dish that stands out. I mean, if we didn't care about how the food looked, we'd be serving it in cardboard boxes. I think it gives me opportunities to have a little bit of finesse, and it doesn't change the way the food tastes, but I think it changes the way that it's perceived."

Furthermore, some chefs combined their artistic talent in cooking with other artistic disciplines, like Alison Trent in Los Angeles. "I do a lot of visual arts on the side. I do a lot of painting, sculpture, and ceramics. I'm an absolute fan of anything visual arts-related. For my event company, Alison Trent Events, I really wanted to make something unique where I was marrying all these things together. It's not just a catering company that's shoving canapés in your face; it's creating beautiful installations using ceramics. It can be stationery and people are just drawn to it. It's food on art, and I think some people have never seen something so avant-garde in terms of some of these plates. We've been eating out of vessels for as long as we can remember, but that connection between what we eat from and what we eat is sometimes lost in the mix of things. I really believe collaboration is the key to moving forward."

Like artists, chefs desire appreciation. Chef Jose Garces says, "One of my creative inspirations is when I see someone enjoying their first bite or taste of my food. Seeing that reaction is like an artist seeing someone appreciate their art."

On the opposite end, chefs believe that the motivation for creativity should have a business reality frame. "Be unique in food style and execution," said chef Ehren Ryan, "but stay close to the core concept of the restaurant."

Chefs need to create unique restaurant concepts to set themselves apart and create media attention. Some have launched special pop-up concepts, teamed up with local farmers, featured rotating guest chefs, partnered with local breweries, turned off the lights to eat in the dark and focus on all the other senses, turned the kitchen into a stage, or explored local history for inspiration.

As an example, chef Brother Luck shared the background story behind his concept for restaurant Four by Luck. "When I came home to Colorado, I was getting ready to open my next restaurant, and I was asking myself what was so unique about Colorado?"

His research took him through the following thought process: Colorado is about Southwestern food, but other chefs have already successfully explored this space. The location is somewhat unique situated at the Four Corners—Colorado, Utah, New Mexico, and Arizona. The region saw the Anglo-Saxon, the pioneers, and the Spanish Conquest, with the trade coming up through Central America, spreading religion and creating missions throughout California, New Mexico, Arizona, and Colorado. Finally, his research taught him about local Native American tribes and their food. "I was reading about the Ute tribe, which was indigenous to the Pikes Peak region where I live in southern Colorado. I read a quote that said, 'Pre-contact, we were experts at hunting, fishing, farming, and gathering, which made us excellent cooks.' I stopped and thought, 'Wow, that's my restaurant!'"

The Four by Luck's website says, "There are four key people who I need to work with to source amazing ingredients: hunters, gatherers, farmers, and fishermen."

"I want people to eat something and not be like, 'That's interesting.' I want them to say, 'That's delicious!'"
—CHEF KIM ALTER

Fourth Motivation: Cooking for Status and Gain Experience

I have often heard chefs say, "Don't become a chef if you want to make money!" This is not the reason people get into this industry. The compensation is modest, at least at the beginning, and a lot of young cooks have student loans to pay from culinary schools. By the time they pay the rent, the insurance, the employees, the purveyors, the equipment and flatware, they don't have much left. Running a restaurant is a business and chefs must do everything possible to make their business profitable. It is not always that easy. Labor cost is going up, turnover is high, and food costs are going up as well, and rent and insurance are not going away.

Customers are getting savvier, which requires chefs to develop more complex recipes to stay on trend. This industry is a single-digit margin business, especially in major cities. Everyone in the restaurant and food business knows that there are important elements that they need to pay attention to in a timely manner, such as weekly checks on cost-of-goods sold, and food cost, monthly reviews of recipe plate costs, menu profitability, and quarterly business reviews with suppliers. While people assume that owning a restaurant is an exciting way to make money from a passion and a way to become famous, in fact, it takes an unbelievable amount of hard week and the ability to withstand enormous pressure and stress.

Like anything else, the approach to business for chefs evolves with the years of experience. At first, young chefs want to acquire status, stand out from the crowd, and put their name on the culinary map. Young chefs want to stick to what they want to cook, ignoring the customer's point of view. The famous phrase comes to mind here, "My way or the highway!"

Chef Hari Cameron started with a menu at a(MUSE.) , in Rehoboth, Delaware that was abstract and deconstructed in profile. He wanted the guests to create their own tasting menu by ordering down the menu. "We were in a place where, half of the year we were inundated with tourists. That was a great thing, as Rehoboth is a beach town. We were a block from the ocean. The rest of the year, it becomes a small town again. We quickly had to listen to our guests and go to a standard format after about a year. Because people just wanted an entree, a big plate, and they wanted to go out and do whatever they were doing with their nightlife. As a young chef, I was very conflicted. It was difficult. The young person in me wanted it the way I wanted it."

Often, beginning chefs want to impose their will on it. Cameron learned it the hard way. He decided to change the menu to adapt it to the core seasonal customer group. They offered "a la carte" and a five-course tasting menu. "If guests wanted to come in, have a glass of rosé and eat cheese, they could sit at the bar and do that. If they wanted a full tour of the seasons, they could do that as well. That was my compromise. I still was able to cook food for people who came in from D.C. and New York, who were used to food that was manipulated, with ingredients that weren't as common."

Another important motivation for younger chefs is working on developing their skills and acquiring experiences. With executive chefs favoring hands-on experience versus culinary education, spending time staging and working at various kitchens, or under specific renowned chefs, becomes critical to building a résumé.

I remember talking to chefs Sayat and Laura Ozyilmaz, who took staging to the extreme as they spent their honeymoon after culinary school touring the U.S. and building their experience and their career as a chef, staging around the country.

With more and more young cooks graduating from culinary schools and getting this formal training, they have been exposed to career coaching and goal-setting processes. Being told at culinary school, or by mentors, to identify what type of chefs they ultimately want to become, young chefs learned how to set up short-term, mid-term, and long-term goals to develop a career path. With this map in hand, they apply for a position that will help them achieve one of their short-term goals, acquire a skill, and then move on to their next goal. If it can be reached within the same establishment, they will probably stay. If not, they will look for another restaurant under another executive chef who will help them reach their next goal.

Fifth Motivation: Cooking for Instant Gratification, Pride, and Leaving a Lasting Impression

Home cooks find instant gratification when they see smiles on the faces of family and friends as they taste their meal. For professional chefs, there is an understanding and a near-obsessive desire to perfect their craft, to create perfect dishes and be able to share it with their guests and see the expression on their faces.

Cooking, especially when done for others, can bring positive psychological benefits, and these positive effects could be enough to get people into the kitchen. Performing the act of cooking for other people is a form of altruism; it can make people feel happy and connected to one another. It is a form of nurturing and a way to boost confidence and self-esteem.

"I want to be inspired by the clients," says Alison Trent. "As I do event creation, like team building exercises for a corporate company or open houses in beautiful locations, I love working one-on-one with the clients to create absolutely stand-out, unique experiences that leave the guests saying, 'Oh wow, I've never seen anything like that before.'

"I can marry all my passions in life—visual arts, installation, cooking in different environments, not being trapped in one kitchen and four walls—and then put everything together. In events like these, people want to meet the chef, the farmers, the beekeepers, or the pastry chef. It's an eclectic group of people that have all come together and are sharing the meal and appreciating every aspect of it. There's so many restaurants you can go to that have really delicious food, but having the experience that you really feel you were a part of something changes people's life in some way."

Achieving Michelin-star level for a restaurant and its team is a real moment of pride, and chef Gabriel Kreuther shared the moment when his restaurant received two Michelin stars.

"I can tell you that the team felt amazingly proud of achieving this," says Kreuther. "This is not just me achieving this. This is the whole team working together since we opened the restaurant five years ago, towards getting the two stars Michelin; it has always been our goal. Right after three months of opening, we were lucky to get our first star, and we were very proud because we never thought it was going to be that fast. It gave extra power to the team to really seek for the next goal, which was the second star.

"We felt funny because we didn't know what to expect, and suddenly at eleven o'clock, I got a phone call from the big director of Michelin who wanted to talk to me. 'We give you the second star, two-star Michelin.'

"I jumped, overjoyed, and went to the lineup and announced it to the team. Everybody was excited, and that evening, all together, we celebrated with a glass of champagne. It was a feeling of accomplishment, but it was interesting because it was an accomplishment for the past almost. We worked very hard to accomplish something, and then we got rewarded for it, but that reward was literally for yesterday."

There are many variables beyond food that contribute to customers' happiness and to transforming any eating-out situation into a noteworthy experience. These factors even weigh differently based on individuals' life conditions, life stages, and need states. In other words, the components that contribute to making a consumer happy at a restaurant will vary considerably. You might be on a first date, celebrating a romantic anniversary, having dinner with your young children, or feasting out with friends.

The environment, the atmosphere, the degree of people interaction, the quality of the staff, the element of surprise, the menu choices, the food ingredients, and the plating, all contribute to the satisfaction level of the clients. When it comes to food, certain individuals will have a memorable experience with straightforward, quality ingredients combined with perfect techniques. Others will search for a sophisticated creative process.

Chapter 2

THE FLAVOR-
MEMORY DATABASE

"Inspiration varies a lot. It can be driven by a need, meaning it's Spring out and we know we need to change the menu. It could be driven by boredom, tired of looking at a dish, or it could literally be like being struck by lightning."
—CHEF DAN KLUGER

List of culinary individuals featured in this chapter:

Chef/Owner **Dan Kluger** from Loring Place in Manhattan and Penny Ridge in Long Island City

Chef **Johnny Spero** from Reverie in Washington, D.C.

Iron Chef, author, entrepreneur, and food innovator **Jose Garces** from Philadelphia

Chef and restaurateur **Tim Hollingsworth** at Otium and C.J. Boyd's in Los Angeles

Chef/Owner **Michael Gulotta** of MoPho and MayPop in New Orleans

Executive chef **Drake Leonards** at Eunice in Houston

Chef/Co-Owner **Brad Miller** of The Inn at the Seventh Ray in Topanga Canyon, California

Chef/Owner **Alison Trent** of Alison Trent Events in Los Angeles (was at Ysabel in Los Angeles)

Executive chef **Matt Bolus** at 404 Kitchen in Nashville

Retired Executive Chef **Andre Natera** from Fairmont Hotel in Austin, Texas

Chef and restaurateur **Jamie Bissonnette** from Toro, Copa, and Little Donkey in Boston

Chef/Owner **Brian Ahern** of Boeufhaus in Chicago

Chef/consultant **Mark Welker**, former executive pastry chef at Eleven Madison Park and NoMad

Executive chef **Jean Marie Josselin** at JO2 on Kauai, Hawaii

Chef/Owner **Brother Luck** from Four by Luck at Colorado Springs, Colorado

Charlotte Voisey, global head of ambassadors for William Grant & Sons based in Brooklyn

Mixologist **Bob Peters** in Charlotte, North Carolina

Chef/Owner **Kim Alter** of Nightbird and Linden Room in San Francisco

Consulting Chef **Elizabeth Falkner** based in Los Angeles

Pastry Chef **Antonio Bachour** from Bachour Miami in Miami

Chef/Co-Owner **Fiore Tedesco** from L'Oca d'Oro in Austin, Texas

Pastry Chef **Emily Spurlin** formerly at Bad Hunter in Chicago

Celebrity Chef and Restaurateur **David Burke** in New York, New Jersey, North Carolina, Colorado, and Riyadh

Chef and **Author Edward Lee**, chef/owner of 610 Magnolia and Whiskey Dry in Louisville; culinary director of Succotash at National Harbor in Maryland, and Penn Quarter in Washington, D.C

Chef and Author **Chris Shepherd**, operating Underbelly Hospitality Group in Houston

According to Google, the definition for inspiration is "…the process of being mentally stimulated to do or feel something, especially to do something creative." I suddenly got a mental image of everyone I had on the show always "plugged in" to the ether. Do they wake up at three in the morning, dreaming of an idea and writing it down on a notepad? Do they have a small notebook in their back pocket and take frenetic notes when they travel? They've probably now replaced the iconic chef notebook by taking notes directly on their smartphone.

There are so many facets to inspiration and so many different ways for a dish or a drink to come about. None of the guest chefs I've interviewed have ever been able, nor had the desire, to settle on a single way. I understand the definition of being "mentally stimulated," but a precondition needs to exist before something can be stimulated and some kind of data had to be stored first in the person's cognitive memory.

Chef Johnny Spero from Reverie in Washington, D.C. explained his sources of inspiration this way: "A lot of it is about tasting and feeling the food. The only way you can do that is to get out there and just taste the world, and build this culinary database of flavors, colors, and textures." Listening to all these culinary leaders over the years, it became clear that their inspiration process was twofold: first they had to feed, consciously or unconsciously, the cognitive memory of their food experiences, and then somehow be exposed to various stimuli that would activate their memory database.

Beyond the seasonal need for change and the fresh produce as sources of inspiration, it was the idea of being "struck by lightning," mentioned by chef Dan Kluger, that intrigued me, and I decided to delve into it further.

"On Sundays, my father would buy my brother and I Kentucky Fried Chicken. That was our lunch after we were done playing soccer and had jumped in Lake Michigan. I always kept that memory, and when I opened Volver in Philadelphia, I wanted to re-create that experience and elevate it. I took beautiful locally raised farm squabs and stuffed the inside breast meat with foie gras and served these with stunning biscuits. The pomme puree was chef Robuchon-inspired with sweet corn sauce. I just put this whole memory of my childhood on a plate."

—CHEF JOSE GARCES

For most chefs and many food enthusiasts, culinary inspiration comes from memories of their youth. I have memories of food that takes me back to my childhood, but, like most of us, I am missing the genius, skills, and techniques to convert fond memories into stunning drinks and dishes.

I was probably no more than eight years old; I remember walking down Main Street in a tiny village in the middle of nowhere in the Northeast region of France with an aluminum can in my hand. And there was only one street in Ville-sur-Saulx, this village where my father was born—it led from the church, at the bottom of the village, to the cemetery located in the opposite direction at the top of the hill, at the edge of the forest. My father used to say that this street was a representation of life: baptism at the church at the dawn of life and the cemetery at the dusk of life. Anyway, I was only about eight years old and very removed from these philosophical questions about life and death. Like every Sunday morning during the month of August, I was allowed to walk on my own to accomplish a mission given by my mother to go to the farm at the bottom of the village and bring her back fresh cream and fresh milk. Back in the early '70s, farms were the only places to get daily dairy products in isolated French villages. People drove to the supermarket only once a week. I always loved looking at the farmer's wife scooping the cream with a big ladle from a large container to generously fill my aluminum pot. Walking back home, I recall opening the lid and dipping my finger into the thick cream and licking it with delight. I made sure to quiver the pot to even the surface of the cream to avoid sanctions from my mother.

But the best part of these Sundays was after church when jumping in the car with my father. We drove to the village bakery to buy croissants, brioches Parisiennes, and my favorite, le pâté Lorrain. The pâté Lorrain is a French dish consisting of marinated meat wrapped in puff pastry. Pure paradise! The meat (usually pork loin, veal, and rabbit) is sliced and marinated in a flavorful mixture of wine, thyme, parsley, bay leaves, and shallots. Before baking, it is completely enclosed in puff pastry. I remember watching the baker bringing the rack full of these rectangular shaped pâtés from the back of the bakery as an aroma of warm pastry mixed with spiced cooked meat filled the entire shop.

Subsequent to the quiche Lorraine made by my mother, the pâté Lorrain was definitely my best childhood taste memory. My mother always started August Sunday lunches by serving a slice of the pâté to everyone sitting around the table. I loved the contrast of the flaky and crispy, golden brown, warm pastry on the outside and the still moist dough on the inside that already absorbed some flavors from the meat, herbs, and wine marinade. This unique aroma and taste is etched into my brain and every time I smell or taste a warm croissant filled with sausage or any other meat filling, it brings me back to my eight-year-old self and my summer Sundays in this tiny village where my father now rests peacefully at the top of Main Street overlooking the woods he particularly loved, and that we often wandered through foraging for mushrooms.

It was amusing to recall my own early flavor childhood memories when listening to the ones shared by the chefs on the podcast. Mine were connected to croissants, quiches, and pâtés Lorrain from France, while my guests recalled having fried chicken with their families. I guess I really deserve the nickname, "Champagne Charlie!"

Similar to Garces' KFC memories, chef Tim Hollingsworth of Los Angeles has memories of fried chicken from his childhood. He named one of his restaurants C.J. Boyd's after his grandfather, Cecil Jordan Boyd.

"He's long gone now. He died close to twenty years ago, and my earliest food memory was on payday. He would go to KFC. That's the date he sprung for it. I'm sure money had a little bit to do with it, and a little bit of health behind eating fried chicken every two weeks was better than eating it every week. One of our catch slogans at C.J. Boyd's is, 'It's payday good.' That was the inspiration behind our restaurant. I wanted to take that Southern fried chicken and apply it to my current life—living in L.A., with all the different cultures that we have here and all the exposure that I have to them and how much I've learned from them and been inspired by them.

"Another memory from my childhood is my grandfather making nachos. He wasn't a chef by any means, but I remember the precision he took with the plate of tortilla chips, putting them in one layer, and on every single chip he placed a slice of cheese. He then microwaved it, and then put a little bit of sour cream, a little bit of salsa, and an olive on every chip. Each of them was a perfect bite. I still think about the amount of patience that it required. He was an inspiration to me."

"There are so many different ways for a dish to come about. Sometimes, I'll eat something at a friend's house or at a restaurant, and this will inspire me to do my own take on it."
—CHEF MICHAEL GULOTTA

A second way that chefs build their flavor memories is eating at other restaurants, and having conversations with mentors, other cooks, and people they interact with all day.

In 1997, my then-boss staged a food experience I will never forget. "Come to the kitchen, I have something to show you!" insisted Roberto, grabbing me by the arm and taking me away from the rest of the group of people who had just arrived in his apartment. Roberto was my manager, and the people gathered in his apartment, in a residential district of Cannes, France, were his direct reports—including me—and our spouses. As we were all foodies, I had recommended organizing a rotating-dinner series in each other's houses and whoever hosted would cook for the others. I thought this would be a great way to bond and create a well-connected team. It was the end of the '90s in France, and everyone in the group loved the idea.

Roberto was from Italy, loved his country, and was proud of the produce from Italy. While working with him, he introduced me to some fantastic wines like Montepulciano, Barbaresco, Barolo, and Nebbiolo. When we dined at his place, we always started the dinner with champagne. These amazing evenings are engraved in my memory.

Roberto knew my passion for food and wine, and several months before this fall dinner, he spoke with passion about the white truffle season in Alba, Italy. Each year, he would go there with an Italian friend and organize a dinner with a fourteen-course tasting menu served with white truffle. He explained that the waiter would present and weigh the white truffle before dinner, shave them on top of each dish, weigh them again at the end of the dinner, and then give the guests the amount of money they would have to pay. I heard about these legendary dinners for a couple of years, as Roberto was trying to convince my wife and I to join. We hesitated for a long time, but we were young and the price of a weekend in Alba, partying with Roberto and his friends, would have been too much for us. I politely declined and still regret it today. It was a unique opportunity that I missed!

While entering Roberto's kitchen that evening, I saw a little smile on his face and a sparkle in his eyes. The pasta machine was still on the table, which indicated that my boss spent the afternoon making fresh pasta for us. He opened the fridge and took out a closed plastic container. He turned towards me, opened the cover, and removed the paper towel to offer to my eyes two gigantic white truffles.

"Emmanuel, you couldn't come to Alba…so I brought Alba to you," said Roberto with undeniable excitement in his voice. We went back to the dining room with his precious, expensive treasure to show to the rest of the group. After champagne, wine, appetizers, and the first course, the time for the fresh pasta came and Roberto delicately and generously shaved the white truffles over the servings. I do not remember the other food that we ate that evening, but when I close my eyes, I remember to this day the pungent aroma and the subtle flavor of this pasta dish. Unconsciously, I stored this experience in my flavor memory bank, and every time I smell the aroma of white truffle, it brings me back to that day on the French Riviera, looking at the shimmering lights above the bay of Cannes, and that unique moment of discovering the precious white truffles, carefully protected in their plastic container like two raw diamonds in a jewelry box.

In fact, 1997 was a great year when it came to recording food memories in my database. I met world-renowned pastry chef Pierre Hermé that same year. It was in Ladurée on the Champs-Elysées in Paris. I had a business lunch with him to discuss the content of a stage session for an event called Des arômes et Des Hommes, "Flavors and the Men who Create Them." More than twenty years have passed, and if I do not remember the specifics of our conversation, raspberry has never had the same meaning for me since that day at Ladurée when I tasted his now legendary Ispahan concept, combining raspberry, litchi, and rose.

These two people had a strong impact on me that year: One was a famous pastry chef, the other was a passionate food enthusiast. They both exposed me to unfamiliar flavors. When I interviewed chef Drake Leonards twenty years after, he said something that resonated with me: "Just being exposed and being around new things and people with different backgrounds will eventually just start rubbing off on you, whether you think it does or not. You will use it later on in life, the day that you pick an ingredient at a local market or use it five or ten years later. You never know where it's going to come into play in your life, but it will rub off somehow, someway."

Similarly, chef Brad Miller shared a great example that took place during one of the episodes of his TV show *Truck Nation*.

"I wouldn't say I would do this in my restaurant, but I was definitely intrigued when I was at the Bread and Circuses food truck in Seattle. They had this nacho cheeseburger where they deep-fried the patty and put all the nacho cheese accouterments onto the burger. It was just amazing! When I took a bite of it, it literally tasted as if I went down to the end of a big, loaded nacho. I really thought it would taste like a burger with a bunch of stuff on it, but the way he put everything together in the meat, the coating on the outside of the burger with nacho crumbs, the fried flavor, the olives, the sour cream, and the guacamole, even with the bun, it tasted like it was a big nacho. I was shocked by that experience. I know that I will never make that Bread and Circuses' recipe in any of my burgers, but somehow, along my lifeline, maybe in a month, maybe in a year, or two, it's going to come into play somehow. Something will spark the memory. I'll be like, 'Oh, I remember when the guy coated this in Doritos and fried it and made it taste like a big load of nachos.' The taste, the process, and the technique might come back to me. That's a lot of what my life is. A lot of things come back to mind. I might not use that exact method or flavor profile, but I'll definitely use it somewhere down the line."

In the same way, Brett Sawyer from The Plum in Ohio City confided to me that much of his inspiration comes from things that he has already eaten. "Things from my past. Memories of certain foods that I loved. I don't like to admit it, but sometimes even certain fast-food items could be a source of inspiration."

When I asked him about any guilty food pleasures, he admitted, "I particularly love the sauce from Big Boy burgers! I like to think about the flavor profiles of stuff and then my process is to figure out similar flavor profiles in those veins. There's no one way that we get from A to Z on a dish. Sometimes it'll be a certain produce coming into season or our farmer will say, 'Hey we're going to have this soon,' or you see it on one of our farm lists so it can start with the ingredient. I will then build the flavor profile around it and figure out what the vehicle is for delivering that ingredient to somebody's mouth. Sometimes it can start with a dish I ate. As an example, I really enjoy going to the northern part of Florida, in the Tampa area. There's a lot of fish houses there, and they all have a smoked fish dip. It's very common but it's something I love. After eating different versions so many times, it was something I really wanted to take on and do my own version."

"Working alongside other artists and chefs that are like-minded is extremely important. There's been such a culture of ego in kitchens for so long, and cooking, and everyone sort of wanting to be the best and so competitive, and knowing you have to be competitive. I honestly think that collaboration is the future of the industry. The only way you continue learning is by being exposed to different things, and being a chef is a profession where you can never know it all. As a chef you should see what other people are doing, sharing recipes and experiences, and I think that's where the industry is heading."

—CHEF ALISON TRENT

I was turning fifty and, unlike most of my male friends and colleagues who chose not to celebrate this milestone, I had decided to turn the occasion into a special moment and an ideal opportunity to bring family members, old friends from France, and new American friends together. We rented a huge house in Vermont with a large, fully equipped kitchen that would allow us to cook all together. To overcome the language barrier, I relied on the international language of food to break the ice. One main event of the four-day weekend took place in that kitchen on the evening of everyone's arrival. Each party had to bring dishes or recipes and ingredients to prepare on site two dishes of their choice, connected to their cultural heritage. After a moment of chaos, everyone organized themselves and, with wine and beer easing the flow of communication, I witnessed this diverse group of people engaged in bizarre conversations mixing French and English words. Everyone became curious about what other people had brought with them, or were cooking. My sister prepared her legendary Burgundy poulet à la crème, my friend Junior Merino created his famous cocktail, Coming-Up Roses, while friends from Germany made their homemade pretzels, and friends from California cooked chilaquiles. It was so extraordinary that I put together a cookbook with everyone's recipes and gave it as a present to all participants.

Two other moments of collaboration during those four-day birthday celebrations were an old world versus new world wine tasting and the exposure to American craft beers for the French visitors. Prior to the event, I connected my brother, who is part of a wine tasting club in Avignon in France, with my friend Junior, a mixologist, chef, and wine expert based in the U.S. Their mission was to work together and identify several wine grape varietals common in Europe and in the Americas and bring the selected bottles to Vermont, educate the group, have a good time, and decide which from the old world or new world would win. It was a long tasting session; our organizers went overboard sharing their extensive knowledge of both white and red grapes, while a lot of the attendees wanted simply to enjoy the wines. The result: new world wines won, to the huge disappointment of my die-hard Burgundy brother-in-law! My four-day birthday weekend celebration in Vermont was a great example of collaboration and exchanges between cultures.

More recently, the pandemic has compelled chefs to work together. People were stuck at home, had to cancel vacation plans, nobody could travel, and the only thing they wanted to do was to get out, but were not able to. Some chefs capitalized on people's longing for the dream of travel since physically exploring the globe or the country was no longer a possibility. Chef Matt Bolus from The 404 Kitchen in Nashville created the Passport Dinners Series, a concept that brings other chefs' cuisines to Nashville residents.

"We started reaching out to other chefs, and the idea was received with a lot of enthusiasm," says chef Bolus. "We brought Andrew Zimmer, Marcus Sanderson, Carla Hall, and other chefs' famous dishes to people in Nashville." Between these chefs and his team, Bolus collaborated on the menus. There was a lot of recipe sharing and trials and tweaking. "One of the things we loved before was having a guest chef, or staging at another chef's restaurant. With the Passport Dinners Series, we were able to do that, and experienced other recipes, which was another point of inspiration to me. I got to work with all these wonderful people, and tried and experienced new things." Similarly, during the pandemic, Kelly English, chef and owner of Memphis' restaurants Iris and Second Line, created sixty wine dinners in collaboration with a local wine store that took his customers around the world (e.g., Barcelona, Portugal, Sicily, Burgundy, Corsica, Croatia, etc.).

In the restaurant world today, collaboration has come to mean special events put on by one or more guest chefs and a host chef to jointly prepare a dinner or a tasting menu.

Chef Trent says, "There's so many restaurants you can go to that have really delicious food, and you walk away thinking, 'Oh, that was great,' but having the experience to really feel like you were a part of something, it changes your life in some way. It takes you out of your comfort zone."

For chefs, collaboration can push them out of their comfort zone and provide new ideas to bring back to their own kitchens.

Chefs and restaurateurs Ken Oringer and Jamie Bissonnette (the duo behind Toro, Coppa and Little Donkey in the Boston area) have known each other for about twenty years and worked together for more than a decade. "Together we kind of do it all," says Bissonnette. "We run the food and the business portion. We help the managers cultivate the teams, and we collaborate. Our catchphrase is, whenever we see each other, 'Hey, do you want to catch up?' It could be about a new dish. Sometimes I'll show up at one of the restaurants where I know that we are going to meet, with a cookbook that I know he hasn't seen, and then we read the cookbook and talk about that, together. We both travel a fair amount independently. For a long time we traveled once or twice a year together, but we would both travel independently more often. We have so much more fun when we're together, because we both just want to see and taste everything. We're like children. I don't think a lot of other people can keep up with us."

"Make sure that whenever you can get time to travel, eat where the locals eat. Find the off-the-beaten-path places, and just keep your eyes open."
—CHEF BRIAN AHERN

Throughout my taste explorations and travels, I have expanded my aroma, flavor, and texture database. While writing this book, I realized that some years I have done more than sixty tastings at restaurants, bars, and food stores around the country, and that I had traveled to more than thirty countries! Several years back, I made a promise to my daughter that I would take her to the country of her choice to celebrate her college graduation. She always wanted to go to Africa, and she decided on Morocco. In 2018, I studied the map of Morocco and started planning our father-daughter trip in the southern part of the country. Chef Mourad Lalou from San Francisco gave me great recommendations and must-visit places from his country of origin. After spending time in Marrakech, we took the bus to Essaouira.

Essaouira had a lot of nicknames throughout history, and my favorite is the "Atlantic Blue Pearl." Until the '60s, the city was known as Mogador, and the harbor, ramparts, and the city walls have been featured in popular movies like *The Gladiator* by Ridley Scott, or the HBO hit series *Game of Thrones*. From the various tourist options the town offered, we decided to learn how to cook with a local in the kitchen of our apartment—a real experience not to be missed.

Fatima sat with us at the dinner table and asked us which traditional dishes we wanted to learn to cook. We selected the couscous and the chicken tajine. I volunteered to join Fatima at the market and noticed surprise and discomfort on her face, but she didn't make any comments and we would learn later the reason for her reaction. I followed Fatima in the crowded and sunny streets of Essaouira along the famous ochre pigment of its ramparts that contrasted with the whiteness of the houses and the bright blue of the doors and shutters, which makes it the blue pearl of the Atlantic. Like all the women in the town, Fatima was wearing a dark caftan—a long lightweight dress—and the only touch of color was her bright pink and turquoise headscarf. She knew her way around and, in a few minutes, she took me from our Airbnb rental to the market in the Medina. We ended up in a larger street with open shops on both sides. Each boutique was only large enough for one or two people to work behind counters that offered colorful vegetables and fruits, bags of spices and dry blossoms, or cuts of meats and poultry. Fatima had an established route for her favorite locations, but I kept regularly distracting her with my never-ending questions and desire to taste everything. I had never seen such amazing pyramid-shaped stacks of black, green, and reddish olives. I wanted to buy everything. I discovered a taste for preserved lemons, and a passion for Moroccan sweet mint tea. Fatima smiled as she watched me speak French with the shopkeepers. I really had a blast in the Medina market of Essaouira.

Back at the apartment, Fatima started preparing the mint tea and we invited her to join us. We inquired about her life in Essaouira, and, in the conversation, we came to understand why she was embarrassed that I joined her at the market. She explained that it was not appropriate for a local married woman to walk alone on the streets with a man who was not her husband.

That day, my daughter and I learned how to prepare a traditional couscous and a chicken tajine with the preserved lemon and olives bought at the market. The small building where our apartment was located had a beautiful rooftop, and we enjoyed our Moroccan dinner under the Milky Way with a bird's eye view on the Medina and the city walls. This food memory will always be associated with the sound of the muezzin calls to prayer that marked the rhythm of our days in Morocco.

In the same way, the time I spent in the market shops of Essaouira opened my eyes to a whole new world of herbs and spices—a main source of inspiration for chefs and mixologists comes from experiencing meals during their travels. Describing his trip to Japan, Anthony Bourdain summarized the experience the best: "It was absolutely life-changing. It was like my first acid trip. It was that mind-expanding and climactic. I came back thinking about everything in a completely different way."

In my conversation with pastry chef Mark Welker (former executive pastry chef at Eleven Madison Park in New York City), he encouraged people to travel. "It's good to get out of the country and see how small the world is, and how small life is. It makes you think differently. It helps you get out of your shell."

Before the pandemic, a growing appreciation of culinary culture had transformed the way people traveled, and food was at the center of many trips. In recent years, food tourism has constantly been increasing. The trend didn't just involve eating at restaurants and drinking creative cocktails at bars but included food tours, cooking classes, food festivals, and other tasting experiences. Unlike most people, chefs use travel, whether it's a trip one hundred miles away or a thousand, as an opportunity for inspiration and to expand their horizons, discover new cuisines and different cultures. "Culinary curation and travels are a big part of how we can create," says chef Jose Garces, "because bringing those traditions back and translating them into a way that works for your market is a talent. It's a skill and something that I feel myself and my team can do pretty well."

Many American chefs have worked or interned in France, Italy, Germany, Greece, or in the United Kingdom. When it comes to Europe, the list of countries and cities famous for their culinary scenes is long. In recent years, two specific destinations—Spain and Denmark—have been strategic for chefs because of chefs René Redzepi from Noma in Copenhagen and Albert Adrià in Barcelona. Let's have a look at different parts of the world that inspired culinary leaders.

The first time I met chef Johnny Spero from Reverie in Washington, D.C., he was coming back from a trip to Europe. All his travel experiences obviously translated into his menu at Reverie.

"The space itself is very much inspired by just a kind of classic and simplistic Scandinavian and Japanese design. I don't want to say it's stark or cold, but we have a lot of natural elements. The concrete walls are still kind of exposed. There are just small amounts of wood, and a lot of natural textures that remind of very simplistic Japanese and Scandinavian designs. The food, for the most part, is modern American, meaning that I can grasp all my different inspirations and travels and put it together on a plate, and no one questions if I'm doing Italian, French, or Japanese. The restaurant's food, stylistically, is me, so you definitely see a lot of my travels and experiences put into a plate where it may not always be a direct dish that has made it onto the menu that I've seen elsewhere, but you can definitely see some of the nuances coming from the different places that I've been to. For instance, we started cooking a lot of our vegetables in Shio Koji (a Japanese cure/marinade made by fermenting grain koji). But they often get paired with other flavors that might be more associated with Scandinavia, like in my scallop dish. The scallops are dressed in Shio Koji with finger limes, and then it gets a mixture of buttermilk emulsion with Époisses cheese, which is a delicious mild Burgundian cheese with a powerful aroma. We make butter in-house that we culture with Époisses, and then we use the buttermilk left over from the butter production to make the sauce. We have a blend of Japanese, Scandinavian, and French with the funky cheese. Most people would probably say that my food looks very Nordic, because that's what they can associate it with."

I traveled many times to Scandinavia, especially Denmark, for business in the '90s. It was long before the era of chef René Redzepi and Noma, but one Danish specialty had an early influence on my way of looking at food. The Smørrebrød, open-faced sandwiches offered at markets and restaurants across Denmark, became my food of choice when taking the ferries from Copenhagen Island to Odense Island, or crossing from Copenhagen over to Sweden. Traditionally, Smørrebrød consists of buttered rye bread topped with cold cuts, pieces of meat or fish, cheese or spread, and basically any leftovers. They have been reinvented and updated since then and became one of the most popular dishes in Denmark, long before the recent popularity of toasts like avocado toasts in the U.S.

When I tasted chef Spero's Scallop Crudo at Reverie, I could connect the dots with the food I experienced while traveling in Denmark, and the classic association of buttermilk and dill. I asked Spero about his time there.

"I went to Copenhagen for two months," he said. "I had all the intention of just staying there for the rest of my life. I was in Copenhagen in the middle of January and February, dead of their winter, and I loved every moment of it. From that moment on, nothing was ever going to be good enough. Noma had changed my entire perspective of food. I now love what chef Christian Puglisi is doing at Relae in Copenhagen, because it's very ingredient-focused, it's not wildly manipulated. It's just pure flavor. My advice for chefs is to spend time in restaurants that are ingredient-driven and for food enthusiasts to dine there. What they do at Relae is beautiful. There are so many other amazing restaurants in Copenhagen, like 108 and Geranium. They are definitely part of the list of the places that inspire me."

Besides Denmark, Spero suggested going to Spain, to the Basque country with their New Basque cuisine, and to Barcelona, with their emphasis on Mediterranean seafood. "Have you been to Disfrutar (restaurant in Barcelona with experimental tasting menus)?" he asked. "When you look at what they do, you can see a lot of similarities to the way that El Bulli was, but it's stylistically, a very different restaurant. And then, obviously, Albert Adrià, who's probably one of the greatest chefs in the world with his restaurant Enigma. Enigma just looks like an incredible experience and presents a different version of what people consider to be a high-end dining experience, where you move from room to room, as Adrià is using the entire building as an experience. It gives people a different viewpoint on how you can do these super-modernist, avant-garde restaurants that are stylistically very different."

Several months later, I talked to another chef passionate about Spain, Jamie Bissonnette. "Ken [Oringer] and I went to a restaurant called Casa Deli in a market in Madrid. We were told they had one of the best tortilla Espanola. It was indeed pretty remarkable. They wouldn't tell us how they make it, but as their kitchen had a window, we stood there watching them making the tortilla. Theirs was cooked for a short amount of time and had not as much of a crust on the outside, and not as dark…it was a little bit blonder. The potatoes and the onions were chunkier, but cooked and added into the eggs, hot. The tortilla was a little bit runny. It was just fantastic. We came back and promptly changed our tortilla recipe at Toro mimicking a similar cooking style. Our restaurant in Boston is inspired by Spain, but when people say that we are a Spanish tapas restaurant, we say, 'kind of.' It's not based on one specific region of Spain. We took the all-star hits of the foods that we've loved from all of our travels in Spain."

What Bissonnette loved about Spanish food culture was how innovative but still simple the food was. "You can really mix any kind of flavors together and you can still have that same spirit of small plates with delicious and impactful bites like tapas."

Bissonnette shared how he and chef Oringer identify food spots when traveling. "When we travel, we leave no stone unturned. We go down every alley, we go into every store, whether it is just a corner store or street food. We look at everything. It has been great to find new ingredients, new restaurants, and we get inspired by everything that we see." I asked him if he and Ken had a process when it came to food exploration while traveling. Joking about it, Bissonnette described their process as "pretty hard." "We wake up in the morning, put on comfortable shoes, and don't come back until we are exhausted, and we just look at everything. I wouldn't say that my success rate is very high for that kind of stuff, but when I do find that one new ingredient, that one new market, that one new dish that I get to try, it makes it all worth it. Ken and I will do a lot of research. We reach out to chefs that we know in areas and ask them if they'll take us around. We reach out to makers and say, 'Hey, we're coming. Can we come do a tour of your facility?' But my favorite way is still to just go somewhere for a week and walk around until I get to know it as if it was my own."

I can relate to chef Bissonnette's tasting adventures as I have developed a process while traveling abroad, or even visiting a city in the U.S. for the first time. Here is the process I fine-tuned throughout the years of traveling and tasting.

"Culinary curation and travels are a big part of how we can create, because bringing those traditions back and translating them into a way that works for your market is a talent."
—CHEF JOSE GARCES

Travel Tips for a Tasting Tour

- Select a destination: country, city, and neighborhood.
- In a non-English-speaking country, I recommend looking for organized food tours run by a local.
- Focus on one type of food or drink you want to experience to make comparisons, or keep variety in the things you eat when you are creating your itinerary.
- Select a variety of types of local eateries that you can use as keywords for your online search: restaurants, delis, food stores, food trucks, pubs, food markets, street food, pop-up restaurants, breweries, wineries, cider house, bars, coffee roasters, coffee shops, bakeries, bread, ice cream shops, etc.
- Search on Google or YouTube for chefs, pastry chefs, bartenders/mixologists from your destination and look for their restaurants and bars.
- Reach out to friends, chefs, and your own network to add to your own list.
- Do online research with the following websites: Eater, Thrillist, Yelp, Google; search on Instagram using the geotag and the hashtag of your city or town and see what locations come up often; airline company magazines (i.e., *Hemispheres* from United), food magazines, travel magazines, and delivery apps.
- When you are in another country, remember to check on local fast-food chains and convenience stores to find the new spices and ingredients you need to learn about and resource.
- Create a first list of locations. Ideally, you want to end up with a maximum of ten locations for one day (five for half a day).
- Create Google Maps, place your identified locations on the map, and save locations as "starred places."
- Check menus online and identify dishes that interest you.
- Identify how much time is needed to get from one location to the next.
- Identify the distance between locations.

- Identify the opening and closing times of each location.
- Decide if you want to walk from one location to the next or use transportation.
- Make reservations where needed.
- Ask ahead of time if the chef can come to the table to answer questions.
- From your Google Maps, create an itinerary that you can share and have it on your phone.
- Order enough food, but not too much to avoid food waste. Keep in mind to pace yourself especially if you are doing a whole day of tasting.
- Take pictures with your phone and use "notes" on your phone to capture your comments on location and dishes.
- Have fun!

During the pandemic of 2020, not having the freedom to travel began to affect my mood, and I welcomed a series of long driving trips in the Spring of 2021. The last time I was in Philadelphia was for the Rising Stars event from StarChefs two years before, and it was time to go back. I met with chef Jose Garces for lunch. He had booked a table at Parc, a stylish Parisian-type bistro along Rittenhouse Square. In between a dozen oysters and an American-style quiche, our conversation focused on our respective travels. We soon discovered that we visited similar places and decided to compare our adventures.

Garces recalled his first international trip at the beginning of his career and how it had impacted his cooking style. When he finished culinary school, he went to cook in Spain. "I got a job through a priest in Spain who owned three restaurants. He was a man of the cloth, but a man of business as well. That experience literally propelled me. I acquired the understanding early that you could travel and really learn about cuisine as part of what you do, as part of your career. The importance of traveling and being inspired became a staple, and for me, when it comes to gastronomy, Spain is unsurpassed."

Garces got a thorough introduction to the ingredients and techniques from the southern region of Spain when he worked at a restaurant in Madrid. He was introduced to several dish variations based on rice flavored with squid ink or saffron, fish fumet or duck stock, and invariably accompanied by a fresh homemade aioli and slices of toasted baguette. The toasted baguette with different variations of flavored aioli became a signature for Garces' paellas.

I told him about my first trip to Barcelona and my exposure to real Spanish paellas. I was on a business trip and my Spanish friend and former colleague, Antonio, invited me to his favorite location in the city for paellas, Siete Puertas. At this internationally renowned restaurant that opened its doors in 1836, we ordered the Rich Man Paella, exclusively made with fish and shellfish. I told Garces that I remembered being fascinated by the way the paella was first brought to our table in a very large paella pan, and then served to us on our plates by the waiters. The restaurant's hostess told us that the table we were at was where the surrealist artist Miro used to sit, and I could imagine that nothing had really changed since the '50s in this establishment.

Garces mentioned he didn't have a lot of money back then and that he got to know more of the classic, home-style Spanish dishes. In his book *The Latin Road Home*, he summarized what set these dishes apart. "First, the ingredients were unparalleled, their quality was superb, and their variety was dazzling. Second, the regional cuisines fascinated me—sharply distinct by virtue of geographical and cultural complexity, deeply steeped in tradition, and, here and there, on the cutting edge of innovation. And the third element was the clincher, the magic ingredient: unabashed pleasure in all things relating to food—components, preparation, consumption, a rare unifying thread that binds these decidedly autonomous cultures."

What impressed me most in Spain was the simplicity of the food. I spent a good deal of time in Spain in the late '80s, from Cataluña, Aragón, La Rioja, Navarra, Castilla León, Asturias, and Galicia in the north to Madrid, Valencia, Murcia, and Andalusia in the south. I told Garces that my favorite city in Europe is Barcelona. "Probably a radical statement for your French compatriots," replied Garces with a little smile. But he agreed with me that Barcelona is a city where people love to socialize outdoors, and the streets and cafés are always vibrant with people day and night. The city provides a long history, and art is everywhere with the iconic works of Gaudí, Miro, and Picasso. "It is warmer than Paris, on the Costa Brava, and the food is served simply," I added ironically. I mentioned to him the quintessential example of Spanish simple food for chef Jamie Bissonnette: the boquerones tapas, anchovies with olive oil. "Spain is such an innovative culinary capital of the world, but it also excels in its simplicity. When you're in Spain you realize that boquerones do not really need anything else but a vehicle to put it in your mouth, whether it's a fork or a piece of bread." Bissonnette emphasized that "we need to learn from that and focus on stripping down some of the overcomplicated things that we do at restaurants so we can focus on simplicity like they do in Spain."

Garces explained that because of his amazing experience learning about the culture and the food directly from Spanish chefs, he understood that the only way to learn about any other cuisines was to go there and visit the country. "I took it upon myself and traveled to Buenos Aires, Uruguay, to Mexico several times, Ecuador, Peru, the Caribbean, and Cuba."

Cuba was a second country he and I had in common. In Cuba, Garces discovered the paladares (home restaurants) in and around Havana. "It was at the dining room tables of modest Cuban homes that I had my best meals and got my introduction to various hearty, full-flavored staples of Cuban home cooking: tostones, moros y cristianos, frijoles colorados, pernil asado, langosta a la plancha, and more."

"Did you have the chance to eat at the restaurant called La Terraza on the Paseo de Marti?" I asked. "They are known for the open grill they have on a rooftop with a beautiful view of the Prado, and if octopus was on every menu in La Havana, the grilled octopus at La Terrazza was among the best I've ever had."

I told Graces that, in 2016, I took my daughter and my youngest son to Cuba. The borders were open at that time, and we had the opportunity to fly to La Havana. That trip was rich in interactions with some truly amazing people and exposure to incredible food. One other reason restaurants quickly moved up my list of favorite places in La Havana was because of their customized Gin & Tonic menu! They featured a great concept where you picked your favorite brand of gin, your style of tonic, and your shape of glass. Then the bartender topped it off by offering you a selection of add-ins including herbs like parsley, herba buena, basil or rosemary, and spices such as pink pepper, licorice, cardamom, cinnamon, rose petal, or hibiscus flowers. Creative, and simply delicious!

Cuba left an imprint on me. I cannot get the colorful names of the four main Havana districts out of my head: Miramar, Vedado, Centro Habana, and Habana Vieja. For many visitors, the crumbling buildings and bustling streets of Centro Habana, crammed between the hotel districts of Habana Vieja and Vedado, are glimpsed only through a taxi window en route to the city's more tourist-friendly areas. Yet in this no-thrills quarter where more than 150,000 people live there was the emblem of Havana, La Guarida Paladar. For past visitors to La Havana, La Guarida had become a must-see experience—I learned that, sadly, the restaurant closed its doors during the pandemic. We met with Enrique, one of the owners of this magical place. He had created a cozy atmosphere with soft lights, fine table linen, candles, and Cuban jazz music. The entrance was off a run-down street, which magnified the effect. You could see the former grandeur of this building with a gigantic wooden door, which opened on two flights of marble stairs.

"Like many other aspects of our culture—music, dance, and religion—our cuisine has African and Spanish roots," said Enrique. "There is also an Indian influence. Like our architecture, you will find a mix, a combination of cultures that have influenced us. Its origins make it an eclectic cuisine. People are familiar with commercial-type "ethnic restaurants", the kind of Hispanic franchises you see all around you, and it's a misconception that these truly represent the scope of various cultures into one identity." Enrique emphasized that the only way to experience a specific foreign food was to travel to the place of origin and enjoy it in the actual country. "We tried to create new recipes that we would be able to keep on the menu. We're limited in Cuba to what we can find at the market if we're going to feature something on a regular basis. We needed ingredients that were easy to find when the markets were open. Look, you cannot get beef all year long, so it is not on the menu all year long. We wanted to keep things fluid so we can prepare consistently good offerings. One of the most successful recipes that we prepare at our restaurant is Tuna and Sugar Cane. We use a lot of coconut and mangos and cilantro and onions. We feature a recipe called Tropical Chicken made with pineapple and papaya."

I personally loved the Papaya Lasagna on the menu. When I asked Enrique about the inspiration behind it, he said, "We are always inspired to surprise the person who is dining at our restaurant—once again, trying to use ingredients native to our country. We grow papaya throughout the year, so fresh papaya is always available. We use the basic fresh lasagna recipe using papaya instead of pasta and it changes the taste and the color and the aroma. We also make duck using citrus compote—lemon, orange, and cilantro, a combination that turns out very fresh tasting, very nice."

I told Garces that as one who loves food, drink, and travel, La Havana was a sensory delight.

I moved on from my trip to Cuba to the one country in Central America that had really impressed me with its quality and creativity of its food: Panama. Back in 2011, I met with chef Adolfo Garcia during a food show in New Orleans. Chef Garcia was known to have brought a new level to traditional Creole specialties by using a creative Latino touch from his Panamanian heritage. I was so intrigued by the way and the passion Garcia spoke about his parents' country and where he lived when he was a teenager that I took my first trip to Panama in 2017.

Before the trip, my historical knowledge of Panama could be summed up in in four lines: The Spanish discovered the Isthmus of Panama during the 16th century; the country became independent in the 20th century; the French started the creation of the Panama Canal towards the end of the 19th century; and the Americans finished it at the beginning of the 20th century.

If you ask most people about Panama's cuisine, they would probably say that it involves rice, beans, and tropical fruit. It is true that there is not a real Panamanian culinary identity, in part because Panama is a relatively young country that got its independence a little bit more than a hundred years ago.

When I prepared my first trip to Panama, I reconnected with chef Adolfo Garcia, and he gave me a great tip to connect with local chef José Olmedo Carles, who was changing the culinary game in Panama City and sharing Panama's cuisine with the world. I felt privileged to sit at the chef's table at his Donde José, a small restaurant with only sixteen seats in a gorgeous nondescript old building at the edge of Casco Viejo. No name was posted outside, so it was easy to walk past. There were only three of us sitting at the chef's table, which felt very exclusive.

"At Donde José, we serve food that talks about Panama," chef Carles explained from behind his prep area. "Our philosophy is to tell stories about our country, its ingredients, traditions, and influences. Every night, we are serving 'stories,' with the aim to share them with our guests and learn something more about Panama." Carles was extremely passionate about his country, its local ingredients and local process, and he definitely liked telling stories.

The first story on the menu was Tortilla de Maíz y Guiso de Tomate Ahumado (corn tortilla with a smoked tomato stew). The wood of a local tree called "nance" was used to smoke the tomatoes, which gave the sauce a distinct characteristic. In the next dish, Sancocho Ahumao (smoky sancocho), pork, the typical ingredient in a sancocho, was replaced by an old hen and finished with cilantro.

The most unusual dish was the dessert. It was a deconstructed apple pie where chayote (an edible plant belonging to the gourd family, popular in Mexico and Guatemala) was used instead of apple, and smoke was incorporated into the whipped cream. The crumble was made of plantains, and dried hibiscus flowers were sprinkled on top. Chef Carles explained that smoke is a prevalent flavor throughout Panama, as a lot of people in villages outside of Panama City still use wood to cook.

During the dinner, I discovered two interesting new fruits: jobo (yellow mombin) and pixbae. The fruit pulp of the jobo is either eaten fresh or made into juice, concentrate, jellies, and sherbets. The fruit exists in other Latin American countries and in Southeast Asia. Pixbae is fruit from a palm tree found in Central America. Jobo was featured in the dish El Ñamfle y sus accompanamientos, a DIY one-bite snack with three elements: a sweet potato waffle, a jobo jam, and a yogurt-based spread mixed with homemade hot sauce, topped with local basil. Pixbae was the fruit layer in a tostado called De aqui, de alla, de todos lados. This dish had multiple layers built on a yucca chip and garlic guacamole, topped with grated pixbae. Every dish was a version of a traditional Panamanian dish, but with chef Carles' unique style and flavor!

In remembering some of the inspiration for his dishes, Garces spoke to me about when he won Iron Chef in 2009. "Some of the battles leading up to that win were in Tokyo. The food was so fantastic that I went back with my kids and did a whole culinary tour. I just loved their food culture and their appreciation for the best ingredients." He once purchased a $300 mango at the Takashimaya department store. "It was beautifully and individually wrapped in a crate. It had some nice foam wrapping around it so the flesh wouldn't bruise. It was amazing. I don't know if I would pay $300 again for it, but it was so good. It was the best mango I've ever had."

I had the opportunity to discover this cuisine in the fall of 2019, when my younger son, Alex, and I went on a father-son trip to Japan. It was on top of our travel bucket list, and we were glad that we went before the pandemic.

Japanese composer Joe Hisaishi's music had been constantly present during our trip, and now every time I listen to it, it brings memories of train rides in the Shinkansen, the Japanese bullet train, that took us from Tokyo, to Kyoto, and then Osaka. The food experience during those fourteen days was amazing. Besides the stunning sushi and a variety of ramen, we discovered Japanese comfort food and street food.

In the vicinity of the Nakamise street, near the Kaminarimon Gate in the Asakusa district in Tokyo, we discovered a little hole in the wall while exploring the small alleys around the commercial streets. A place with no more than ten tables specialized in Okonomiyaki and Monja, types of do-it-yourself Japanese pancakes. They provided the ingredients and we cooked them directly on a griddle, which was built into our table. The menu was only in Japanese, but there were some infographics on the wall that helped us navigate the offerings. Alex and I decided to go for the house specialty: Okonomiyaki (flour, egg, cabbage, tempura, clams, dried shrimp, egg, and pickled ginger) with a side order of enoki mushrooms.

After our okonomiyaki experience, we stopped by the Asakusa Kokonoe shop, near the Senso-ji Temple, also well-known for its Manjū, small steamed and fried cakes. We loved their crispy and puffy texture. They had a variety of fillings such as bean paste, green tea, sweet potato, pumpkin, sesame, cherry blossom, and custard. I loved the sesame and green tea Manju the best.

Before leaving for Osaka, I took my son to the Tsukiji fish market, and we spent the whole morning with a local Japanese guide. Chef Spero had recommended a guide as the best way to communicate with the vendors. Spero talked about his experience at five o'clock in the morning on the "tuna floor" where buyers from all over the world are purchasing fresh tuna. After our guided tour, Alex and I spent more time in the market, and we picked some seafood and street food in the outer market for our lunch: the best uni (sea urchin), grilled squid skewers, oysters, grilled octopus, together with a glass of freshly whipped green tea latte made simply with milk, matcha green tea, and sugar cane syrup.

Another great Japanese food moment was the selection of our bento-box (called ekiben) before the bullet train ride to Osaka. If most of the train stations in the U.S. offer only fast-food restaurants and pizza, it is a very different picture in Japan. A giant food court was located in the lower level of the Tokyo train station. Most major train stations have entire floors dedicated to food kiosks and restaurants. Many people in Japan commute by trains, and a lot of them choose to bring ekiben with them on the train and eat while commuting at almost 200 miles per hour.

Like many other passengers, we unwrapped our boxes forty-five minutes after leaving Tokyo station and enjoyed pork tonkatsu, chicken teriyaki, and a different variety of onigiri—triangle-shaped rice packets wrapped in dried seaweed sheets filled with salted salmon roe and tuna mayo.

The most intriguing street food item we found was in Kyoto in the tiny, covered streets of the Nishiki Market. Take tomago—glazed baby octopus stuffed with boiled quail egg stuffed into the head, grilled and served on a stick with kewpie and shoyu. Chewy, sweet, and salty all at the same time.

I liked takoyaki much better—octopus balls made with wheat flour batter and diced octopus, tempura scraps, green onion, pickled ginger cooked in a special cast iron pan. These octopus balls were brushed with takoyaki sauce, sprinkled with green seaweed and dried bonito flakes.

While in Japan, I began to understand why so many American chefs were inspired by the flavors from this part of the world, and I remembered chef Jean Marie Josselin (a renowned French chef who was one of the pioneers of Hawaii regional cuisine) saying that the first country that really inspired him was Japan.

"They respect the farmers. They understand that there are seasons and things work for certain reasons. It inspired me and I tried to do it with the farmers in Kauai. … It was something that they have done in Japan for years."

Chef Brother Luck, from Four By Brother Luck in Colorado Springs, worked at different restaurants while traveling in Japan and one thing he loved about the country was the way people embrace everything that is intrinsic to Japanese culture, including nature, from oceans to land. "It's all revealed in the Kaiseki menu cuisine," said Luck. "These four seasonal multi-course menus rotate all year. It was really special. There's a beginning, a middle, and an end to every season in their philosophy. I was really inspired by that." Japanese Kaiseki dining represents the quintessential haute cuisine of Japan, taking ingredients at the peak of their freshness, presented simply, without artifice, and with a specific seasonal theme. The kaiseki dining experience typically begins with appetizers, followed by sashimi, cooked dishes, a rice course, and a dessert, with optional palate cleansers in between the courses.

Chef Garces spoke about the influence of Japanese culture on his cooking. "I always wanted to cook food with all due respect and appreciation like they do in Japan. We had an opportunity to open Okatshe restaurant in Atlantic City at the Tropicana hotel, which was my take on a Japanese Izakaya. It was more of my take on the best things that I loved about Japanese cuisine, which were small plates. Dumplings, ribs, pickles, Karaage (deep fried technique), ramen, yakitori (chicken skewers), sushi, and maki…all into one menu. I had so much fun with it!"

When I asked Garces if he had been to other countries in Asia, he briefly mentioned his trips to Macau, where he was fascinated by the fusion of Cantonese and Portuguese influences in their dishes. He encouraged me to explore South Philly where the food influences from Southeast Asian countries like Thailand, Cambodia, and Laos can be spotted in street markets and restaurants. In fact, I had just visited south Philly. I had been invited to a food pop-up from Bao.logy at the rooftop bar Bok bar. Bao.logy is a street food Taiwanese place located between Rittenhouse Square and Logan Square. I tasted fluke crudo with ginger, scallions, chilis, sesame oil, and rice vinegar, and cold noodles with sesame peanut sauce, cucumbers, and carrots. But my favorite was their grilled hamachi collar (the collar of the yellowtail located just above the gills and below the head).

"Other Asian countries had a strong impact on chefs," I reminded Garces. Chef Kim Alter based out of San Francisco had taken a trip to Taipei and told me that it reminded her a lot of San Francisco. I thought about what Alter had shared with me. She said, "It was very hot and humid, and the produce was beautiful. Even though I would never probably have fried blood or octopus cheese balls on my menu, it was interesting to go out to the night markets, try different taste profiles, and get excited about everything and see just how that part of the world eats. Taiwan cooking and going to the night markets changed my approach to cooking by utilizing new ingredients and thoughts. For instance, sugar wasn't used as much in sweets, so I think about that now when I am doing desserts. It also made me rethink how I do my menu, like finishing with a broth instead of having a broth in the middle. Little things like that which only travel and experience can do."

Chef Johnny Spero was also influenced by traveling to Singapore, Cambodia, and Vietnam, and chef Hari Cameron traveled through Thailand and indicated how really eye-opening it was in terms of diversity between the different regions, and so different from eating Thai food in the U.S. He remembered, "I loved the way they balanced their dishes integrating all the elements of sweetness, spiciness, umami, blossoms, bitterness, and sourness."

Traveling with someone who knows the area is always best. I recalled that chef Gulotta went to Thailand with his chef de cuisine (Paul Chell) from MoPho.

"It was fun to be there with him," said Gulotta, "because he always got excited. 'Oh, we got to go to this stall. Oh, we got to go see this lady.' He was down to just walking each city and trying everything. One morning, we got up at 7 a.m. to get to taste khao soi, which in Thailand is a brothy curry soup with lots of noodles; whereas in Laos it's a broth, almost like a pho, with almost like a scoop of bolognese in the middle that you slowly mix into the noodle soup before eating it. It's just a very transformative, wonderful, restorative dish that you have early in the morning. The best one in the city was at this one lady's stall where you had to get there super early, and it was just this amazing experience where each bundle of herbs was hand-tied with a piece of stripped lemongrass. That really influenced us when we came back to New Orleans.

"Bangkok was an amazing experience as well, so we put a boat noodle dish on Maypop's menu that has stayed on forever. I got to have my first real tom yum there, and tom yum has now been a part of both restaurants' menu (MoPho and MayPop) since we got back. We are serving really great tom yums using Louisiana seafood. We are making our own noodles in house and everyone who had it thought it was amazing. I would not have been able to do this if I hadn't traveled there and had the real dish. Sometimes I wonder if MoPho would not have been an entirely different restaurant if I had been able to go to Southeast Asia before opening it."

After my lunch discussion with chef Garces, I continued to think about other chefs' travel experiences to Asia. I had recently spoken to chef Elizabeth Falkner about her trip to China before the pandemic. She went from Beijing to Chengdu in the Sichuan Province.

"The Sichuan Province had such a massive impact on me," recalled Falkner. "I had always known that this would be kind of an amazing culinary area and history, but the Sichuan peppercorns and the profile of spices or the mala in their cuisine is just so haunting and delicious and memorable. I'm playful with a lot of things. I might use some Sichuan chilies and peppercorns in a vinaigrette with orange flower water while making a salad with mung beans. And when I was in China, I came up with a dessert idea using creamy soft tofu. But it is very unusual in a dessert there. You would never go to China and have tofu in a dessert. It doesn't exist. I made a black sesame, fermented black bean caramel sauce and then a black sesame streusel, and then serve that with just kettle, creamy tofu. Tofu feels like panna cotta to me. Also, Chinese fermented black beans in the caramel sauce in dessert is so unusual, but it's salty and it has umami."

Later that day, I recorded a podcast with pastry chef Antonio Bachour (an American pastry chef based in Miami). It was the day before his trip to Dubai and I looked forward to hearing what dishes he found there. Of late, Dubai has become a source of inspiration for chefs. Bissonnette came back from a trip to Dubai with a myriad of new spice blends and local ingredients from the souk. "There's a couple of people in the souk that are from Iraq and Iran, and they specialize in wild, high-altitude mountain honey." The honey from the Kurdish Mountain in Turkey, Iraq, and Iran is in high demand.

"I think honey is such a dynamic ingredient," continued Bissonnette. "The honey they have is unlike anything I've ever tasted before. It tastes more like fruit molasses and less like typical honey. It's got great acidity and it's just wildly different than anything else. It's a mix because it comes from wild hives. It's extremely dangerous to harvest it because the bees are not used to humans. It's like three times as expensive as any of the other honeys that we could get from the same people. But this one particular style is just remarkable, and they come from different parts of the mountain ranges, so each one has its own terroir, with its own completely different flavor."

"Traveling to Dubai opened my eyes to new spices, flavors, and culture," agreed chef Kim Alter. "With traveling, you get out of your element. When you're in the restaurant every day, your head's down, you're working a station, you're doing the same thing, you're seeing the same people. You get in a routine. That's how you get consistency, but when you get taken out of that environment and you go to Dubai, for instance, and you get to see how they work with lamb brains—I wondered how I could apply this to my menus in San Francisco. It made me think of ways to implement those items into my cooking style without changing my voice in my cooking. Honey, curry, paprika, black cardamom, I didn't discover these there for the first time, but I wanted to use them more. I would season broths with the black cardamom husks, I would use a different curry in my vadouvan mixture. It is in Dubai that I really started to appreciate how different honey was in every country, state, or city."

To sum up, most culinary professionals I talked to attribute their food memory database to four origins: childhood memories, eating other people's food, collaboration with other chefs, friends, or other professionals, and from their travels. What makes them different from you and me is their ability to activate this food memory database and leverage their skills, techniques, and experience to create new dishes and drinks.

While listening to these professionals, it became clear that several stimuli were responsible for firing their flavor memory bank. Chef Brad Miller, from the Inn of the Seventh Ray near Los Angeles, had the perfect way to describe his experience. "I guess the process is the same with every chef, but for me, it works this way: I'm at the market, I see ingredients, I taste them, and literally, a bomb goes off in my head. 'What could I do with that? What could I pair it with?' That's mainly what takes place in my mind, because I've already gone through all my food memories."

When I started my podcast and considered all of the topics with which I wanted to engage my guests, identifying some of these "sparks" that set off the fire of their creativity and activate their flavor memory bank was top of the list. I wanted to explore the notion of "being struck by lightning" as chef Dan Kluger described it. After many discussions, I found that there were four sparks that activate food memories, four stimuli that went beyond the primary reality of cooking with seasonal food or exposure to local produce at the farmers' markets. These things kept coming up in our conversations: music and songs, colors from nature and art, cookbooks, menus, and social media, and dreams.

Spark #1: Music and Songs

For most of us, hearing music or a song may bring back a unique memory that involved food. For me, hearing the call to prayer will always evoke memories of the market shops of Essaouira and the lemon chicken tajine my daughter and I enjoyed on the rooftop of our Moroccan apartment. Listening to the Summer arrangement by Joe Hisaishi will forever bring me back to my trip to Japan with my younger son and the exploration of street food in Tokyo, Osaka, and Kyoto. But for chef Andre Natera, listening to classical music fires his creative juices, helps him to get inspired and create new dishes for his restaurants Garrison and Revue at the Fairmont hotel in Austin.

Likewise, chef Jamie Bissonnette shared that he can be inspired by a song, and playing music helps clear his mind by occupying his brain space with something non-food-related. "I've been playing music my whole life. I'm still very, very bad at it, which is why I'm a chef, but I still love to play. Sometime, my hands will be just moving on the guitar, I'll be thinking of a song, and then my mind will wonder. If I'm playing a Led Zeppelin song for instance, I can start thinking and wondering about where they were when they wrote that song and what the lyrics are in the song, and all of a sudden I am wondering 'Why am I thinking about Vikings? Why am I thinking about salt cod?' I will put my guitar down and, on the computer, will be looking up what the Vikings were eating and how they were sustaining themselves and go like, 'Oh, wow, that's a really cool thing. Let's do that.' And next thing I know, I will be calling my friend in Iceland, 'Hey, can you send me any of that fermented shark?'"

Bissonnette likes to listen to jazz records, and sometimes in the lyrics somebody will talk about food. "Blossom Dearie, an old jazz crooner from the '50s, often talks about food. Or Action Bronson, though he's hip-hop, he still has a lot of jazz in his soul, the way he talks and raps as a modern hip-hop artist, and he also used to be a chef. So, hearing him talking about olives from Tunisia, right after he references duck prosciutto in one of his songs, will get my mind going—duck prosciutto and olives together, yeah, that might work. I just love that. I love finding food references everywhere in the world."

When it comes to inspiration from listening to songs, chef Fiore Tedesco explained, "I got in the shower and a song came in my head and it was a Neil Young song from the album *On The Beach*. It immediately triggered a visual from my childhood memories. My cousins grew up in Nahant, Massachusetts, and there's a beach called Forty Steps Beach. I remembered being on that beach looking out straight ahead to the lighthouse, the rocky cliffs around, and the ocean lapping up onto the shore. The Neil Young song then connected to that visual, which then connected to the idea that it would be so fun if I could make a dish to articulate this feeling I was having. In the span of a couple of minutes, I came up with the idea of a tower of scallops and foie gras, layered as a torsion, almost like a candy-stripe torsion of those two elements, with cockles and periwinkles lining and representing the rocks and the seashore, the scallop and foie representing the lighthouse, and making a blue algae puree as water washing on the beach. I got out of the shower, and I started writing this idea down. I called the dish 'On the Beach' because of the Neil Young album. Then I thought, 'What if I made a series of dishes for every one of my favorite Neil Young albums? What a cool thing that would be to do.' That night, I wrote out a whole menu of my Neil Young dinner with the seven dishes inspired by these albums. Still that night, I wrote out a menu for the Talking Heads, The Police, and The Misfits."

"I came up with the idea of a tower of scallops and foie gras, layered as a torsion, almost like a candy-stripe torsion of those two elements, with cockles and periwinkles lining and representing the rocks and the seashore, the scallop and foie representing the lighthouse, and making a blue algae puree as water washing on the beach."

—CHEF FIORE TEDESCO

Spark #2: Colors from Art or Nature

When asked about their sources of inspiration, my guests' most common answer was frequently "everything can be a source of inspiration." Besides music, another major trigger for culinary professionals' creativity involved visual perception. Nature and changes of season wonderfully inspire mixologists.

"Just the colors and the aromas that I see in nature, especially when I travel, inspire me," explained mixologist Charlotte Voisey (global head of ambassadors for William Grant & Sons). "Anything new that interrupts my normal is an opportunity to be inspired and creative."

Similarly, Bob Peters, renowned mixologist in Charlotte, North Carolina loves edible flowers. "Mother nature offers the most beautiful things in the world. If I can showcase that stuff with, maybe a pop of a garnish, that's prettier than anything I can make, and it's simple and elegant and beautiful. I love purple and in North Carolina, there is a flower that grows during a micro season, and it's something that sort of just appears on the side of the road, it's actually kind of a weed that grows on trees. You'll find clusters of these beautiful purple flowers attaching themselves to these big, beautiful trees in the canopy. It's called 'wisteria.' They have the most beautiful, absolutely stunning, but still sort of mild aroma, almost like artificial grapes. I make wisteria tea and a syrup that goes well with gin, vodka, or Blanco tequila. I brightened the flavor with a bit of lemon juice and a sparkling to create this incredible drink, which is so beautiful and delicate for the spring."

In Austin, blossoms inspired chef Fiore Tedesco from L'Oca d'Oro as well. "The color of a flower, or something that's blooming right after a rainstorm makes me pause and think. It might be this bright pink flower that reminds me of the color when you air a beet puree, which is such a beautiful intoxicating, bright pink color. It almost looks like Willy Wonka food—it doesn't seem real. To apply that color palette to something vegetal and healthful, wholesome, and earthy is really appealing. I start to work outward and try to make a dish out of that. I use a lot of visual cues from the world around me."

My first interaction with chef Kim Alter centered on colors. It was June in 2019 during the San Francisco Rising Star event by StarChefs where I was doing a tasting trek with customers. Chef Alter kindly welcomed our group to her restaurant, Nightbird, located in the Hayes Valley district of San Francisco. Nightbird is an elegant boutique restaurant with a massive wooden door displaying a giant carved owl, the logo of the restaurant. Right away, I loved everything about that place. The decor was simple yet refined, and the colors and textures used reflected natural elements. Chef Alter was known to offer tasting menus and to change themes every three to four weeks. "We try to make it fun, and we've never run a menu twice," says Alter. "We always try to come up with something new."

That night in June, the theme was "Colors" and each course represented a color in the pride flag. From that tasting menu, I remember vividly three colors from three dishes that were gracefully handwritten by the chef on a simple white card: green for the Halibut, Green Zucchini, and Green Garlic dish; brown for the Flannery Beef, Morels, and Summer Truffle dish; and finally purple for the dessert Blueberry, Chamomile, and Custard.

Similarly, pastry chef Emily Spurlin from Chicago thinks in terms of color and associations, particularly groupings and families. "Foods that have complementary colors or foods that are in the same color scheme would be a good match for the initial ingredients." In addition, she also likes the "if it grows together, it goes together" method. She explains, "Quince is in the rose family, and I really like using rose in moderation in desserts. I think it's really lovely and it is tied together in my brain that Persian cuisine uses both quince and rose. That kind of association leads me into a new direction of other flavors I can play with in the Persian cuisine space."

When it comes to associations of colors, chef Tim Hollingsworth from Otium in Los Angeles found inspiration in museums and art galleries. "When I am in a museum and see a painting on the wall with a specific color palette, I often think, 'Wow, those are very striking colors together. Let's imagine that in a dish. What are my green things? What are my red things? What are my yellow things? What are my black things? How can I make it strike?'"

Any expression of artwork such as a piece of pottery or a plate is where chef and restaurateur David Burke based in New York City discovers his inspiration: "A lot of things come into play when it comes to my sources of inspiration." He told me that he might go to a food show or a housewares show and look at all the new plates, pots and pans, and something will spark his imagination, and he could create a dish just so it fits on a specific plate.

In the same way, chef Alison Trent gets inspiration from the vessels used to plate the food. "I do a lot of visual arts on the side, painting, sculpture, and ceramics. Anything visual arts-related, I'm an absolute fan of, and I am marrying all these things together for inspiration. I recently did a dinner at a ceramic studio that people were really blown away by. They got the experience of making a pot themselves, learning how to throw a pot on the wheel, and then they eat from these absolutely incredible ceramic art pieces. We've been eating out of vessels for as long as we can remember, but that connection between what we eat from and what we eat is sometimes lost in the mix of things."

Spark #3: Cookbooks, Menus, and Social Media

A friend recently asked me what the one thing was I usually bring back from the places I travel. The answer was easy: cookbooks or cocktail books. I have collected about eight hundred books that I've been hoarding over the years. It became an obsession, almost an addiction. A lot of them are signed by their authors. If you estimate that a cookbook contains on average one hundred recipes, I have about eighty thousand recipes to choose from. Like many food enthusiasts who love cookbooks, I flip through them and select recipes to cook over the weekend. But what I care for the most are the personal stories of their authors and what compelled them to become chefs and how their personal stories influence their cooking and creative process.

While foodies use cookbooks to cook recipes, chefs tend to use them as a source of inspiration for a new dish. Chef David Burke once told me that he had a library of 1,200 cookbooks. "I normally never need them to find inspiration, but if I pace through a few books, I might earmark a few pages. I may see braised endives and think that I haven't seen that for a while, and maybe I put that on the menu somewhere or I just refresh my memory."

Modern cookbooks are almost like art books with their stunning pictures, and for chef Tim Hollingsworth, inspiration can come from looking at the visuals in cookbooks, magazines, and pictures of food on Instagram.

"One thing I've noticed about myself is that I get really inspired by looking at other people's work and being wrong about what they made. I can glance at a picture and be like, 'Oh, there's this, this, and this.' Then I read over the recipe, and that's not it at all, but that would be really good if it was that. It generates a dish in my head, then I go and try to map it out. For many years, it was about taking something that was very classic, doing it well, and then maybe reinterpreting it a bit, and presenting it in a different way."

Charlotte Voisey looks a lot at food menus to inspire her flavor combinations for her cocktails. "I think it's only natural that when you see food flavors come together, you can understand how similar things can work in drinks, particularly the sort of garnish on food and pastry. It might be salads, appetizers, and desserts that often give me a lot of ideas for cocktails. I also look to see what other people in my profession are doing and looking at interesting new menus, anytime a good bar has a new menu launch. Even if you don't have the recipe, that's better because then you just have an idea of flavors that work together. Then you can build your own recipes."

Just as cookbook sales survived the era of digitalization and online recipe searches, and thrive today, social media just adds a new source of inspiration for culinary professionals. Chicago-based chef Brian Ahern says, "I'm not the biggest social media guy in the world, but I like to peruse the Instagram of restaurants that I like or places that I used to work at, of chefs, of their bartenders, or managers that I used to work with. I look at what they are doing and how they are doing it."

When reopening Reverie in Washington, D.C., Johnny Spero posted a nice display of cookbooks on Instagram, and this reminded me of what he said during our conversation: "I have a ton of cookbooks that I like using for inspiration, but there's something about actually going to the place where they're created, where those ingredients come from, and experience them firsthand. Clearly, I didn't do well in school, so books don't teach me—firsthand experience does."

Celebrity chef, restaurateur, and author Edward Lee had a slightly different point of view about cookbooks. "Yes, everything is an inspiration, but going to eat at a restaurant or looking at cookbooks or Instagram feeds are, for me, probably the least inspiring situations because you're seeing stuff that's already created. Maybe someone is going to steal a dish idea, but that doesn't really inspire me. It just keeps you informed as to what other people are doing, but I don't think inspiration comes from there. Seeing art, reading a poem, walking through the woods, that's what inspiration is. And if you couple that with knowledge, then you have something of a creative process going. Some days it works and some days it doesn't."

Nevertheless, in each episode of my podcast, I ask my guests in the series of rapid-fire questions the top three cookbooks that inspired them the most throughout their career. The three cookbooks mentioned most often are: *The French Laundry* by Thomas Keller, *On Food and Cooking* by Harold McGee, and *La Technique* by Jacques Pépin.

Spark #4: Dreams

The most surprising source of inspiration came from a conversation I had with chef Fiore Tedesco.

"It might sound a little funny," whispered Tedesco, "but the ideas that I have for creating dishes or creating food come to me in the ether." Tedesco had invited me to a collaboration dinner in Manhattan where he served his creative dish of Beet Risotto, Short Rib, Ginger Mascarpone, Pickled Apple, and Lemon Verbena. "This dish came to me in a dream," explained Tedesco. "I woke up in the morning, and I started tinkering with it last year. I've played with different versions of it. The dream was not super articulate about what to put together, but there was something about beets, apples, and ginger and I was surrounded by blades of grass that somehow reminded me of home and reminded me of beef. … When I woke up, I wrote everything down.

"Another side of how this dish came about was taking what came in the dream and putting it through different prisms. My restaurant is very much inspired by my grandmother, who passed away twenty years ago, and about the comfort of the way that she made food for me. The comfort of her affection was really displayed through her cooking and the hundreds and hundreds of meals that she would prepare for me. In the wintertime, she would make a very simple beef knuckles and rice soup. I put the dream I had through the prism of that very comforting soup that my grandmother would make for me and made a risotto. I made my subsequent dish out of those two ideas."

I loved Tedesco's story but not many people experienced true creative sessions from dreams. I personally go through moments when my mind wanders as I am not ready to create what I want. They are moments of daydreaming. Recently, chef and restaurateur Suzanne Goin from Los Angeles explained to me that she still needs go through two hours of procrastination, alone in her home, before coming up with ideas for a new menu.

My personal flavor memory database has been loaded with so many food experiences, from childhood, inspiring dinners with mentors, family, friends, and travels in more than thirty countries. I am grateful that I was able to attend more than sixty food and drink tastings within the past ten years.

To illustrate the inspiration process and how home cooks can draw inspiration from their own flavor memory bank, I decided to focus on one of my favorite childhood memories, and it only took me less than ten minutes to come up with four variations based on the French quiche Lorraine. To refresh everyone's memory, a French quiche Lorraine is made of eggs, creme fraiche, milk, nutmeg, salt, pepper, smoked stripped bacon, and homemade pâte brisée for the crust. Would these variations of ideas have been considered really creative? According to what chef Edward Lee shared with me, they are not, but I am not a chef either, and as a food enthusiast, I still can leverage some of the sources of inspiration culinary leaders use to enhance my creativity in the kitchen.

- One idea I had is a direct steal from my conversation with pastry chef Antonio Bachour, from Miami. He substituted the traditional quiche pâte brisée with a croissant-style crust! My French DNA loved that, though it may not be an easy one to execute perfectly for a home cook.

- Thinking back to my memorable dinner in Cannes and my first exposure to white truffle, I could combine this experience easily with my quiche childhood memory and create a white cheddar and white truffle quiche.

- Since I now live in America, I could play with any combination of meat, fish, and vegetables in a quiche recipe base. I could take inspiration from my travels and come up with a Scandinavian version, substituting the smoked bacon with a mix of fresh and smoked salmon, a part of the milk with buttermilk, and add goat cheese and dill.

- For a Spanish inspiration, I could create a fusion between a Spanish tortilla and French quiche by adding roasted onion, scallop potatoes, manchego cheese, and olives.

- And finally, taking inspiration from my trip to Japan, I could marry the okonomyaki and the quiche concepts, and use shredded cabbage, green onion, add a dash of oyster sauce in the egg mix, substitute soy-milk cows for milk, use standard bacon instead of smoked stripped bacon, and drizzle the end product with Kewpie mayo, pickled ginger, and Bonito flakes before serving.

This was a relatively effortless exercise for me and I could quickly see in my head how I could easily combine or substitute ingredients based on the inspiration and idea that came to my mind. Some people will probably say that I was "intellectualizing" the exercise, and I would agree. I did, and I loved doing it. But like chef Bissonnette rightfully said, the best creative outlet is to just start cooking and have fun with it. "Don't overthink it. Sitting in front of a notebook and writing things down is great, but I will have more impact with things if you just put me in the kitchen, give me a bunch of ingredients, and say "start cooking!" I become way more creative than I would be if I was just looking for recipes, reading books, looking at pictures and my notes from my travels.

When it comes to inspiration in cooking, the sky's the limit. As chef Chris Shepherd from Houston explains, "I tell people all the time that the only thing that holds you back is yourself. And that's the honest truth. The only thing that you can say no to is yourself. Because you have to try and push to try to learn, and you'll find inspirations anywhere and everywhere."

Chapter 3

FARMERS, FORAGING, AND ROADSIDE RICHES

"Celebrate Mother Nature's seasons. There's an opportunity for people to have a better understanding of when food is in season and how to celebrate that."
—FARMER LEE JONES

List of culinary individuals featured in this chapter:

Chef **Hari Cameron** former chef/owner at a(MUSE.) in Rehoboth, Delaware

Chef/Owner **Gabriel Kreuther** from two-Michelin star Gabriel Kreuther restaurant in New York City

Farmer **Lee Jones** from The Chef's Garden in Huron, Ohio

Chef **Sam Freund** from White Birch in Flanders, New Jersey

Chef **Johnny Spero** from Reverie in Washington, D.C.

Chef **Shamil Velazquez** from Delaney Oyster House in Charleston

Chef/Owner **Alison Trent** of Alison Trent Events in Los Angeles (was at Ysabel in Los Angeles)

Chef and restaurateur **Tim Hollingsworth** at Otium and C.J. Boyd's in Los Angeles

Executive chef **Jean Marie Josselin** at JO2 on Kauai, Hawaii

Chef/Co-Owner **Fiore Tedesco** from L'Oca d'Oro in Austin, Texas

Chef **Jonathan Zaragoza** from Birrieria Zaragoza in Chicago

Chef/Co-Owner **Drew Adams** of Meloria in Sarasota (was at Bourbon Steak in Washington, D.C.)

Chef/Owner **Michael Fojtasek** of Olamaie and Little Ola's Biscuits in Austin, Texas

Executive chef **Drake Leonards** at Eunice in Houston

Chef/Co-Owner **Brad Miller** of The Inn at the Seventh Ray in Topanga Canyon, California

Chef and Author **Edward Lee**, chef/owner of 610 Magnolia and Whiskey Dry in Louisville; culinary director of Succotash at National Harbor in Maryland, and Penn Quarter in Washington, D.C

Chef and Author **Chris Shepherd**, operating Underbelly Hospitality Group in Houston

Chef **Trigg Brown** from Win Son in Brooklyn, New York

While parking, I already began to see people with white chef coats folded on their arms, carrying boxes and bags and walking towards the Brooklyn Expo Center to get set up and prepped for upcoming culinary demos, hands-on workshops, beverage tastings, business seminars, or food competitions. Each year, StarChefs comes up with an overall theme that drives the content of the three-day event. In this Fall of 2019, the StarChefs Congress' theme was New Foundations: Flavor + Technique + Business. In 2018, it was Cooking with Respect: Better People, Better Food; in 2017, the focus was on Cook Your Culture—The Techniques, Knowledge, and Flavors That Define You; and before that, the theme—my favorite—was Open-Source Cooking: The New Era of Collaboration and Connectivity.

That day, I quickly climbed the steps that led to a series of meeting rooms where I had scheduled an early recording for my podcast with chef Hari Cameron from Rehoboth Beach, Delaware. That fall, Cameron was the chef and owner of a(MUSE.), since sold—a fine dining restaurant that used local, Mid-Atlantic ingredients and both classic techniques and modern culinary preparations with both a la carte and a five-course tasting menu.

I just had time to finish my setup when Cameron energetically entered the room and introduced himself, and we dived right into our conversation. He explained that the role of a chef is to enhance the produce by extracting its flavors. Without great ingredients, chefs cannot make great food. "You can't take a crappy product and make it into something wonderful." I realized that, but any home cook knows that the reverse is not necessarily true. Even if you follow a recipe, the outcome depends on how you adapt the recipe to the ingredients you have available.

While I was listening to Cameron, I remembered a previous conversation with chef Gabriel Kreuther: "You can have a great tomato but still need to enhance it by preparing it a certain way, depending on what you decide to do with that tomato. Same with fish or meat, depending on how good the cut is, how old the meat is, or how old the fish is. That's why a recipe is never perfect, because if that piece of fish has more water retention than another piece, it's going to cook differently. The same is true with meat—dry-aged has less water in it, so it cooks much faster."

When I was packing up my recording equipment after Cameron left for his upcoming cooking demonstration at the Congress, I was thinking that I was so accustomed to buying any type of produce year-round that I forget that not all produce is created equal. Not everything is always in season. The produce that I have always available in supermarkets was grown for two main reasons: size and durability, but not for flavor. All these culinary leaders assure me that fresh food, locally produced on a small scale, is more nutrient-dense and tastes better. Eating with the season would give me access to more produce variety, and provide access to farmers and farmers' markets.

Several months later, in the quarantine phase of the pandemic, access to fresh produce was challenging. Searching online, I found local farms in New Jersey that would deliver their fresh fruit and vegetables to my doorstep on a weekly basis.

One of my friends introduced me to The Chef's Garden in Ohio when the owners pivoted their business to shipping boxes of veggies around the country. I hosted Farmer Lee Jones, owner of The Chef's Garden, as a guest on my podcast a couple of days after receiving their first package. I was astonished by the quality of their spinach in particular. Since that day, I can no longer purchase spinach from a standard retail store. I know it may sound a bit pompous that my spinach has to come from a farm, but the stuff you buy in plastic bags from the stores has no body and starts to deteriorate and turn yellow after three to four days in the refrigerator.

"The spinach that you got in your box," explained Farmer Lee Jones, "is the spinach we're harvesting right now, that we planted last fall. It's actually a variety that we call 'iced' spinach. It freezes at night. It has crunch, body, texture, flavor, and vitamins in it. It's just full of health." Jones was telling me that they had tested the spinach a few days before with a refractometer and they scored as sweet as a Red Delicious apple!

If chefs and mixologists have their secrets for sourcing the freshest and most flavorful ingredients to include in their signature dishes or drinks, and if not all produce is created equal, I was hoping that my guests would share some of their secrets with me and give answers to some of my questions. What should I consider when buying ingredients when I cook at home? What does local really mean for them? How do I discover local food around where I live? Is buying organic food more important than buying local food even if it is not organic? Can I trust all "farm-to-table" labels and statements?

Through my conversations with these culinary leaders, I wanted to understand why it was important to source food locally, and how they cultivated relationships with growers. Some chefs have been foraging for unique ingredients. Are they foraging for their restaurants? How do they get inspired to create dishes with foraged food? Is it legal for me to forage too? Along my conversations, I found out that the word "local" had various meanings: some looked at it literally as "near me," others considered it as "regional," and others interpreted it as a locality of culture—meaning "from a specific location" or "from a specific country."

I live in New Jersey, which is known as the Garden State. There is a rich agricultural tradition in central New Jersey, and it is the perfect place for a farm-to-table dining experience. Chef Sam Freund from White Birch restaurant cares deeply about the food that he serves to his customers. His restaurant is located in the farmland part of the state, an hour's drive from Manhattan, and he grew up near farms not too far from there. As he remembers, "Growing up, I don't remember buying eggs from a store. We just went up the street to the farm, and I still keep that mindset today."

The concept of his restaurant is focused on working with local farmers and seasonal market ingredients that are found within an eight-mile radius from his restaurant. "We aim to serve our community and impact the culinary landscape of Northern New Jersey." He was surprised that few local restaurants utilize what they have available in their backyard. "I really want to bring the real farm-to-table idea to this part of the state—everything from the restaurant's decor to working with local farms. No one around here is really doing that."

Freund was concerned that not enough people supported local farms. "Without them our restaurants are nothing. The more we support them, the more they are going to support us. When you get produce from purveyors and not from farms, honestly, you don't know who's handling it. With these local farms, I can literally pick out this produce myself. The more people support local farms, the better off restaurants are. The busier they are, the busier we are."

Freund recognized that it is not easy, and it takes a lot of work to go to these farms and build relationships, although he admits, "That's what you have to do to survive in this industry." He described how he gets excited every spring to start these relationships again and begin working on his restaurant's spring menu.

A couple of years ago, Freund started the Farmer Dinner Series. Each dinner featured a farm with which White Birch restaurant worked; the special menu he created used produce from the farm, and the farmer was present and celebrated during the dinner. I attended one of these dinners honoring Let It Grow farm, located in Chester, New Jersey. The tasting menu consisted of four main courses: herbed pappardelle with sugar peas, braised beet greens and kale pesto; roasted halibut with red pearl onion, baby fennel, and butter lettuce puree; aged NY strip steak with potato croquette, roasted farm vegetables, and garlic scape compound butter; and a strawberry shortcake with holy basil chiboust, buttermilk biscuit, and sugared parsley.

Let it Grow farm actually grew a couple of plants just for White Birch. "They brought a seed catalog. We picked out what we wanted for the restaurant and they planted it for us," Freund said. "That alone again says a lot about this industry. It's a full team effort."

Chefs developed relationships with farmers, and farmers usually work with chefs by sending them weekly lists of current available produce or animals. Sometimes chefs are inspired by the unusual products that are available each week. I recall a conversation with chef Johnny Spero, from Reverie in

D.C., admitting, "I like working with weird stuff. Once, a farmer from Culpepper in Virginia had some birch trees on his property, and he had birch bark that I could make gallons of birch syrup from. I took all of it! We made a dessert on the menu that was pretty much dedicated to him. We turned the bark into ice cream, and then we used birch syrup to sweeten it and served it with spruce, root beer, and charcoal. I was wildly obsessed with that dish." The farmer also made pine syrup and brought Spero a bunch of big pine cones. "Those are kind of fun, finding ingredients that are not new, by any means, but new for us, and trying to do a new take on them. This is what excites me!"

The work chefs Freund and Spero are doing with farmers is awesome, but in the past decade, there has been a lot of controversy about the term "farm-to-table." This movement began more than two decades ago with good intentions: food made from locally sourced ingredients, often natural or organic. The movement's intent was designed to change the culture around how we eat. However, with capitalism and bad marketing strategy through the years, this movement lost its meaning and the term got overused.

Chef Shamil Velazquez from Delaney Oyster House in Charleston, who attended the Culinary Institute of America with a concentration in farm-to-table, shared that this whole movement has been blown up by all the major food and food service companies. "As a chef, it is our due diligence to make sure that we are working with local farmers, local fishmongers, oyster farmers, and do our part in society, rather than leaving the carbon footprint of getting stuff from the other side of the world, when it's right here."

Chef Alison Trent from Ysabel in West Hollywood has also built these relationships throughout the years and she has learned the ins and outs of the farming industry. "Their job is brutal. It makes my job as a chef look like a walk in the park. They need our support, otherwise they won't survive. With property value going up, farmers are staying in the industry out of respect. They could easily sell their farm and probably live off the proceeds for the rest of their life, but it's about maintaining their integrity as farmers. I just have the utmost respect for people that go down that path." Trent shared that some of her closest friends came from and through work. "It is all about aligning yourself with like-minded people that care about A, the environment, and B, good food."

This support that exists among chefs, farmers, or purveyors goes both ways. During the pandemic, many farmers and purveyors suffered from the interruption of the food chain. I remember watching an Instagram Live between chef Tim Hollingsworth from Otium in Los Angeles and Celine Labaune from the company Gourmet Attitudes, as Hollingsworth was doing a cooking demo using the beautiful black truffles provided by Celine. Hollingsworth talked about his long-time friendship with Celine and the relationship they developed through the years.

"I started talking to her and ordering truffles from Gourmet Attitudes twenty years ago. There's a trusting relationship. She's truly a friend. I think that when a friend calls me looking for help and support, the last thing I want is for my favorite truffle provider and supplier, and a good friend of mine, to go out of business after she's been great with us for so many years." Hollingsworth explained that even if Celine was not close to going out of business, it was important for him to show love, and to support her and other suppliers who didn't necessarily have the restaurants backing up their business during the pandemic.

"Without them our restaurants are nothing. The more we support them, the more they are going to support us. When you get produce from purveyors and not from farms, honestly, you don't know who's handling it. With these local farms, I can literally pick out this produce myself. The more people support local farms, the better off restaurants are."

—CHEF SAM FREUND

I have been fortunate enough to take several trips to Hawaii and of all the islands, by far, my favorite is the island of Kauai. I have developed several culinary rituals when I am on Kauai, and one of my must-stops is the restaurant JO2 in Kapa'a with chef Jean-Marie Josselin.

The exhilaration about any trip I organize always starts during the research phase. I cannot go anywhere without doing prior investigation with multiple online sites, magazines, and books—a very annoying obsession if you listen to my kids! Before my first trip to Kauai, I picked JO2 as a key food location and read everything I could find about the chef. The fact that he was originally from France, had spent thirty years in Hawaii, and for many years placed local vegetables at the center of the plate, intrigued me. On my first trip to JO2, I took my time tasting chef Josselin's dishes, all of which were as pleasing to the eye as they were on my tastebuds. Poached Carrot Dumplings with taro basil coconut sauce, Stir-Fried Local Japanese Eggplant with almond sate, Spinach Watercress Roll with black sesame sauce, and Mizo Marinated Salmon with soba noodles and ponzu sauce were a few favorites among other delicious small plates. At the end of the dinner, when the rush in the kitchen was over, I asked chef Josselin how he prepared and seasoned the delicious carrots, eggplants, and spinach in his dishes.

"Nothing sophisticated. I let the produce speak for itself. You have to realize that Kauai is not like New York, Boston, or Los Angeles. Everything that we get at the restaurant is grown within fifteen, twenty minutes of the restaurant," explained Josselin. "One of the biggest things for me in the last twenty years was to work with farmers, and try to bring Hawaii up to the mainland standards."

In 1991, he and eleven other chefs started the Hawaii Regional Cuisine movement, which celebrated local farmers and producers, long before "farm-to-table" became the buzzword it is today. His first step when he opened his previous restaurant in Kauai was to meet with farmers. "I did all the farmers' markets on Kauai. Every time I saw a new guy, I approached him and invited him to the restaurant. I started to build a network of farmers that wanted to work with me to try new vegetables."

Josselin explained that it was a challenge as the weather changes frequently and there are a lot of pests in Kauai. "It could be ninety degrees one day, and it can rain for two weeks after that. There's a lot of challenges, but the farmer network that I put together was willing to work with me."

He bought a lot of seeds for himself, and worked with the University of Hawaii to develop seed types made to grow in tropical parts of the country. Step by step, they started to build a garden, and then a market that he could buy from. "Suddenly, I had Cavaillon melon, eight different types of carrots, thirty-six different types of tomatoes. It took a couple of years to do that. When I worked on the JO2 project, I knew that it was going to take a while. JO2 was an evolution from a protein-run restaurant to slowly getting into a vegetable-centric restaurant. That was my vision six years ago. I wanted to take, step by step, all the fish, all the meat, all the animal proteins off the menu and draw everything only from the farmers."

Beyond building simple business or friendly relationships, chefs truly collaborate with farmers around the country and each year explore a new variety of produce and ingredients and ask the farmers if they would grow specific vegetables for them.

Farmer Lee Jones recalled the creation of The Chef's Garden with his father and the beginning of long-lasting collaborations with celebrity chefs from all around the country. "It started with chef Jean-Louis Paladin, a highly-touted chef from France. He was very gregarious and outspoken. Basically, his message was that our food was bad in America. 'If you want to grow for me, then let's figure out how to grow properly.' A lot of American farmers were really doing quite well at that time and they were wondering, 'Who was this guy coming into our country telling us we needed to learn how to better grow things?' It really was off-putting to a lot of people, but it did resonate with my father."

Jones said Paladin was pushing for growing without chemicals, without synthetic fertilizer, and growing to enhance the flavor of the produce. "What he was suggesting had existed in America before, we had just lost our way and moved away from that with the convenience factor of production agriculture that drove the economic engine in the US. We produce food cheaper than any other country in the world, as it relates to our income." Jones and his father followed what Paladin preached and Paladin knew that if he didn't give them enough work to keep them in business, they couldn't do it. "He got on the phone and called other chefs like Daniel Boulud, Alain Ducasse, Jean-Georges Vongerichten, and a lot of other European chefs that had come to America and asked them to support us. They took us under their wings and allowed us an existence and the ability to grow food the right way." Jones added that these chefs didn't necessarily know which were the best varieties to grow, so they didn't dictate to the farmers. Instead, "What they told us was, flavor, quality, and consistency were their key priorities."

These people are challenging the status quo as well as having people's best interests at heart while taking a sustainable approach. Other farms around the country are collaborating with chefs and grow, harvest, and eat according to the seasons. They follow sustainable agricultural practices and have worked in the past decades to reintroduce native heirloom varieties of vegetables or grains. For years, chef Sean Brock has worked alongside Glenn Roberts, owner of Anson Mills in South Carolina, to revive Carolina Gold rice and extinct varieties of heirloom corn and wheat.

Alex Weiser is one of the most famous farmers in the Los Angeles area. His family has been in the business for decades. When I talked to chef Trent, she mentioned that she was supporting Weiser Farms and organized dinners in collaboration with them. "Alex works closely with the Tehachapi Grain Project growing these incredible grains in California. These grains are actually much better than grains we're getting from other states in the country." The mission of the Tehachapi Grain Project is to restore, preserve, and grow non-GMO heritage organic grains for home cooks, chefs, bakers, and brewers.

Chef Fiore Tedesco from L'Oca d'Oro in Austin grew Calamint (also known as Nepatella in Tuscan cuisine) with La Flaca Farm. "They were really wonderful. They worked really closely with us when I had an idea to grow a weed or a flower." These ingredients are key to Tedesco, who finishes a lot of dishes with different flower buds and herbs that really bring a lot of light and liveliness to his dishes. "I'm always doing research and tasting through a lot of different herbs. Some of them do not readily exist. We started growing Nepitella Calamint at La Flaca Farms so that we could use it with a mushroom dish that I was working on."

The farmers who follow sustainable agricultural practices are working in harmony with nature rather than trying to outsmart it. Farmer Lee Jones told me, "It's like when you go to the doctor and get blood work drawn. From that blood work they can tell you if you're high or low in iron, or if you're high or low in calcium. They can read what's going on within your body. We do the same thing with the soil. Even the commercial chemical growers do it. In fact, chemical companies will supply that service for farmers, and they'll do the soil test, the analysis, and then suggest what application of synthetic fertilizers needs to go on. This is where our approach and theirs differ. We do the soil analysis and based on the deficiencies that we find within the soil, we plant specific crops."

Jones explains that different types of plants will accept varying types of energy from the sun. They even have a seventeen-variety cover crop mix that they use to give something similar to a multivitamin treatment to the soil. Then they let the land sit fallow and let the plants grow. "If you can visualize the leaves of that plant as antennas or receptacles, they accept the energy through the leaves into the stems, down to the roots, and then into the soil. Then the year after, when we plant the turnip or the beet, the carrot, the radish, or the zucchini, it picks that back up, and eating it strengthens our immune system." Jones compares today's chemical and commercial farming to Western medicine. "Once we get sick, a doctor prescribes penicillin or amoxicillin. They always treat the symptom. I compare that method of farming with what we're trying to do today, which is more like the Eastern culture. We want to get the body in balance to defend against the disease in the first place. So, we have healthy soil, healthy vegetables, a healthy environment, and healthy people."

But following sustainable agriculture principles versus industrial farming and humanely raising meat, versus mass-producing meat, costs more money. Quality products will cost a few dollars more per pound. Chef Tim Hollingsworth from Otium restaurant in Los Angeles said, "I think it's also important for people to understand how expensive these products are. To get lamb from a butcher, versus a grocery store, is more expensive because of the way the farmer goes about raising it. It's not mass produced, and it's an exceptional product. The same thing applies when that box of vegetables comes in from The Chef's Garden."

"You need to buy quality products and quality products cost money," says chef Kim Alter from Nightbird in San Francisco. "These farmers are artisans, and their meat is coming from the best cows, and the cheese is made by someone who has spent their whole life doing it. Sometimes spending that extra two dollars is going to change your entire dish because of the quality of the cheese and getting the tomato from the farmers' market. It might be a dollar more than what you would get at a standard grocery store, but it's going to be the most beautiful tomato, and you're paying for the quality. I think buying the best ingredients is number one when you're doing something simple."

For some chefs, the collaboration with farmers means an integral part of their vision for their restaurant, and it takes farmers and producers and a community of people to make their vision come true. Chef Fiore Tedesco confessed that the important question to him was how to honor them. "How do you create your restaurant concept in a way that makes everyone's life richer—or even how not to compromise anyone's life—in the pursuit of a restaurant success?" It is a very complicated question as most restaurants are propped up by the industrial food system. "What I want is to be attached to these people who are growing the produce, whether it is a small farm or a very large farm. I want to be connected to their stories and know what my place is in that system and know what their place is within my system."

When he and his business partner were coming up with the idea of their Austin restaurant L'Oca d'Oro, they really put that question front and center. "Once you put the question of the quality of everyone's livelihood at the center of the concept, you realize that this industry is not based around the restaurant's success. It's based around the restaurant trying to survive in a pretty tough environment and making sacrifices to all those other places, so that you can survive. We realized that, for us, to work the way that we wanted to, by celebrating the farmers and the producers, and the people that work with us, we had to work away and swim against the stream to make our vision come true. If we take tipping as a service charge and embed that in the price of our menu, it gives us a greater opportunity to remove ourselves from the way people are generally paid within the hospitality's business. Basically, it is distributed evenly to all the workers in the restaurant to ensure that everyone that works in our restaurant is paid a living wage. We've been operating that way every day since we've been open."

For Tedesco, the goal is to make a sustainable restaurant that nourishes people in a healthy, holistic way. This means that he is allowing his twenty-five employees to live sustainable lives. They are making a living wage and they can make responsible decisions for themselves. This model supports farmers in a way that helps them reach those same goals for themselves. "Whatever is left over for profit, that's great, but it is not the main goal, and I'm sorry to our investors, it is not purely a profit-driven business, and we will not ebb away at our values for the sake of a couple of extra dollars."

I realized after talking to Tedesco that chefs and food entrepreneurs cannot approach a food business or a restaurant as a stand-alone operation. It is part of an ecosystem, and creating real collaboration and partnership is the only way forward to achieve a win-win situation.

Funny fact: Farmer Lee Jones mentioned the one positive outcome from the pandemic is the growing popularity of people having their own gardens. There were more family gardens planted during the pandemic than at any time in the history of the US. Jones mentioned that it was like after WWII when America had victory gardens, and everyone planted gardens because resources were short. "During the pandemic we saw people on Instagram planting and growing their own veggies and cooking them. Families were doing it together. Parents were interested in planting a garden, and kids wanted to be out there to help Mom and Dad in the garden."

Jones explained that because they started gardening as a child, and learned how intriguing it was to understand that carrots come from the soil and that they can harvest them, cook them, and eat them, it established a connection with where the food comes from, how it's grown, and how much work it takes to grow it. "We created a whole entire generation of new gardeners!"

"Get to know your local producers and farmers, have conversations with them, introduce yourself to them, and support them every week. They'll tell you what to buy and how to cook it. It all starts with establishing a connection with people. That's what home cooks need to do, they need to get out, support local farmers, local markets, local butchers, and build these relationships and change the food culture that we currently have."

—CHEF JONATHAN ZARAGOZA

As I do not have the space nor the motivation to grow my own vegetables and raise my own chickens, I will follow the chefs' lead and work with local farmers. But I will go foraging for some unique ingredients.

In the past five years, American chefs have been rediscovering foraging and are helping others learn to forage for food. It seems that the surprise-and-reward aspect is one reason foraging has become so popular. Twenty years ago in France, chef Michael Bras in the Laguiole region, and chef Marc Veyrat in the Alps, were foraging long before it became cool. Bras is still one of the most influential, forward-thinking chefs on the planet. More recently, Chef Rene Redzepi, from Noma in Denmark, put foraging back in the forefront of their food culture. Foraged ingredients are at the heart of Redzepi's work. Each seasonal menu at Noma is based on a different theme inspired by wild Scandinavian ingredients. The restaurant features seafood in winter, fresh vegetables in summer, and wild game and forest picks in fall. In the U.S., chef Dan Barber also forages for herbs and nuts in the eighty acres of farmland around his restaurant Blue Hill Stone Barns in New York state.

In 2019, I approached chef Drew Adams, the executive chef at the Four Seasons in Washington, D.C., as I was curious about his motivations for foraging, even though he had access to such beautiful and luxurious ingredients at the Four Seasons. "It's a good excuse to get outside," he told me with a smile. Adams explained that besides the fact that foraging gives him access to wild ingredients, it also offers him the opportunity to learn and discover new flavors. Foraging gets him outdoors, removes him from his day-to-day routine, changes his perspectives on things, and contributes to his productivity and inspiration.

"I started doing it probably six years ago," said Adams. "It gave me a lot more appreciation for the product that I'm working with. The first thing I found was ramps in the spring, and just got excited about it. You want to do everything you can with your cooking to make sure you really showcase the product you collect. The more I learned about foraging, the more I realized how little I knew about how many edible things were out there. Each year, I find something new, and it's just very fascinating to me. It's like when you were younger, and everyone wanted to be the kid on the block that had that new toy! I liked to be that kid."

Foraging also gives Adams unique access to products, like ground nettles, mustard greens, and different types of edible flowers, which aren't necessarily readily available elsewhere. "In the spring, we have this field that is covered in violets. I make violet syrup and candied violets that we use as garnishes. We get wild persimmons as well. They grow locally, dry on the trees, and they taste unbelievable. It's like eating candy! There are hundreds of different things that I can find in the woods that I can't buy from local purveyors."

In the early spring of 2019, my younger son and I went to Washington, D.C. to meet with chef Adams and experience his program, "Foraging and Feasting." It was one of those father-son trips that I loved to organize. The program is an all-day experience that started with an a la carte three-hour guided tour by chef Adams and finished with a multi-course tasting menu using versions of the day's finds paired with wine.

Arriving early at the Four Seasons in Georgetown, chef Adams welcomed us with a massive basket of homemade pastries, croissants, and a freshly poured mocktail. We were off to a good start! To my big surprise, we took a Town Car with chauffeur to the woods along the Potomac River. During the ride, it was a nice opportunity for my son and I to get acquainted with chef Adams.

I asked him, "So, Chef, is everything safe when it comes to foraging? Certain plants and mushrooms can be harmful for humans."

He smiled at my caution and said, "I never ended up at the hospital. When I was a kid, I ate some mushrooms and got really sick, but that was a long time ago. That's the only real time I think I've actually gotten sick from picking something up." Adams talked about his passion for mushrooms now, and how he doesn't pick anything about which he is uncertain.

"I'll go home, and I'll look it up," he said. "The hardest thing for me is mushrooms because there are so many different species out there, and I'm only good with five of them, maybe. Each year, I learned about more types. Morels and chanterelles grow here. I actually had some Porcini mushrooms growing in my front yard this year, which was pretty wild, and I usually get woodier mushrooms like chicken of the woods or oyster mushrooms while foraging."

I enjoyed the three hours in the woods, looking at nettles, ramps, mushrooms, and other herbs whose names I forgot. My son immediately connected with chef Adams, and discovered a unique aspect of the life of a chef that he had never considered.

This time in the woods brought me back to my childhood when I was foraging morels, chanterelles, and porcini mushrooms with my father in the forests and countryside of France. When I shared my memories about this nostalgic time with my father, Adams said, "That's really cool. It happens that I have received plenty of beautiful morels at the restaurant. I am going to change one of the dishes for your dinner tonight and make something with morels and a wild onion foam!"

I was already salivating about the morel dish and thinking that my father would never have imagined that his youngest would be reminiscing about our time together picking mushrooms forty years earlier, nor would he have believed that it would be while I was walking in the woods near the capital of the US.

As we were following chef Adams along the paths in the woods, he pointed at a stand of thin, tall trees and asked, "Do you know what those are?"

Seeing the ignorance on our faces, he continued, "They are pawpaw trees. They grow around D.C., northern Virginia, western Maryland, and even up to southern Pennsylvania as well. They produce a fruit called the pawpaw. The fruit comes out for about three weeks to a month out of the year. It usually starts anywhere from mid-August to the beginning of September, but if you're not out there every day looking at them, you can easily miss them. It's a green fruit, probably about an inch and a half, two inches in diameter, maybe about three to four inches long, with a similar shape to a jellybean. It tastes like a mix of mango, banana, and avocado. It's one of the northernmost tropical fruits in the country."

Adams continued walking and explained that he had become obsessed with it over the years. "Do you know the French chef Cédric Grolet? He is an incredible pastry chef and does all these fruit dishes that mimic the shape of the fruit. He'll do a strawberry stuffed with a strawberry mousse. He'll spray paint on it and the result looks a hundred percent like a strawberry. He does it also with peach, pear, or apple."

Adams explained that he worked together with his pastry chef Chelsea Spalding on something similar with pawpaw. "We started conceptualizing the dish. We found this company that makes silicone molds. We got them to make us a jellybean mold. Then we cast the mold out of white chocolate, we stuffed it with pawpaw mousse, pawpaw chutney, some candied hazelnuts, and then we spray-painted it to look like a pawpaw. We served it on top of some chocolate soil and pawpaw ice cream." For Adams, exploring the possibilities that this new pawpaw fruit suddenly offered led him to a whole new world of opportunities. That is the fascination of the unknown. Whether it's tasting new products, shopping for new ingredients, discovering new destinations when traveling, meeting new people, or experiencing new business models, there is an excitement of discovering the unknown. It opens up possibilities to enjoy something new, and it forces you to grow.

On the car ride back to the Four Seasons, I asked him, "With all the regulations around foraging, are you able to bring products from foraging to the restaurant?"

He shook his head and said, "Because of the law, you're not supposed to really forage anything and bring it in. Fortunately, I have good relationships with a lot of local providers that have foragers. So, I just buy a lot of these same products through them. Whereas some of the more privately owned restaurants would just get backdoor drops from local foragers."

Back at the Four Seasons, Adams treated us to a tour of the kitchen before starting to cook our memorable tasting menu. While in the kitchen, my eyes caught a glimpse of the menu that Adams had created especially for us taped on the counter's white tiles. The feasting part of the Foraging and Feasting program turned into an eighteen-course menu!

"Eighteen courses?" I asked him, surprised.

He replied, "I went a bit overboard for you, Emmanuel. I know you and your son will appreciate it."

In the dining room, it seemed that half of our large table has been magically dressed-up by forest elves with a thick layer of moss of different greenish colors, and wild mushrooms and morels spread around with tiny white and pinkish flowers. Later in the evening, we learned that this undergrowth decor, that seemed to come directly from a fantasy movie, had been prepared by the chef himself to set the scene for his gastronomic performance.

Each course of the menu featured a foraged product. Here are the eighteen dishes that we savored:

- fermented ramp sourdough bread with honey ramp Benne seed butter.
- fried oysters with sorrel cream and hone.
- scallop crudo with wild onion oil, barrage, and wild fennel.
- a tartine of spring veggies, uni with creme fraiche.
- hash browns with pickled quail egg and sorrel.
- rockfish crudo.
- Faro with morel, poached egg yolk, wild garlic and wild onion foam.
- pork lettuce wrap with Serrano, ice plant, and fiddlehead.

- Carolina Gold rice with sorrel flowers.
- pork belly sliders with Japanese milk bread.
- pickled green tomato, wild onions, kewpie mayo, grilled mustard greens.
- grilled mushroom with cauliflower, green garlic cream, chive oil, and benne seeds.
- grilled quail with mushroom cream.
- fried cauliflower mushrooms.
- chicken thigh balloting with stinging nettle sauce, potato pearls, and nasturtium, sank with barley miso.
- golden enoki, truffles, and way beef.
- sorrel panna cotta with parsnip cake, pea tendrils, and whipped sorrel.
- and finally, rhubarb dip n dot's, with macerated strawberries.

My son couldn't believe his eyes or his taste buds. We both would never forget that day! And the use of quails, benne seeds, and Carolina Gold rice in Adams' dishes brought a Southern flavor to our tasting, reminding us that we were already in the South.

When I was a kid, my parents bought me a board game designed to introduce children to regional food specialties from France. The board was a map of the country featuring each region and their main cities. A collection of tokens represented unique agricultural production like oysters from Normandy or fruits from Provence, and food specialties such as local cheeses—Muenster from Alsace or Époisses from Burgundy—or famous dishes such as cassoulet from the southwest region and cheese fondue from Savoy. To win the game, you had to make a maximum of correct associations of tokens to French regions on the board. I loved that game, and after playing it multiple times, I knew everything about French local ingredients and regional food specialties.

Talking to chefs and farmers across the U.S., I discovered that local food is an important component of the health and sustainability of our communities. With the expansion of farmers' markets, community-supported agriculture, and farm-to-table restaurants in recent years, it is encouraging to see that the support of local food systems is growing. Knowing where your food comes from and the farming practices that produce it are important factors in choosing the best way to source ingredients. Local farmers focus on soil health and crop rotation. Organic farmers banned pesticides or herbicides and instead are committed to using sustainable practices to benefit both land and community, as compared to conventional, large-scale agriculture.

To learn about the food culture in this country, I have had to look beyond the nationwide food service chains and fast-food brands that represent a food standardization reality of the country. Throughout my travels, I have discovered the unique specialties from each region:

- sweet potatoes, squash, peanuts, and barbecue styles from the South.
- soybeans, oysters, melon, and gumbos from Louisiana.
- rice, benne wafers, and grits from the Low Country.
- corn, chicken, crabs, and Philly Cheesesteak from the Mid-Atlantic.
- berries, walnuts, and Marion berry pies from the Pacific Northwest.
- and almonds, avocados, dates, and pizza from California.

I remember tasting fried peanuts for the first time in Charleston, at the outdoor farmers' market in Marion Square. Located downtown, this green space hosts a once-a-week for Low Country farmers, growers, and artisans.

I love spending time in the alleys of the farmers' market and chatting with the locals in every city to which I travel. I had a lot of first food experiences that day. I discovered kiwi ice cream made from locally grown kiwis. I tasted local fruit preserves. I patiently watched the Low Country kettle corn being handmade in small batches in large copper pots and smelled the beautiful aroma of the almost burnt caramel. I took a tasting tour with a local, and got the opportunity to taste their famous hush puppies—these are small, savory, deep-fried round balls made from cornmeal-based batter.

I had the opportunity to learn much more about peanuts when I interviewed Ted Lee on my podcast. Ted and his brother have a company named The Lee Brothers Boiled Peanuts Catalog. I developed an interest for the South while reading their cookbooks, and I had always wanted to meet them. I was really excited that Ted accepted to be a guest on the show. He explained that he and his brother originally created their company to ship boiled peanuts and other Southern staples like grits and fig preserves that were at that time very difficult to source in other parts of the country.

Peanuts are a roadside snack in the South and are also known as goober peas. You walk into a gas station and there usually is a pot of warm peanuts in their shell on the counter.

I have an affinity for a great peanut dish created by chef Michael Fojtasek from Olamaie in Austin. I love Fojtasek's restaurant. He serves refined versions of hush puppies, hoppin' john, cornbread, and pork chops, and offers boiled peanuts in a pretty unique and interesting way. Fojtasek pressure cooks the peanuts and pairs them with a benne oil-honey mustard, pickled mustard seeds, local thickened buttermilk, and a green pea hummus with garlic and Texas olive oil. With his incomparable biscuits, I consider this boiled peanut dish as one of his signature dishes.

"The story behind these boiled peanuts is really remarkable," said Fojtasek. "Since we opened Olamaie, I always wanted to serve some kind of boiled peanut, but how to do it in such a way that isn't as messy as the roadside side ones, because essentially you get the brine (the salt solution) all over your hands when you're eating them."

Fojtasek explained that he tried to buy green peanuts for a couple of years, but it was not sustainable because, for one, green peanuts are very perishable, and two, they're typically harvested in huge quantities and no one was open to portioning off the smaller amount a restaurant would need.

"A couple of years ago," says Fojtasek, "James Brown from Barton Springs Mill opened an organic mill in Austin."

Fojtasek explains that Brown contracted farmers to grow wheat or corn for him, and he paid them in advance of the season. They established an agreed upon price and he received their crop. He also decided to buy peanuts from them, because peanuts were a great crop to put nitrogen back into the soil to repair the soil after growing wheat. To support the idea of crop rotation as well as soil fixing, he paid them to plant peanuts so that he would have a great wheat product from them. So, he bought the peanuts together with the wheat they produced.

"He offered these peanuts to a lot of folks," says Fojtasek, "and I think we're the last restaurant standing on a lot of them because they're rather labor-intensive. But what he does is he buys the peanuts, or the farmers harvest them and then they turn a bunch back into the ground, but they also harvest them, and they dry them just to shelf stable (food that can be safely stored at room temperature in a sealed container) so they're not roasted, like what you would get at the ballgame."

The Southern revival trend has been in the eyesight of chefs and the public for several years now. Since I arrived in the U.S. in 2002, I have observed Southern food growing in popularity, and it is no longer simply about fried chicken or barbecue clichés—don't get me wrong, I love fried chicken and the variety of barbecue profiles from one region to the next. Today, there is a celebration of local and regional ingredients. I have seen other well-known regional cuisines like the ones from New England or Louisiana being celebrated by chefs, but it is only recently that I noticed the cuisine from the Mid-Atlantic gaining traction. I feel it is sometimes overlooked as a cuisine. At the StarChefs event, chef Hari Cameron told me, "I think we have a lot of history and rich heritage in the Mid-Atlantic region. There are now a lot of great chefs in D.C., Philadelphia, Maryland, and Virginia that are putting their flag down and making Mid-Atlantic cuisine their own."

I asked him, "How would you define the staples of the cuisine from the Mid-Atlantic?"

Cameron highlighted the waterways and the Chesapeake Bay: "The tradition of sitting around the table with a steaming pot of crabs with Old Bay seasoning, drinking some light beer, and eating corn. The staples of the summer!"

He quickly added, "When people think of Delaware, they don't really think of crab. That's a Maryland thing. But we have crabs in all of our waters as well. We call it 'chicken necking.' We actually take a chicken neck and throw it over in the water and just net the crabs. It's a net lining."

Listening to Cameron reminded me of my best experiences eating blue crab. Annapolis, the capital of Maryland, just an hour east of Washington, D.C., is tucked away in one of the indentations of the Chesapeake Bay. I took my brother and my sister-in-law there for a week when they were visiting from France, and one day we ended up having lunch at Cantler's Riverside Inn—a restaurant nestled at the water's edge that welcomes their customers either by land or by sea. We sat at the terrace where the wooden tables and benches filled up as the customers arrived. The tables were covered with newspapers and after ordering "buckets" of blue crabs, our waitress brought us, to our great surprise, wooden mallets together with the classic forks and knives. The second moment of consternation was the delivery of the bucket overflowing with grilled crabs, which was emptied directly onto the newspaper!

Our tablemates, amused by our disconcerted look, were happy to explain the instructions: once the shell is crushed on the "tablecloth" with a wooden mallet, the best tool is finally your fingers! Our excitement allowed us to quickly acquire the necessary dexterity to extract the blue crabmeat from their shells. This moment turned out to be as tasty as it was unusual and convivial; the communal tables favoring exchange. Before the end of the meal, we knew everything about blue crabs and about the life of our table neighbors.

I often travel to New Orleans for business and have spent ten days touring the state on my own. I loved every one of my trips there. Compared to the noisy and dirty nights on Bourbon Street, I definitely prefer spending time in the small jazz bars on Frenchman Street, including the Three Muses, d.b.a., or the Spotted Cat. But when it comes to craft cocktails, my local spots are Tonique with Mark Schettler behind the bar, and Jewel of the South with Nick Detrich and Chris Hannah.

I followed the recommendation from the locals that to really appreciate the atmosphere of Louisiana, I had to spend time in the Bayou. I rented a flat boat in Henderson, a few miles from Lafayette, and at dawn I ventured out alone on the Atchafalaya swamp under Highway 10. Through majestic cypress and tupelo-covered swamps, I wandered my way through endless waterways. In the morning fog floating above the water, I frequently noticed burbles and ripples from the water and imagined water snakes and alligators nearby. As my motorboat penetrated the winding waterways, I surprised several great egrets and blue herons that took off by my side. When the swamps were no longer mine alone to enjoy, and families were picnicking on little islands, I decided to return the boat. I started to get hungry myself and drove back to New Orleans, where I had booked a cooking class at the New Orleans School of Cooking on St. Louis Street. That day, I learned the definition of the Holy Trinity in Cajun and Louisiana Creole cuisines, which is the base for several dishes in the regional cuisines of Louisiana. It consists of onions, bell peppers, and celery—in the same manner that a sofrito is used in the cuisines of Spanish and Caribbean cooking. I cooked and ate my own gumbo, jambalaya, shrimp, and grits.

When I met chef Drake Leonards in Houston several years later, I connected right away with his cooking, which was rooted in Southern Louisiana classics with some Texan interpretations. "One of our dishes is a crispy quail," says Leonards. "We're very fortunate here, the hill country's Bandera Farm is just a stone's throw away from Houston, and they raise the most beautiful quail, and we do a classic buttermilk fry with it."

His restaurant Eunice is a modern Cajun-Creole brasserie. Leonards makes a batter of flour, Creole spice, and buttermilk to dredge the quail in, and he fries them like chicken. The result is most delicious. They take the McIlhenny pepper mash—the same pepper people make Tabasco sauce with—and blend it with local artisan Texas honey. "That's, to me, a Cajun-Creole-Houston sort of dish that we're able to pull together from everywhere," says Leonards. "There is something from South Louisiana, something from just right outside of Houston, and we create a great dish that is uniquely modern Cajun-Creole."

I also discovered at Eunice the Cajun caviar served with burrata, pepper jelly, and a side of biscuits. It has become one of their staple dishes. The Cajun caviar comes from the Choupique fish in the Atchafalaya Basin. This is a great illustration of a high-low concept that's trending—the cream cheese and pepper jelly which is connected to this traditionally easy-going dish served with crackers and dressed up with burrata and local "Louisiana caviar." "We are trying to take the best of what we can get our hands on locally and still keeping that traditional Southern Louisiana vein to make sure that it still ties back to Louisiana."

As I continued on my travels through the food culture of the US, I discovered that the state of California is a paradise for chefs and mixologists with its cornucopia of fresh produce. The state produces two-thirds of the nation's fruits and nuts, and about one-quarter of what the state produces is exported around the world. "We have the best ingredients, and everything's local, and everything comes from the best farms," says chef Brad Miller. "We have the most amazing farms out here. That's why you see a lot of chefs from New York and Chicago moving here and opening restaurants. They fell in love with our farmers' markets."

The coast of California offers great seafood as well, and during one of my early trips to San Francisco, I discovered the Hog Island Oyster Company on Route 1, north of San Francisco on the Shoreline Highway. They have several restaurants, and one of the most popular is located in the Ferry building in San Francisco, but nothing compares to an early morning stop at the Hog Shack in Marshall, and hand picking your own oysters for breakfast. The last time I went there, they still had their Shuck-Your-Own picnic program, and I was able to shuck my oysters while peering out over the Tomales Bay. Nothing is better than that. Unfortunately, they had to stop the program as they could not control the amount of non-recyclable and non-compostable waste generated each day by people stopping by.

One of my trips to California took me to Cabazon. I spent some time with friends in Chino, forty minutes west of Los Angeles. They took me to a pow wow, celebrating Native American culture and heritage. I spent the afternoon among colorful costumes, with feathers and fabulous beading, that were a sight to behold. Besides being surrounded by Native American jewelry, pottery, and clothing, I tasted Indian tacos, tamales, and frybread for the first time before attending an evening of traditional dances. The recollection of that singular day reminded me to invite Native American chefs to my podcast to celebrate indigenous cuisine.

In 2018, I explored the southwestern area of the Appalachia. Chef Milton Travis is a name that comes to mind when thinking about the revival of Appalachian cooking and the local ingredients from the Appalachian region. It is only since late 2010, when the region was frequently featured in media articles, that people understood how special this region was. The Appalachian trail is rich in plants, fruit, and fungi such as hickory nuts, sassafras, huckleberry, pokeweed, ramps, sumac, wild grape, wintergreen, chicken of the wood, morels, and pawpaws.

I went from Atlanta to Asheville, North Carolina, driving through Chattanooga and Knoxville. This was a research trip about understanding the revival of Southern cuisine, and a brainstorming exercise to come up with new dishes and drink concepts for industry manufacturers. The objective was to develop a new line of natural flavors and seasonings for Symrise—the company I work for.

A cross functional team of flavorists, food technologists, research chefs, sensory analysts, and marketing specialists took a flight from Newark, New Jersey to Atlanta and jumped on a minibus. We had spent a month prior to the trip conducting interviews with local chefs and researching restaurants, bars, and food spots that represented the best of what the region had to offer, and would help us understand what the key ingredients and the new influences of the new food and drink scenes in this region were.

Chef Edward Lee told us, "Start in Virginia and go west to Kentucky. Go south to east Texas, then draw a line across the Gulf coast to northern Florida. Then, trace the line back up to Virginia. That's the cultural South. Basically, you have a number of different regions. There are the Mountain South—states that cross Appalachia: Virginia, North Carolina. That's basically mountain cuisine—a lot of pickles, pork products, dried corn products, dried beans, stews. South from there is low country cuisine. That's coastal cuisine—from Georgia to the Carolinas—a lot of seafood but also a lot of pork. If you keep going south you get to Louisiana, Alabama, with a much more Cajun/Creole, French influence. Gumbos, crawfish boils, étouffées are a very different type of Southern cuisine. Going west into Texas and the Great Plains, you see a lot of beef and a lot of barbecue. Mississippi delta—northern Mississippi and those plains have great agriculture—you see rice and the Mexican influence with tamales and corn. Going up to Kentucky, you get a lot of cured meat, hams, and bourbon, the original spirit of the South."

Pimento cheese was an important food trend that started after 2015. This popular dip or spread, typically made with sharp cheddar cheese, mayonnaise, and pimiento peppers, had risen by more than sixty percent in new items on the menus across the U.S. and was very popular among foodies and Southerners.

In Atlanta, we tasted our first pimento cheese at Empire State South with chef Hugh Acheson, who put a contemporary twist on classic Southern ingredients. The pimento cheese was combined with bacon marmalade as a savory and creamy spread served in a glass jar. We loved the touch of sweetness from the bacon marmalade. We continued our tasting at Empire State South with the farm egg with crispy rice dish and the Carolina Gold rice grits with mushrooms. We couldn't be in Atlanta without eating at Holeman and Finch from chef Linton Hopkins, where we tasted our second pimento cheese with bread and butter pickles, the Johnnycakes with Benton's bacon, poached egg, duck liver, and sorghum, and a slice of sticky toffee pudding with salted vanilla ice cream. Our last stop in Atlanta was at the Bar B Que place at the Heirloom Market where we got some of those great smoke aromas and tasted the smoked brisket and smoked marinated beef short ribs. Interestingly enough, we experienced some Korean influences with kimchi and gochujang.

We left Atlanta and stopped at Two Ten Jack in Chattanooga to check the Japanese influence in the South, with yuzu (a Japanese citrus), shochu (a Japanese distilled beverage), tea, or plum nectar used in craft cocktails, and crispy Brussels sprouts with miso vin and rice crispies. We used the time in the minibus between stops to talk about our tasting experiences and brainstormed new ideas that we could leverage for future discussions with customers. On our way to Knoxville, we stopped at the renowned Benton's Country Ham in the Smoky Mountains. Their business started in the late '40s, and the unique slow-cured hams are famous around the country and used as key ingredients at many restaurants. When we entered Benton's location in Madisonville, Tennessee, it was hard to imagine that this place was nationally known. It felt like a rundown retail operation from the '60s, with a series of not-so well-organized glass cases displaying packages of vacuum sealed ham and bacon, cardboard boxes full of Benton's bacon ends, and wooden structures where different kinds of meats were hanging. Before leaving, we had a private tour of the facilities and went in the refrigerated rooms, the curing room, and saw the smokehouse. The smoke aroma was omnipresent. A smoke smell hit our nostrils as soon as we entered the store, and remained on our clothes back in the minibus, and stayed with us until we hit Knoxville.

In Knoxville, we stopped first at Knox Mason with chef Matt Gallaher and tasted the fresh pork rinds served with Bourbon barrel-smoked paprika and Tennessee Sunshine hot sauce, the deviled farm eggs with rooster sauce, and Tennessee Chow Chow—a local condiment made of green tomatoes, cabbage, bell peppers, onions, spices, and apple cider vinegar. We also tried another mason jar with pimento cheese (which is made with Sweetwater Cheese and served with Saw Works beer bread and Wickles pickles), the smoked trout Gillette's, caramelized Visalia onion dip, a fantastic Mac and cheese, and finally, the Heritage Farm Pork Belly with Jack Daniel's fired apples and Benton's bacon.

We stayed at regular chain hotels for most of the nights, but one evening we organized a stay at the Dancing Bear Lodge in Townsend, Tennessee. Centered in the foothills of the Great Smoky Mountains, Dancing Bear Lodge is known as east Tennessee's ultimate basecamp, offering charming Southern hospitality with individual lodge cabins. We arrived at night and the Appalachian Bistro at the Lodge had prepared a special dinner for our group. The dining room was all wood and stones and a long wooden table was set up with stone boards carrying deviled eggs, pickled shrimp, benne seed bacon, smoked blue cheese, pimento spread, country ham, cherry pineapple compote, and pickled vegetables with wheat crackers and herb biscuits. The next boards featured four slices of king salmon, each served with preserved lemon, chive risotto, sugar snaps, and beet mascarpone cream. That was followed by lump crab-stuffed trout with a celery root puree of sugar snaps, chanterelles, and truffle butter. From the garden, we tasted a baby beet slide with warm walnut-crusted blue cheese, macho, and strawberry vinaigrette, a wild rice-stuffed poblano, and sunny-side up egg and Brussels sprout slaw. We finished the evening around a fire pit roasting marshmallows and making s'mores.

We ended our three-day trip in Asheville, North Carolina, having breakfast at Biscuit Head with delicious golden biscuits served with different styles of gravies: espresso gravy, fried chicken gravy, pork sausage gravy, housemade chorizo gravy, and sweet potato coconut gravy. We tasted one more pimento cheese spread with jalapeño, and some sriracha maple sausage. We particularly enjoyed the hot sauce bar with Banana Buffalo, Wicked Biscuit Sauce, Sweet Heat, Grilled Jalapeño, Blueberry Jalapeño, Hababango, and Cat Scratch, to name a few, and their homemade jams made with peach rosemary, sour cherry, sweet potato chai, mango, and grapefruit marmalades. These are only some that I remember.

Another year, my travels in search of regional flavors took me to the region between Albuquerque and Santa Fe in New Mexico. One early morning, I drove to the Kasha-Katuwe Tent Rocks National Monument—the name means white cliffs in the language of the Native American Pueblo Nation—and I arrived at the gate just before 8 a.m. when the park opens. No one else was there besides the guy at the entrance, and I found myself hiking alone. I took the Canyon trail, a one-way trek into a narrow, "slot" canyon with a steep climb to the mesa top. Some section of the trail was so narrow that I could only place one foot at a time on the ground and help myself through the canyon by bracing my arms on both sides of the vertical walls of the canyon and pulling my body along. It was worth the climb to admire the beautiful views of the Sangre de Cristo, Jemez, Sandia mountains, and the Rio Grande Valley. The wind was blowing on my face while I admired the unusual conic formations of rocks resulting from a series of volcanic eruptions that occurred between six to seven million years ago.

My early morning hike had given me an appetite, and I was ready to discover some local food. Back on the road, I decided to stop at Albuquerque's landmark Duran Central Pharmacy, located on the famous U.S, Route 66. Inside, the pharmacy was a New Mexico diner featuring some of the best tortillas of any restaurant in New Mexico. Duran's tortillas are made to order, the way *abuelitas* (grandmothers) in New Mexico have done it for generations. Their green and red chiles are considered the best in New Mexico, and are based on the local Hatch chile. I ordered the stuffed sopapillas: two sopaipillas with beans, cheese, and a choice of red and (or) green chile. The waitress advised me to go with the "Christmas" option, with both red and green chile. If the red chile dazzled on the plate, the green chile was the star of the dish. It had a nice balance of piquancy and roasted wholesomeness.

The next day, I rented a bike and ventured along the Rio Grande banks, and on my way back to town, I caught sight of a white truck on the side of the road with a series of colorful circles and a logo that read "PopFizz." Intrigued, I stopped and entered a little shop next to the truck and discovered a store manufacturing *paletas*, Mexican popsicles made with a lot of fresh local fruits. I probably lost all the health benefits of my bike ride that day by taste-testing a bunch of paletas—Jamaica raspberry, mango chile, pineapple habanero, pecan cajeta, and avocado.

Instead of taking the freeway to Santa Fe, I chose to drive the Turquoise Trail National Scenic Byway through the mining towns of Golden, Madrid, and Cerrillos. State Road 14 carves through rolling juniper-dotted hills, and I stopped at many art and crafts shops and third-wave coffee shops along the way. Before reaching the Georgia O'Keeffe Museum in Santa Fe, one of the main reasons for my trip there, I stopped along the road at a taco and breakfast burrito truck, El Chile Toreado. I ordered the barbacoa, al pastor, carnitas, and carne asada tacos. I read it was one of the best places for locals to eat, and I was not disappointed.

I didn't realize that there was still a stigma about food trucks at that time. Many people still believe that the food cooked and served at food trucks is not going to be amazing, much less fresh. I know that is absolutely not true, as I was lucky to attend one of the last Vendys Award Food Festivals on Governor Island, the long-running and biggest food truck event in New York. (The Vendy Awards began in 2005 and ran its last edition in 2019.) In several hours, I had the opportunity to go on a global-gastronomy tasting tour with South India's vegetarian crêpes, Venezuelan dishes made with plantains, soul food such as fish and chips and shrimp and grits, Afghan comfort foods, Colombian *arepas*, Vegan bites, Southern Chinese comfort food, and traditional Moroccan food. It was an amazing experience that stimulated all the senses.

Since attending the Vendys Awards, I never miss a chance to research the food truck scene at each American city I travel to. There are today about 25,000 food trucks around the country, and they represent around $1.3 billion in business.

Getting food from food trucks is a no-brainer for younger generations. Millennials are more inclined to experiment with different foods, and the Gen-Z crowd doesn't question it, as they were born with the variety of options offered by food trucks. The novelty offered by food trucks attracts many customers who do not want traditional restaurant menu items. Customers are looking to experiment with new cuisines and flavor combinations. Urban locations where population density is high, and where per capita disposable income is higher than average, are places where you see most of the food trucks. Portland, Austin, Denver, Los Angeles, New York City, Houston, Philadelphia, and Nashville are some of the top cities with many food trucks.

I watched the show *Food Truck Nation* on The Cooking Channel, where chef Brad Miller traveled across the country to discover the best food trucks. I decided to have him on the podcast as the expert to answer my lingering questions: What are the best cities for food trucks? Will a culinary degree or a chef experience position you for success? What are the top three success factors to be successful in this business?

I sent a direct Instagram message to chef Brad Miller's account, not expecting too much, but to my surprise he sent me a nice message back agreeing to be on the show. Miller was a great guest, and I quickly came to understand why he is great on TV. His bubbly personality came across clearly in his podcast episode. He confirmed the top cities mentioned above, and added that Indianapolis, Minnesota, and North Carolina have great food truck scenes as well.

"It's amazing the level of cooking that's on these trucks. It is actually shocking," says Miller. "People think that food trucks are, like, down and dirty food, always super fattening, and that everything is fried." On *Food*

Truck Nation, Miller wanted to show it was absolutely not true, and that there were really good cooks who served great food from a food truck.

Many food entrepreneurs are starting their business with a food truck, and using it as a soundboard to test their food before opening a brick-and-mortar restaurant. It is obviously less of an investment than opening a restaurant. The average cost of getting a food truck and all the necessary permits ranges between $50,000 and $60,000, compared to $1 million to $2 million needed to open a restaurant.

When it comes to the top three success factors, Miller explained, "A food truck should be wrapped in fancy colors and have something that really catches people's eye. That will get people to walk up to the food truck, when they are walking down a row of twenty-five food trucks. People will walk up to the weird one!" This is the opposite of what a restaurant should be.

The second factor of success is obviously to serve amazing food. Miller's advice is to focus on doing one thing and making it perfectly. "That just goes for anything in the world, stay hyper focused on anything you're doing and become great at it. People that have mac and cheese trucks, when they just focus on mac and cheese, it is some really good mac and cheese. Same for barbecue trucks; if you focus on a certain style of barbecue or if you only do pork, or you only do beef, then you have the best result."

The last criteria is to have food that people can hold and eat with one hand while walking around.

And to my question if people need to be a chef to succeed in the food truck business, Miller answered, "Absolutely not. So positively not."

The last time I was in Austin, I remembered Miller's statement that the best food truck focuses on one type of food only. When I explored East Austin, Rainy Street, and South Congress Avenue, I indulged in vegan tacos at The Vegan Nom, Mexican traditional tacos at Veracruz All Natural, grilled cheese with a twist at Burro Cheese Kitchen, and decadent dessert at Gourdough's Big Fat Donuts.

My experiences in California, Louisiana, the Mid-Atlantic, Texas, New Mexico, or in the Low Country are just a few examples of what the regions in the U.S. can offer. Each state has its unique food and local ingredients, either based on weather conditions (California), longstanding diaspora (Vietnamese food in New Orleans), or indigenous communities (Albenaki in Vermont, or Navajo in Arizona).

Local ingredients or local food mean something different to people. For some, "local" is defined by the distance between where the food is grown or produced and the place it is consumed. For others, it relates to the characteristics of a particular place, and the culture of a region or country. For some chefs, local means locality of culture.

Here is a series of examples to illustrate key cultural staples:

- Sesame oils are commonly used in East Asia, South India, Japan, and the Middle East, whereas olive oils are used in the Mediterranean countries;
- Hong-Kong is known for XO sauces and India for its chutneys;
- Sinigang is a cultural staple in the Philippines;
- Soy sauces are used in East Asia; and
- Fish sauces flavor regional foods in Southeast Asia.

When I met chef Chris Shepherd from Underbelly Hospitality in Houston, he shared with me his interest in various cultures. As he explained in his book, *Cook Like A Local*, most people connect local with the carrots they grow in their garden and the strawberries that are in season at their market. For him, local means more than the locality of ingredients. It means the locality of culture. Take fish sauce, for instance. Shepherd is passionate about it, and I mentioned to him that fish sauce is not an easy product to come to like, and that for me it is an acquired taste. It's not something that you can easily enjoy; it has to grow on you.

Shepherd agreed and explained that people have to understand that fish sauce doesn't really step into the forefront of a dish. "It gives you that rich umami kind of salty characteristic that you're looking for. You need to learn how to manipulate it to be able to *not know* it's there, but to *understand* that it's there—and that's the key. You can take a bunch of herbs, a bunch of chilies, honey for sweetness, some garlic, some citrus, and you add fish sauce to that puree. You marinate that with beef, poultry, or fish. Once you cook it, the taste is there, it is in the background, and it starts to grow on you. People should really try it!"

Shepherd made clear that not all fish sauces are created equal. "Try fish sauces side-by-side, and you start to understand the ingredients—mainly anchovies and salt—and you start to look at the levels of sodium. Cheap fish sauce is not worth the time. Make sure you're buying quality."

Then he talked about the importance of learning how to balance a dish using fish sauce. "You have something that's so super funky, that you need something sweet and something spicy to tone it back. You need some acidity. This is about learning balance. Fish sauce is the perfect element to inspire you to learn balance in a dish. Most people cook with salt, pepper, and maybe a little bit of lemon or lime juice, or by adding something to a dish to finish it. It's more about understanding the balance of sweetness, sour, spiciness, and…the 'funk.' Fish sauce is a perfect ingredient for young cooks, especially to train their palate and to understand balance and flavors."

Olive oils are a staple from the Mediterranean area, and in the past five years we have seen an explosion of olive oil tasting bars around the country. Instead of directly picking a bottle off a shelf, customers are able to sample oil "on-tap" before making a purchase. American consumers started to understand the variety of nuances in olive oils. When I met chef Trigg Brown from Win Son in Brooklyn, New York, he explained to me that, similar to olive oils, we do not see a lot of different brands of soy sauce in the U.S. People are not aware of the different taste profiles between soy sauces. "I hope people can start looking at soy sauce that way," says Brown, "because a large portion of the world uses it to season their food. People should learn more about soy sauce, and they should taste the different varieties to understand what kind of soy sauce to use. They should find out more about other fermented soybean products too."

Brown talked about a soybean paste that people used in Taiwan. "It's really salty, but it's thicker than soy sauce, a lot more balanced, with a depth of flavor. It's a little sweeter and contains fermented Koji Greens." He was really excited to work with this paste, and to get his hands on a high-quality product. "When you're using a sauce from a generic brand it's just not that attractive."

I look at fish sauces and soy sauce with a different perspective after my conversation with Shepherd and Brown. It forced me to consider bringing "funkiness" into my home cooking, and I now keep a bottle of fish sauce handy in my kitchen. It is perfect for chicken wings dishes!

As I was driving to my local farmers' market, I recalled my conversation with chef Shepherd and realized that the range of sauces, spices, and condiments in my fridge and kitchen cabinets were drastically different from the ones of my siblings in France. It may sound obvious or trivial, but it also represents my evolution as a person and as a cook. After almost twenty years in the U.S., and conversations with hundreds of culinary leaders, I have been exposed to many new influences. As quality produce is usually the first step in the creative process of a new dish or a new drink for chefs and mixologists, and as sourcing the right ingredients is critical for the flavors of the end result, I explored my farmers' markets and food stores in a thirty-minute radius from where I live. I conducted online research, read local food blogs, and the New Jersey edition of *Edible* magazine. I created my personal top choices list. The next time I went shopping at the fish market, I asked Mark behind the counter for his recommendation. "You should get the sea scallops, we just got them." Scallops are one of my favorite seafoods. My mother used to prepare them in the shell with béchamel sauce, button mushrooms, and gruyere cheese, and gratineed them in the oven. I was looking for inspiration to prepare them differently.

Chef Cosentino confessed that he doesn't have a lab or a separate lab kitchen to create and experiment. "I just go to the farmers' market and taste things." Likewise, chef Fojtasek has his Saturday morning routine when he hits farmers' markets after his tour of the farms. "My creativity usually starts with an idea that happens in those places." I wanted to experiment on my own with what these chefs shared with me and see what would come out of it. I continued on my way to the farmers' market from one of my Saturday morning shopping tours (I have multiple). I bought red onions, habanero chiles, finger limes, Meyer lemons, Cara oranges, cilantro, and yellow, purple, and red cherry tomatoes. Looking at the vegetables, I remembered a wonderful ceviche with scallops I was served at Garrison in Austin. The inspiration came from scouting seasonal and regional ingredients.

What are the next steps for culinary leaders after the selection of the ingredients? Where do chefs and mixologists find their inspiration to turn these ingredients into an amazing dish or delicious drink? Back in my kitchen, I decided to prepare the marinade for the ceviche with all the ingredients and just added the sliced scallops at the last minute, like Peruvian chefs do with their fish ceviche. I do not like to have the acidity of the lemon "cooking" the delicate flesh of the scallops too long. Before adding the scallops, though, I added a few drops of fish sauce and soy sauce. On top of the scallops, I sprinkled furikake, a Japanese seasoning made of toasted sesame seeds and other ingredients that differ according to the region it is from. I love ceviche, and since that day I make ceviche once a week.

Chapter 4

A MOSAIC OF CULTURES

"It's fascinating how food can be a really powerful narrator of culture."

—CHEF LEVON WALLACE

List of culinary individuals featured in this chapter:

Chef **Andrew McLeod** from
Avenue M in Asheville

Chef **Levon Wallace** at
FatBelly Pretzel in Nashville

Chef/Owner **Gabriel Kreuther** from
two-Michelin star Gabriel Kreuther
restaurant in New York City

Sylvia Barban, Executive Chef and
co-owner of the Italian restaurant LaRina
in Brooklyn, New York

Chef **Bonnie Morales** from Kachka
in Portland, Oregon

Chef **Shamil Velazquez** from the Delaney
Oyster House in Charleston, South Carolina

Pastry Chef **Antonio Bachour** from
Bachour Miami in Miami
Pastry Chef **Philip Speer** from
Comedor in Austin, Texas

Sayat and Laura Ozyilmaz formerly
at Noosh in San Francisco

Chef **Carlo Lamagna** from Magna
Kusina in Portland, Oregon

Chef and Author **Edward Lee**, chef/owner of
610 Magnolia and Whiskey Dry in Louisville;
culinary director of Succotash at National
Harbor in Maryland, and Penn Quarter in
Washington, D.C

Chef **Erik Ramirez** from Llama Inn
and Llama San in New York City

hef Andrew McLeod introduced me to chef Levon Wallace from Nashville. "You absolutely need to talk to Wallace; he is great at telling stories and you should have him on your show."

I set up a Zoom call with Wallace to introduce myself and get to know him. My first visual of Wallace was not what I expected; the lighting of the room he was sitting in was so dark that his face appeared pale due to the glare of his computer screen. He was wearing a black hoodie which barely hid a thick black and white beard that was sticking out.

He looked at me and smiled. "I really liked your conversation with chef McLeod on your podcast, and I'm pleased to meet you. What do you want to talk about? I love to talk about food!"

We quickly connected and Wallace mentioned his recently opened pretzel business, called "Fatbelly Pretzels." With the loss of a new chef job opportunity at the start of the pandemic, Wallace had found himself procrastinating in his home and cooking for his family to fill the time. One day, he baked soft pretzels for his kids. "I decided to do what I know how to do best, which is do something for someone else. It usually works, nine times out of ten, to get me out of any kind of situation." He and his wife Kim noticed the moment of joy that these pretzels brought to their family. "We were having a good time with these big belly pretzels and my wife had this great idea to have a bake sale the coming weekend." As people started showing up, Levon and Kim set up a Facebook page, and less than a year later the business was doing well. "Every time we handed someone a pretzel, the person got so excited as it seems that everyone's got a story about pretzels."

Prior to creating his company, Wallace was an executive chef at various places, from fine dining to boutique hotel restaurants and fast casual places around the country. In this first conversation, I came to discover that Wallace was more than a chef—he was also a food historian and cultural detective. He had a deep desire to understand the fabric of a dish and to know how each element came to be on a plate, or in a recipe. He respects tradition, but he's also not a purist. He wants to get to the root of something before he allows himself to experiment with it and get creative, by combining ingredients to make something new and interesting. To my surprise, when I asked him about his sources of inspiration, I learned that Wallace had a Mexican background. "Isn't my name Levon Wallace a dead giveaway that I'm of Mexican heritage?" he commented ironically. "I grew up eating those foods. The more I dug my heels into it, the more I discovered that it's a complex and beautiful cuisine, but it's also almost comical how some of the techniques are so primitive. I think that's what makes it so good—because it's elemental and simple. So, my inspiration usually comes from keeping things as simple as possible, and on top of that I add the layers of experience and environmental inspiration."

Wallace looks at food as a tool for cultural understanding. "I think that food is a really powerful narrator of culture. Who was here before? Who came here? What happened next? Where are we going? All the food scenes are all so different and beautiful to me, but what I love about them is that they all tell a story. That's what food does, food tells the truth. A dish can be used as a tool for cultural understanding."

In the summer of 2021, I decided to conduct research in the New York Public Library to better understand the impact immigration had on food in this country. I had an initial phone conversation with Rebecca Federman, the head research librarian from the New York Public Library, who was passionate about food. She advised me to focus on immigration after the 1965 Immigration Act. From her point of view, this federal law, signed by President Lyndon B. Johnson, had a ripple effect on what defines today's food landscape in the United Sates. As a follow-up to my phone conversation with the librarian, I decided to visit the library in person to start my research.

The Big Apple was roasting under an intense heat wave and the humidity was so high that it made the temperatures feel like the triple digits, making it a perfect day to spend several hours in the cool atmosphere of the New York Public Library. I had been there many times as a tourist, on my own or with family and friends from France, as the main building on Fifth Avenue is one of the top-rated sights in Manhattan.

While climbing the outside steps in front of the Schwarzman Building, I mentally addressed a good morning to Patience and Fortitude, the two marble lions that guard the front of the building. After the security check in the huge marble lobby of the Beaux-Arts library, I climbed the impressive staircase to the third floor, to find the rather majestic Rose Main Reading Room. The size of the room is comparable to two city blocks, with fifty-two-foot-high ceilings. Like the inside of a cathedral, the impressive architecture naturally inspires silence. After checking at the inquiry desk, one of the employees handed me the books I had reserved online. Reading through the pages of these publications affirmed my opinion that the American food culture is made of many flavors—locally, ethnically, and politically influenced—and reflects social and cultural trends and population migration.

The food landscape has been constantly evolving and that's what fascinates and excites me about being here in the U.S. People call it a melting pot of culture, but I personally prefer the description of the American population as a "mosaic" of cultures. It seems that American society is moving towards the salad bowl concept, where colorful individual pieces are fitted together to make a single entity. With a similar pattern, food trends suggest that cuisine has evolved from fusion cuisine and non-traditional mash-ups—where fusion rhymes with confusion and cultural appropriation—towards chefs mixing a fundamental understanding of techniques with an essential respect for tradition and local ingredients so that the finished dish is greater than the sum of its parts.

The 1965 Immigration Act abolished the National Origins Formula, which had been the basis of U.S. immigration policy since the 1920s, and this changed the face of America and, therefore, the way Americans eat. Before 1965, most of immigration came from Europe and China. After 1965, there were many more immigrants from Asia, Latin America, Africa, and other parts of the world.

The easy access to a diversity of food and cuisines is one aspect I love about living forty minutes from New York City. Besides shopping at immigrant food markets, scouting through bodega aisles, and eating out at restaurants, I particularly enjoy going to Smorgasburg, an open-air market in Williamsburg. The ferry ride from Pier 11 in Manhattan always stimulates my appetite and gets me ready to go on a tasting tour of the open-air food market. With more than a hundred vendors, I stay focused in my selection and rotate my food choices at each visit, but I always end the food feast with a Mango Chamoyada (chah-moh-yada) from the vendor La NewYorkina. Chamoy is a savory sauce-condiment from Mexico made from dehydrated fruits such as apricots, mangos, or plums (or a combination of these), chili powder, salt, sugar, and a little citrus juice. It is sweet, sour, salty, spicy, and a little tart—a perfect combination of flavors! Traditionally in Mexico, sideroad carts sell fruit slices like watermelon or mango as snacks, and drizzle Chamoy and shake some Tajín (salted acid chile powder) on top. La NewYorkina's stand in Smorgasburg blends Chamoy with a fruit ice of your choice (for me it is often mango), shakes Tajín on top, and inserts a long tamarind candy in the cup. An excellent treat that I take with me while continuing my food exploration of the streets of Williamsburg. Walking out of Smorgasburg, I cannot stop thinking about the 1965 Immigration Act and, in a way, this open market is somehow a result of it. The diversity of vendors is the perfect illustration of the food of this country: the immigration story and the constantly evolving American palate.

In my conversation with Wallace, I alluded to the fact that I was amazed about the evolution of the appeal for spicy food in the past fifteen years. "When I arrived in 2002," I said, "spicy food was barely a trend. The word 'spicy' had only begun to appear on menus and packaged food labels. Suddenly, everything became 'spicy.' Salsa began to outsell ketchup, and according to Mintel (a global market research company), five percent of all sauces and snacks launched in the U.S. market between 2002 and 2010 had 'spicy' on their label."

"Then specific chiles became popular," added Wallace. "It started with jalapeño, followed by chipotle—not the food chain but the smoked-dried form of the jalapeño chili. And in more recent years, I have seen mainstream food markets offering different types of chiles, like habanero, poblano, ancho, and morita peppers."

"This happens throughout the country, even as far as Hawaii," I told him. "Last fall, while ordering breakfast at a local joint in Kihei on Maui, next to the local Loco Moco—a traditional Hawaiian breakfast with eggs any style on a local beef patty over a bowl of rice, topped off with brown gravy—and the ubiquitous acai bowls, I found options on the menu to add chorizo to my scrambled eggs, or order huevos rancheros."

Wallace nodded, and after a pause, I added, "I remember my French family, in the early years after moving to the U.S., asking me, 'How would you define American cuisine?' None of my answers would satisfy them, as each time I was giving them an answer, they would comment that I was mentioning either Chinese, Italian, French, or Mexican influences." They would always say, "See, there is no real American cuisine!" I confessed to Wallace that twenty years ago I did not have the knowledge of American culinary history that I have now, and I couldn't tell them how immigration played a critical part in that story. "My only point of reference at that time was France and other Western European countries with long culinary traditions and heritages." Throughout my twenty years in this country, I told Wallace that I embraced the fact that American food is the food of immigrants.

"Words like chop suey, sushi, curry, tacos, and kimchi have slowly become part of the American popular imagination," agreed Wallace, "the same way you now found chorizo and huevos rancheros while you were in Hawaii!"

I brought up to Wallace that the blending of food influences took time before being part of the mainstream American mindset. So-called "ethnic cuisines" were initially not celebrated by American tastemakers, such as food columnists and restaurant critics. To some extent, previous generations of chefs had shaped the twentieth century culinary culture in two divergent spaces: prestige and necessity. The prestige from certain foreign foods, at first limited to French and so-called Continental cuisines, eventually expanded to Italian and Japanese towards the end of the century. The first space is fundamentally depicted in aesthetic terms of taste and skill, while the second is understood as a matter of basic needs.

"I have noticed," I said to Wallace, "that Americans often refer to ethnic and cultural foods as a monolith without acknowledging the existence of distinct nuances and regional cuisines, such as French cuisine or Filipino cuisine." I explained to him that there is not really a French cuisine per se, as each French region has its own distinct dishes and cooking preparations. "Nevertheless," I continued, "French influence in North America can be traced back to mid-sixteenth century and can be found in products that Americans consume on a regular basis. Baguettes, for instance, can be found even in the cuisines of ethnicities with previous colonial ties to France, like Vietnamese bánh mì. Other examples are vinaigrette, the hollandaise sauce on Egg Benedicts, béchamel sauce, Roux, Boston Cream Pie (created by a French chef), French fries (that are in fact from Belgium), crêpes, cheese fondue, 'fleur de sel,' Roquefort, clarifying butter."

"And ratatouille, Emmanuel, don't forget about ratatouille!" interrupted Wallace.

We agreed that French cuisine acquired its reputation of refined cuisine and that it was Julia Child who democratized French cooking and made it accessible for mainstream America to try in their home kitchen.

"Then Jacques Pépin opened his first restaurant, La Potagerie, in New York City," I added, "and then Eric Ripert with Le Bernardin, and Daniel Boulud with his eponymous restaurant continued to pin French fine dining on the New York City map."

I told Wallace I hadn't had the privilege of speaking with those three chefs, but "I was honored to welcome chef Gabriel Kreuther to the show."

I referred to my conversation with Kreuther and my dining experience at his eponymous two-Michelin star restaurant on Bryant Park in Manhattan that serves French, and more specifically, Alsatian-inspired food.

Kreuther explained that Alsatian cooking represents the homeyness of German food, mixed with the refinement and the finesse of French cooking. "It's almost like a fusion before anybody talked about fusion food. It's really digging into my roots, and then blending in my world travel, the love of food from different cultures, and different techniques. But always with that little Alsatian spirit in it." Kreuther further explained that the Alsatian spirit can be the product itself, the way it is seasoned, the way of using acidity or smoke.

"There is always a little link to Alsace in the background." The kugelhopf is a yeast-based Alsatian cake, traditionally baked in a distinctive circular mold. As my mother used to bake homemade kugelhopfs for dessert, I was taken by surprise the first time I ate at Gabriel Kreuther's restaurant and was offered a warm, savory, house-made kugelhopf with whipped chive fromage before my meal.

Gabriel Kreuther also proves that there is still space for consistency and precision in fine dining. He has a desire to teach people to value older cooking techniques that might be out of vogue. His emphasis on tradition seems to have come from his experience in learning from his family, who are from a region of the world that values culinary tradition. It translates into his desire to bring old knowledge and techniques into modern cooking to ensure these traditions are valued and remembered.

"The techniques we're using are not crazy techniques," says Kreuther. "It's cooking techniques. We really cook at Gabriel Kreuther. We don't just drop bags in the water and twenty minutes later open it, that's not happening. Everything is still done the way we would, say, the old-fashioned way. What's important to me is to teach people how to tame the fire—basically, how to use the fire, the heat, every source, every single cooking style. I always used techniques that were either very old techniques or techniques that were forgotten—and that you bring back and people laugh at you."

I liked the fact that Kreuther created a desire for a more casual attitude towards food and especially French cuisine. Thinking about what defines a food culture, the Alsatian example from Kreuther demonstrates that it is a blend of influences, and that these influences can be clearly explained by the history of a country or a region. Alsace is a region that has changed nationality four times in a century!

"Everything is still done the way we would, say, the old-fashioned way. What's important to me is to teach people how to tame the fire—basically, how to use the fire, the heat, every source, every single cooking style. I always used techniques that were either very old techniques or techniques that were forgotten—and that you bring back and people laugh at you."

—CHEF GABRIEL KREUTHER

"After talking to chef Gabriel Kreuther," I said to Wallace, "I was wondering how important it was to stick to cultural traditions when chefs are cooking. I decided to look for a chef who represents another European country having a reputation of refined cuisine." I targeted Italy, as Italian chefs, like French chefs, pay strict attention to rules when cooking.

"Do you know chef Sylvia Barban?" I asked Wallace. "She was a *Top Chef* competitor, and she is the co-owner of the Italian restaurant LaRina in Brooklyn."

Barban incorporates flavors and techniques from different parts of Italy, like butter and olive oils, and I described my conversation with her.

"In the north of Italy, obviously it is colder than in the south," said Barban. "Most of the cuisine is based on butter, and the result, like polenta, is heavier, richer, and warmer in flavors. Going towards the south of Italy, where you get closer to the ocean, you just have another breeze and menus are focused on fish, seafood, and olive oil. I feel like my cuisine is kind of the same, inspired from the regions of Italy."

Barban moved to the U.S. in 2012, and she combined the Italian tradition of using what's fresh and local, using American ingredients.

"My approach is obviously from what is local and what is fresh. A lot of times I prefer using products that are local rather than something that will fly in from Italy. Especially when we have something that is great from here. Sourcing locally is very important. I use things that are in season. We don't have Brussels sprouts in Italy, nor certain types of pasta mixed with butternut squash, for example. I use what is in my surroundings and what I traditionally ate when I was little and during my life, and just mix the two things together."

Going to the market is a good part of her inspiration.

"There's so many ingredients here that I've never seen in Italy. I'm like, 'why can't I just use this with my pasta?' I find a way to still be Italian using products that are from here."

A great example of the melding together of Italian traditions and American flavors is her smoked spaghetti aglio e olio with garlic, Calabrian chilies, and hazelnuts.

"I call it my life in a bowl. Aglio e olio is very traditional in Italy. It's garlic and olive oil with pasta spaghetti. It's the type of pasta that you make when you have like a lot of people over and you don't have anything in the fridge. But in Italy, we always have olive oil, garlic, and chili flakes. I took that inspiration and use garlic and Calabrian chilies because my mother is from Calabria. I also added hazelnuts because they are from the north of Italy, and as we are in America, the best representation is the smokey flavor. So, basically, I smoke my pasta."

The way Barban smokes her spaghetti is still a mystery. Almost like a secret family recipe that they pass down from generation to generation. I could almost picture Barban in Italy when she was younger, preparing Sunday meals in the kitchen with her grandmother.

"My grandmother, on my father's side, was from Venice. She was the one taking care of me. She would teach me how to cook. That's how I started my journey, making roasted potatoes and Carnival fritters. I was always spent a lot of time with her. She got sick because of stomach cancer when I was ten years old. 'Grandma is not cooking anymore. Who is going to cook now for the whole family? Who is going to unify the family and have a big feast every Sunday?' I asked. 'I want to do that.'

"I decided that I wanted to make people happy with my food. I started to cook and learned as many recipes as possible from both my Venetian and my Calabrian heritages. I would spend a lot of time in the summer in Calabria, with my aunt. The food was so good and amazing that I would always ask for a recipe."

During my conversation with chef Barban, I noticed her juxtaposition of being an Italian, always adhering to rules when cooking, and the fine line she strikes creatively with exposure to new ingredients in America.

"I don't have cream in my kitchen. When I was in school, my chef would tell me, 'You know who uses cream? People who don't know how to cook pasta, they are the ones who use cream!'"

I told Wallace that this comment reminded me of my mother's specific viewpoint on what a traditional French quiche Lorraine recipe must be.

"I can relate," answered Wallace. "French etiquette towards food has always been particular, and French chefs often viewed as traditionalists and trapped in their own culinary heritage. French cuisine had always a unique place, and has been equated with gastronomy prestige."

I told him that in my reading, I saw that the first *New York Times* "Guide to Dining Out in New York" in 1964 listed eight restaurants in its top three-star category. Seven were French. And there was a time when "ethnic" food in the U.S. meant mainly Chinese, Mexican, and Italian. These top four represented about seventy percent of everything "ethnic." We both agree that in the past twenty years this picture has changed dramatically, mainly because of the following three reasons: a demographic shift, the influence of the foodies, and the succession of two new generations, millennials and Gen Z.

The exotic appeal is not limited to unknown foreign cuisines but can also refer to unconventional or unusual culinary combinations. Food professionals and food enthusiasts constantly push the boundaries of what is considered daring, bold, and exotic.

I do not like the word "foodie," and I told Wallace so. "I do not consider myself as one, but see myself more as a food enthusiast."

We discussed that the word "foodie" appeared for the first time in 1980s media, and nowadays more than half of the American population consider themselves foodies, and the so-called "trendsetter foodies" total around thirty million, representing about twelve percent of the adult population. Food enthusiasts embody the cutting edge of consumers who are passionate about food when they shop in grocery stores, cook at home, or go out to eat in restaurants, and post pictures of food on social media to share their passion, while somehow not making others feel bad about what they eat.

I noticed that one element of immigrant food that resonates with the food enthusiasts is its authenticity. For most of them, authentic food is just food that is prepared simply and that shows a connection among the producer, the chef, and the food.

For foodies, authentic food is made the way it was traditionally made with traditional ingredients. In their mind, people connect authenticity with ethnicity. The craving for adventure and intense flavors pushed mainstream consumers to further explore immigrant cuisines. It especially resonated with younger consumer generations like millennials and Gen Z.

For millennials, healthy and fresh food have become priorities, and they are on the hunt for flavors that excite and reflect their appreciation of cultural diversity. Millennials are described as open-minded and curious, and they like trying new flavors and immigrant cuisines.

"Do you know that Gen Z is the most ethnically diverse generation in U.S. history?" I asked Wallace. "This is the last generation that will be a majority Caucasian, and where the Hispanic teen population is the fastest growing."

Their interests in food gravitate around authentic immigrant food, healthier and plant-based menus, and restaurants that serve both traditional gastronomic and street-food-inspired dishes.

Wallace and I discussed how food trucks started to become popular in 2008 during the last recession, and how the explosion of food trucks was a result of two simultaneous things: the new popularity of social media for foodies as a tool to share their passion, and the need for customers to connect with their local community and fulfill their desire for local tastes.

Through my research at the New York Public Library, I discovered that we had to wait until late 2015 for the food industry literature to show a burgeoning interest in exotic cuisine. Wallace and I both recalled at that time the recipe-filled cookbooks morphed into more food-focused memoirs, integrating the chef story and how their cultural heritage influenced their creative process. A new generation of chefs, children of immigrants, had begun to transform the American food scene.

"In the course of the first three seasons of my podcast," I said to Wallace, "I hosted about fifteen chefs, including yourself, who either emigrated from various parts of the world or were second-generation American chefs."

These fifteen, and others like them, drafted the new face of America's cuisine. American food was and still is greatly influenced by where cooks grew up and from where their family originally emigrated. It is this cross-pollination of cultures that is influencing today's culinary landscape.

"Who else did you get on the show?" asked Wallace.

"One of my early guests was chef Bonnie Morales from Kachka in Portland, Oregon."

"Kachka? What a singular name," noted Wallace.

I explained that chef Morales paid homage to her grandmother and her roots through her exploration of food.

"My grandmother was escaping a ghetto during World War Two," Morales explained. "She left in the middle of the night, and the following day everyone in her town and her entire family was killed. From Belarus, she made her way towards Russia, fleeing the German occupation. There were still controls along the way, basically German-appointed Russians. One of these checkpoints caught my grandmother along the way and accused her of being Jewish, and she said, 'No, no, I'm not. I'm a Ukrainian peasant making my way.' That was her story. She was Ukrainian trying to get to her in-laws in Russia. They said, 'Well if you're Ukrainian, then how do you say duck in Ukrainian?' In Russian it's "утка" so they asked, 'How do you say утка in Ukrainian?' but she didn't know Ukrainian. She spoke Yiddish at home and probably knew a little bit of Belarusian, but really everyone there spoke Russian besides Yiddish. She decided to take a stab at it hoping that maybe the Yiddish word was the Ukrainian word, because she knew there was a little bit of overlap. She said, 'Kachka.' And it turned out that was the correct answer. They let her go. It turned out that kachka is the same word for duck in Ukrainian, Belarusian, Yiddish, and Polish—probably in other languages as well in that region—but not in Russian. That story is just one of many stories in my family of her surviving and other people surviving, and that became really important to me to honor her."

Like many second-generation American chefs, Morales learned to value her culture through food, and when her future husband appreciated her childhood food, it prompted her mother to cook more traditional foods, which, in turn, inspired Bonnie to become more interested in them.

"I grew up being pretty embarrassed of the food, not really wanting anything to do with it. I brought my husband, my boyfriend at that time, over to my parents' house. And whenever I had friends or a boyfriend coming over, I always gave them a warning about the food that would be strange. 'You're not going to like it. I'm sorry, you might want to come over already fed.' So, I gave him all those same sorts of warnings. And when we were in the car driving back, he just stopped and said, 'It was amazing!' My mom caught wind of this, and he would ask her questions about food, and she started inviting us over for dinner just because she was whipping up some dishes that she hadn't made since before my parents emigrated. He basically lit this fire in her, and then in me, to sort of reevaluate and rediscover what I just took for granted for so long."

Her perspective altogether changed, and it inspired her to create the restaurant Kachka, which is rooted in the food that she grew up eating—sort of a homage to the family history as her parents emigrated from the Soviet Union in 1980. Morales assumed that the food she grew up with was wrong because it was Russian.

"That's something that has changed in me since. I don't make that assumption anymore that just because it's Russian or from the Soviet Union that it's automatically wrong in some way."

Like other second-generation chefs, she grew up turning her nose from traditional food of her family. It was almost as if her ancestors were chasing her through food, trying to prove that as a chef, there was something she wasn't seeing. Then finally, her partner's interest began to dislodge her misconceptions and sparked appreciation. Talking to Morales, two questions popped into my head: Where do our perceptions about certain cuisines come from? What does it take to change our ideas about what's "good" and "bad"?

Morales shared that she found competitive advantages in people not understanding Russian food. "People might have no knowledge of it, but in many ways, that's better than what we are up against. People have a very negative connotation of Russian food. They assume food shortages, lots of spoilage, and canned vegetables. Often, they think about meat and potatoes. This is the picture that shows up in people's minds. It is not a positive one."

Food is the way she found to connect the many facets of her cultural identity: Russian, Belarusian, and Jewish. She brings all of that together, along with other regional traditions, to begin to shape a culinary identity for herself that's more inclusive than her initial cultural identity. When political and geographical lines are redrawn, how do people hold on to and reinterpret their culinary identity?

Morales pulls from many different influences when it comes to her creative process. "There's so much cross-pollination across all of the republics that I can harvest from a larger perspective of the Soviet Union as a whole. My parents were cooking a little bit of a mix of Georgia, Azerbaijani, Latvian, and Ukrainian food. Nobody really had a name for it because they're all part of the Soviet Union. That's kind of what Kachka is, rooted in that mash-up."

I told Wallace that it was at Kachka in Portland that I fell in love with Zakuski—the appetizer section of the menu. Dumplings are considered hot Zakuski in Russian cuisine, and Kachka has a full section of its menu dedicated to dumplings. One I especially was fond of was the Ukrainian specialty, the sour cherry dumpling varenyki.

For chef Morales, dumplings of any kind are an easy way for people to be introduced into any cuisine. "I can't think of a single cuisine that doesn't have some form of dumpling. It's a great way to start a meal. As a young girl, the cherry varenyki were ones that my mother would always buy at the Russian Market and keep in our freezer. As a teenager, when my parents were going out, that is something I could make myself. It became my favorite thing. When I was working on that dish for the restaurant, I was very much inspired by that memory."

Remembering home by re-creating culinary memories is a common trait of immigrants. Their culinary narratives, saturated with nostalgia, often bring back immigrant memories, and imagined returns to the homeland. Chef Morales uses the word "reverence" to depict the feeling of deep respect for her heritage.

"I think reverence is very important," said Morales. She gave the example of the traditional sour cherry varenyki, based on sour cherries, flour, and water.

"I could take all these ingredients and make something totally different. I could dehydrate the cherries, make a cracker instead of the dough, and take the butter and powder it," said Morales.

"That's not to me the essence of the dish and how I would enjoy it. I don't like to change things that way. That could be an interesting cerebral exercise, of course, but that's not what we're here for."

Morales explained that she viewed the re-creation of the dish as a design problem. Growing up eating these sour cherry varenyki, she knew that there were structural problems with them. Already, the fresh cherries brought a watering challenge, and then throwing them in boiling water brought even more water to the dumplings. The dough sometimes had thicker parts, sort of clumpy thick knotted sections. Morales found the solution using a specific dumpling maker that eliminated the risk of making any knot with the dough.

Morales also wanted these cherries to be more cherry tasting. "I can use delicious dehydrated sour cherries and rehydrate them in sour cherry syrup and make the filling out of that. I'm still totally one hundred percent honoring the dish, but it tastes like more concentrated cherry."

"I can totally relate to chef Morales' quest to re-create the perfect taste memory of her mother's cherry varenyki," agreed Wallace. "She unfolded the original recipe, learned about each ingredient, and leveraged modern culinary techniques."

I expressed to Wallace that Russian food helped Morales stay connected to her family roots, change people's opinion about "Russian" food in Portland, and ultimately build a career and strong cultural connections.

A few years later, I interviewed two chefs, both with a Puerto Rican heritage: chef Shamil Velazquez from the Delaney Oyster House in Charleston, and pastry chef Antonio Bachour from Miami. Both described Puerto Rico as a family- and food-centric culture, and when it came to their inspiration, both mentioned their family and local produce.

I had the opportunity to travel to Puerto Rico in 2019. It was a short stay and I spent most of my time walking the streets of old San Juan tasting coffee and cocktails. The colorful houses reminded me of past trips to Old Panama City and La Havana in Cuba. Puerto Rico is very diverse when it comes to food. The three main influences are Spanish, African, and the native people.

"I took those influences from just me being there with my grandmother, my mother, or other family members cooking," said chef Velazquez. "I come from a family where everybody cooks. It's just one of those things that you get taught from a young age to learn how to cook white rice. It's the first thing they teach you. But those influences were more of me being with my family and me learning different dishes. They shaped me a lot as a chef today."

Pastry chef Bachour's parents had a bakery business on the island.

"My father was a businessman. The family bakery was across from my house. I was there from the beginning of the bakery, going every day to watch the pastry chef work. I fell in love with the passion these people had for their work. I have never in my life seen people working with that much passion and love. In those times, they were not working for money; they were working because they loved what they did."

Bachour is very inspired by Puerto Rico. It comes through in the flavors he chooses to work with and the bright colors he highlights. His desserts are "Puerto Rico on a plate." His passion is also a direct result of witnessing and growing up around a culture that infuses love and energy into its culinary traditions. From his heritage, he is drawn to take inspiration from what's available around him.

"Stimulus for me is everywhere. It can be from a flower, a painting, or from coworkers working with me coming up with a great idea." He pointed to the red shirt I was wearing and said it could inspire him to create a new dessert. Colors are essential to Bachour's work: "For me, color is everything in life."

In 2019, he published a book called *Bachour in Color* with recipes that range from entremets, tarts, petits fours, and macarons. Another influence he had from growing up on the island was easy access to an array of fruits.

"I love mango, passion fruit, coconut, and banana. I cannot make a dessert in my shop case without these fruits. Eighty percent of my influence is coming from the island of Puerto Rico. We're eating everyday tropical fruit that you can see as you walk on the streets. They fall down from trees," he added with a smile.

This proximity to food and his ability to inspire joy in people is why chef Velazquez became a chef. "I grew up with two breadfruit trees and a banana tree in my backyard. My grandmother had her mango tree, and other family members had avocado trees. For us, it was very important to share, 'Hey, this is what I have, what do you have to share?' It's a true farm to table culture! Food was always present. It was just there. In Puerto Rico, it is always about the food. I just really enjoyed being with food and seeing how food brings different emotions in people. Seeing how happy it makes people when they eat it. It's not only for sustenance or health benefits, but also for the joy of being able to share a meal with somebody. That was very special to me." Velazquez started applying to the Culinary Institute of America when he was in the ninth grade. "More than anything, I knew that it was the school I wanted to go to."

Later in life, both Bachour and Velasquez discovered new ingredients from other parts of the country and the world that they integrated into their family recipes and culinary heritage, but they both believed in maintaining traditions—not very different from what I had early heard from my conversation with chefs Kreuther, Barban, and Morales.

"We need to keep the classic desserts alive," said Bachour. "With the classic desserts, we remember our childhood, our family, our grandparents, our moms, and our fathers. I always like to keep classic desserts with a new interpretation, because I want people to remember as we are always thinking about the past and about family."

Similarly, Velazquez has two dishes on the menu that are directly connected to his grandmother: the salt cod empanadas and the Flan de Abuela. In fact, he was in denial about putting the flan recipe on the menu. "Every restaurant in Puerto Rico has some sort of flan on their menu. So, to me, it was a big 'No Way!'"

As people were asking him to have this flan at Delaney Oyster House, he remembered that his grandma's flan was always the most expected dish in their family gathering. So, he took his grandma's recipe and modernized a bit and got great feedback from everybody who tried it. He tweaked the texture and elevated the flavors with citrus and nut brittle, sea salt, and lime zest sprinkled on top. For the salt cod empanadas, he remembers his grandmother would make bacalao guisado (codfish stew) during Holy Week with white rice, potatoes, and olives.

"I decided to take that recipe, flip it around, and put it inside empanadas rather than serving it with white rice and avocado. That's an example that takes one of our traditional dishes and modifies it a little bit to make it more modern but keeping it true to what it was. My inspiration has always been my family because my food is what I come back to. We gathered pretty much every other weekend together just to eat. It's very important for the whole family to get together, have a couple drinks, and then have some good food. And that's a big inspiration for me."

I shared with Wallace that from their culinary heritage, both Velazquez and Bachour were used to leveraging ingredients that were available around them, but I got a different approach when I talked to pastry chef Philip Speer from Comedor in Austin. I discovered someone who looked at his heritage as sourcing ingredients that are true to the tradition and true to the culture.

I had pastry chef Speer on the podcast and talked to him on a Zoom call but never met him in person until one of my recent trips to Austin.

Each time I come to Austin I have a morning routine to walk five miles on the trails downtown along the Colorado River. One day, I bumped into

Speer, who was on his morning run. Even with a mask on because of COVID-19, I recognized him. His tattoos gave him away! I told Wallace that during the recording of the episode with Speer, I learned that after battling with addiction issues, Speer created a community of support for people with mental health needs and recovering from addiction. His routine morning run is part of having a new meaningful life.

"Are you coming to Comedor during your stay?" Speer asked me, after greeting me with a firm handshake.

"Yes, I already booked a table for tomorrow's dinner. I will be there with some friends."

"I am looking forward to seeing you there, and I will treat you well. See you tomorrow!" said Speer, waving his hand as he resumed his run.

After our conversation on the podcast, I was looking forward to tasting his desserts at Comedor. Speer has a Latino background. "My family heritage is half Mexican on my mother's side. We grew up very much experiencing that Mexican culture and more specifically, the Texas style of Mexican culture." Speer's cultural upbringing is based largely on family connection and gathering around food. He's infused those cultural roots in the care he demonstrates for his employees and the desserts he puts on the menu.

The next day, I met my friends at Comedor for dinner. As we walked in, the entrance opened into a huge thirty-two-foot vaulted ceiling made of glass, atop an indoor courtyard. "That indoor courtyard," says Speer welcoming us to our table, "came from a lot of inspiration from trips to Mexico City. When we worked with our architect, we really wanted to bring that feeling, as we really enjoyed the culture and lifestyle together from different parts of Mexico, but specifically this Mexico City particular style."

Speer continues to share their approach to food at the restaurant, and the importance of sourcing some of their ingredients directly from Mexico. "We wanted to build with tradition and soul in the techniques in which we presented everything. We use the greatest corn from different small farms in Mexico, sourced by Tamoa, which is an organization in Mexico City that brings us the best of all the surplus heritage corn from different small farms and communities throughout Mexico. We're using those ingredients that are true to the tradition and true to the culture. However, some of the flavors may go outside of the traditional realm of what you think of Mexican food, but not in a way of fusion or anything like that, just as a way of celebrating the products that are local to us, with that same intention of Mexican soul and tradition and technique."

After sharing the Tuna Aguachile, quesadilla with Texas cremini mushrooms and huitlacoche (a fungus that grows on corn) and bone marrow tacos with friends, chef Speer treated us to two of his desserts: Atole, with heirloom corn, and Piloncillo, a masa Shortbread; and a Tamal de Chocolate, with caramelized milk ice cream, and Amaranth (an ancient grain that is similar to quinoa). "I love blending cultures through food," explained Speer while putting the chocolate tamale on our table. "One of the fun desserts we do is our chocolate tamale. It really brings flavors and ideas from not only places I grew up, but also places some of the other chefs grew up, because our approach to food at Comedor has always been collaborative."

The team at Comedor had been able to translate their Mexican heritage beyond food through the architecture of the place, reflecting some of the interior courtyards from Mexico City. I loved the experience there and it reminded me of a similar feeling I had having lunch at the restaurant Noosh in San Francisco, where chefs Sayat and Laura Özyilmaz oversaw the food and beverage program. A couple of years prior to 2020, Middle Eastern food had taken over the U.S., and fast-casual restaurants serving hummus, falafel, and pita bread, and spices like harissa, cardamom, and za'atar were found on many restaurant menus across America. I loved spending time with chefs Sayat and Özyılmaz. Their concept when they created Noosh was all about blending. The Middle East inspired the ambiance of the restaurant. They believe in hospitality that showcases an understanding of the guests and an atmosphere that celebrates that.

"We put olive trees into our bar that provided shade in the afternoon," said chef Sayat, "and it was one of the most gorgeous times during the day. Our wide-open windows let the breeze in on a cool day in San Francisco. It was one of the most amazing feelings, it just felt like you were in the Mediterranean." From their own personal relationship—he is Turkish, and she is Mexican—to their food, which spans across very different cuisines in the Middle East and Mediterranean area, they've found a way to make things work together. It's a way of finding peace and collaboration through the medium of food. Laura Özyılmaz is a great example that you must be from a place to really understand the culture through the cuisine. The concept is inspired by Sayat's Turkish culture.

"We named the restaurant after my grandmother," said chef Sayat. "We care about cultural anchors, something that sort of rests in history and culture in a logical place. Noosh is not just an Armenian and Greek word, but it's also a Farsi word, part of an expression that means 'Cheers.' 'Nooshe jân' is how you basically say 'salud' in Farsi."

It inspired the kind of food they've created: a borderless cuisine.

"We've expanded boundaries that existed only after the beginning of the twentieth century and have created a borderless cuisine that celebrates the whole region," added chef Sayat. "We're breaking a lot of walls in people's minds, and it means we're serving Hungarian wine with Turkish food; you're putting Moroccan preserved lemons on a lamb kebab. A Georgian dish is shaped like a Turkish flatbread. People are getting really confused. And I think our staff basically untangled all of it in explaining and scripting everything to the guests. That idea of borderless cuisine and the value we bring by expanding it to not just food but also the wine menu, the cocktail menu, the non-alcoholic beverages—and being able to explain these sorts of relationships to guests—has been the biggest way we've elevated casual Middle Eastern foods to a higher level."

Sayat is using his culture to bring story to his food.

"Let's create something that is unique and powerful. It tells a compelling story because, hummus is hummus. But hummus with a story is a lot more convincing than hummus without a story."

Sayat and Laura Özyılmaz found a way to blend cultures. One example I have in mind is the use of marigold flowers in their cooking. The use of blossoms in dishes as key ingredients rather than for garnish has been a big trend in recent years and marigold was part of that trend after orange blossom and nasturtium. Marigold is used both in food in some Eastern Mediterranean countries and in Mexico as well.

Laura shared that "Georgia is the only country that uses marigold flowers as a part of their cuisine. And the reason why I get very excited about this is because we use marigold flowers in Mexico for rituals and for ceremonies."

I explained to Wallace that the blending of cultures with Sayat and Laura Özyılmaz was based on the love they have for each other and for their respective origins. More often than not, the blending of cultures results from dramatic events.

This brings me to my conversation with chef Carlo Lamagna from Magna Kusina in Portland, Oregon. Filipino cuisine represents a great example of how historical influences through invasions and occupations enriched the local food culture. Some people would probably say this distorts the origins. But how different would Filipino cuisine be without the blending over time of Malay, Islamic, Chinese, Spanish, and American influences? With colonial ties that flourished for more than two hundred years under Spanish rule, elements derived from Mexico are also detected in Filipino cuisine.

For Carlo Lamagna, bringing Filipino food into the mainstream is a way to create awareness around the large Filipino presence in the U.S. Rather than remaining in the shadows, it's a way of saying "We're here!" and honoring his family by bringing this food to the mainstream. His food is a response to centuries of cultural assimilation in America.

"A lot of the reasoning that Filipino food has not made its way into the mainstream," says Lamagna, "is that the Filipino community itself was forced to assimilate into any culture that they move into. They might find themselves holding back on their heritage, or holding back on the culture and food that they're used to, because they wanted to be indiscriminate—they may prefer to remain in the shadows, not causing a stir. That phrase of 'Oh, we don't want to be a bother' actually applies well to the Filipino community."

Lamagna is inspired by the two cultures of his parents.

"In the Philippines, I grew up Ilokano (member of the Malayo-Polynesian branch of the Austronesian language family, the third most prevalent language of the Philippines, after Tagalog and English). A lot of the dishes I eat stem from the ancestral home of my father and my mom. Even though they're both Ilokano, they came from two different parts of an island. One from the most northern tip, which was seafood heavy, and one that was a little bit more inland, which was based on a lot of dried fish and more meat. I draw inspiration from understanding those particular flavor profiles."

I was curious to have his perspective on authenticity. With more than seven thousand islands, how can you find authentic food from the Philippines? Looking at it from a foreigner's perspective, I might sometimes have the tendency to look at someone else's cuisine as a homogeneous monolith, versus a pluralistic melting pot based on regions.

"I think authenticity depends on the individual," answered Lamagna. "There are many subtribes and sub-regions within the Philippines. Ingredients change. Adobo is a good example. It's a very popular dish that is well-known around the world. But what people don't realize is that every region and every island in the Philippines has its own variations. And every family has their own variations. To say 'Oh, this adobo isn't adobo' is, in a nutshell, incorrect, because that adobo to me is going to be what is authentic to my palate and to my upbringing. Someone who grew up in the south might add coconut milk, or soy sauce, or might not have x, y, and z in their version. It's the variations that define what truly authentic is."

Authenticity then only exists within the country of origin. Lamagna added, "I don't think that the word authentic should have any place in the current vernacular of anybody opening a Filipino restaurant outside of the Philippines."

With the multiple influences that the Philippines went through over the centuries, I asked if Lamagna would consider Filipino cuisine as fusion cuisine.

"It is not a fusion cuisine, it's an evolutionary cuisine. When you say fusion, I think P.F. Chang! Fusion is taking two things that don't belong with each other and forcing them to stick. Basically, I think that Filipino cuisine is an evolutionary cuisine. It evolves just like any other culture. It evolves and withstands the test of time. If you start with the initial indigenous people of the Philippines, and you move forward in history, you'll see that those indigenous ingredients and foods and dishes have remained. The only thing that has happened is they evolved with the introduction of cooking terms, other ingredients, or flavor profiles, whether it was soy sauce from the Chinese immigration and Chinese trade; the introduction of farm-raised pigs from Spain, traveling on the boats; or whether it's coming from Mexico. Some of the indigenous techniques and ingredients from Mexico made their way into Filipino culture."

"It is not a fusion cuisine, it's an evolutionary cuisine. When you say fusion, I think P.F. Chang! Fusion is taking two things that don't belong with each other and forcing them to stick. Basically, I think that Filipino cuisine is an evolutionary cuisine. It evolves just like any other culture. It evolves and withstands the test of time."

—CHEF CARLO LAMAGNA

Like many second-generation American chefs, Lamagna went back to his heritage late in life. The final conversation with his father before he passed away made him realize that he had a place in this world, and he made a promise to him to pursue Filipino food professionally because, as he explained, in all the years he had been cooking, his dad was always telling him, "Why don't you do Filipino food?"

"It took a tragic moment in my life to realize it, but it really pushed me to go that route. It's been an amazing journey, genuinely it has been so much fun, experimenting and failing at so many dishes."

Lamagna is focusing on bringing Filipino food to the masses. Filipino immigrants by nature, like many other immigrants from Asia, were trying to fit in. Their food was mainly made at home quietly, rather than blending into the culinary fabric of America. Immigrants made a conscious attempt to fabricate authenticity at home to create a sense of belonging.

"They wanted to hide," confessed Lamagna. "They felt like their food was just their own, they didn't really want to share it, and that the other communities would not care for it."

He felt that there was a lack of support from the Filipino community to bring their food out into the open. "The Filipino community held themselves back, and instead of supporting each other—instead of saying, 'Oh, this is great. This person is trying to feed the community'—they thought, 'Oh, why would I bother paying X amount of money when I could just make that at home?'"

In Portland, Lamagna introduced something new to Filipino cuisine: familiar but not exactly traditional.

"What I'm excited about with Filipino food right now is that we can explore it. It's not going to please everybody, though—piss off a lot more people than I make happy," he added with a grin.

Cooking other types of food reinforced techniques he learned in Filipino cooking. "I've trained under so many different chefs and cooked many different cuisines, whether it was new American, French, German, Italian, or Spanish. The advantage with cooking Filipino food is that I've seen so many similarities and given names to techniques that I already knew, and even kind of upgraded those techniques. At the end of the day, it really helped me find my own path in Filipino food. I consider Magna Kusina as a modern Filipino restaurant serving modern versions of traditional dishes."

In some way, what chef Carlo Lamagna is doing with Filipino food in Portland is what chef Edward Lee was doing years ago with Korean food in Louisville. Chef Lee's food at that time was very focused on a collaboration between cultures, particularly Korean and Southern. His inspiration was a combination and melding of cultures.

"I eat a lot of Korean food, as it is the food of my childhood. It's always in my mind. But then, I also love Southern food. So, the two vocabularies are always kind of present in my head. Southern food is very spice-driven.

It's very bold, it's full of flavor, and so is Korean food. And so, the two work well together."

His inspiration came from watching and cooking with his grandmother.

"I think cooking with my grandmother was something that I always enjoyed. She cooked all our meals. My parents worked full-time jobs and my grandmother cooked. We didn't have a lot of money and there wasn't a lot to do back in Brooklyn. So, we spent a lot of time at home just watching her cook. And I still remember it to this day."

Chef Lee is always trying new things and he's not afraid to take chances, nor to fail.

"We have traditions, and they work for a reason. But if we don't try new things, then we always get stuck. And then traditions sort of get stagnant or stale. The collards and kimchee dish on the menu is, I think, a perfect example of the two things that have never been in a bowl together. When I ate collards for the first time, it reminded me very much of a Korean seaweed soup that we eat, and it's very nurturing, very satisfying and comforting, and as a kid I would always put kimchi in it. So, it just made sense to me. I didn't know if the people would like it. And then we tried our menu and lo and behold, everyone loved it."

Another example of common elements between Southern culture and Korean culture is barbecue. The technique is different—Korean barbecue is grilled over live coals—but it is also an essential part of Korean food.

This idea of charred or smoky or burnt flavors is very important in both cuisines.

I love chef Lee's unique perspective on the concept of authenticity.

"Whenever you say something is authentic, it implies that this other thing is not authentic. And to me, that doesn't belong in the food world. Authenticity basically implies truth, or realness, or superiority. And to me that just doesn't exist in the food world. I like to say there's hundreds of traditions, but there's not one that's more authentic than the other. So, traditions can be as small as something that you do in your own family home, or it can be a regional or national tradition. And those are fine. But no traditions are better than another."

—CHEF EDWARD LEE

The South has seen a major revival when it comes to cooking. Chef Lee is one example among many. From Eastern Texas to North Carolina, including Georgia, Alabama, Tennessee, Kentucky, and South Carolina, pockets of immigrants have influenced how local chefs are cooking.

During my Zoom conversation with chef Levon Wallace, we talked about the American South. "I've had this ongoing love affair for the past over ten years now," said Wallace. "It is such a beautiful, rich, albeit painful story about its food and foodways and where it came from, and how it evolved to what it is now. Southern food is not all fried chicken and barbecue. It's far from that. There's a beautiful history of food preservation in the Appalachian parts of the country. There's that beautiful rice culture, that's just peppered with African history along the coast, you know, the low country."

He talked about the foraging and the homemade Southern pantry: "Then there's the other pantry, which is like the homemade pantry. Whether it's dried mushrooms that we found when we were hiking, or salted or preserved vegetables or fruits. I love that part of Southern culture. I know that it exists in every culture, but I get very excited in the spring and summer months here. Not so much about what's coming in fresh, but rather what's that going to look like. And what's it going to look like put in a can for me to eat in the fall?"

His style of cooking is about digging deep into the basic cultural elements, then getting creative by combining them to make something new and interesting.

Wallace is looking for what connects us, rather than what makes us different, and adjusts his perspective to look for the similarities rather than the differences. His obsession about ingredients and dishes led him to unpack and unfold it like a kid that takes apart a radio to see how it works on the inside. This deep understanding of a dish helps him to take it further and achieve a balance between tradition and creativity.

"There was one particular festival that I was at several years back in Arkansas," recalled Wallace.

"Originally, I was going to make a salsa matcha, which is a pre-Hispanic oil-based salsa. Usually, it's based on dried seeds, dried chilies, and oil. "

"And out of nowhere it hit me, what's really good is chili crisp! And this is very similar to Chinese chili crisp."

Wallace explained that he was also making some smoked chicken at the time. He smoked the chickens and tore the skins off and threw all the skins in the deep fryer—they were going to be a snack for the staff.

"I was thinking to myself, 'wait a minute now, here we have this Southern American, arguably African dish, right?' The barbecued smoked meat and chicken. And then, I had this Mexican idea, with the salsa macha. But then I gave it a nod with the Chinese chili crisp. So, I took those fried smoked chicken skins—basically this was like a chicken chicharrones at that point— and I busted those up. I made the salsa macha, with the inclusion of fried peanuts, fried soybeans, and fried sesame seeds, along with the dried chilies, the herbs, and the fried garlic, and combined it all together to make what I called a Mexican chili crisp.

"It was fried chicken skins, fried peanuts, fried sesames, fried dried chilies, and it had this beautiful umami, crunchy, smoky spicy condiment that we ended up serving with a chicken tostada. And to give another nod to the African culture, I added a little bit of preserved watermelon. The preserved watermelon and the smoked chicken gave a nod to the Southern African roots; the chilies and the salsa based on peanuts and sesame give the Asian profile. It was just Chinese Southern Mexican without being annoying, without being weird. It was delightful."

I told Wallace that several years ago Chef Jose Garces had a similar approach with Latin food. His passion for Latin food started when he was a child, cooking with his grandmother when she came to visit the family in Chicago during the summer. A very similar thread of cooking from an early age and learning from family (again, all from women) strongly impacted his interest in food and cooking. Later, he traveled through Latin America and the Caribbean doing culinary curation and finding inspiration. A major part of his creation process is based on bringing those local traditions back and translating them in a way that works for the U.S. market.

Ten years later, another chef with a Latin heritage focused on balancing creativity and tradition in Brooklyn. Chef Erik Ramirez opened his first Peruvian restaurant, Llama Inn, in 2015. Peruvian cuisine is influenced by both the biodiversity of the country and the mix of cultural influences. When Ramirez opened Llama Inn, I instantly fell in love with his quinoa salad with banana, avocado, bacon, and cashew. We had the opportunity to continue our conversation about Peruvian cuisine.

"You have the indigenous," says chef Ramirez, "then you have the Spanish, African, Chinese, Japanese, and German. And then there's the biodiversity, if you look at the country, and the way that it's broken down. You have the coasts, the Sierra, the Andes, the forest, the rain forest, and then in the south, it is desert. The results of all these microclimates are these amazing local ingredients—3,500 varieties of potatoes, corn, quinoa, lupin beans, and one of the most popular fruits in Peru, the lucuma."

Chef Ramirez introduced me to lucuma about ten years ago, when he was chef at Raymi in Manhattan. Raymi was a modern Peruvian restaurant that celebrated the multicultural spirit of Peru. The restaurant has since closed, but it was my first introduction to Peruvian cuisine. The first time I ate there I sat at the bar and tasted salsa criolla in chicharron sliders, aji Amarillo, and aji rocoto (the two popular Peruvian chiles) in Tiraditos and Ceviches. I was introduced to chef Ramirez, and he invited me to tour the kitchen and look at various ingredients.

"Do you know lucuma?" asked Ramirez.

I had not even heard the name before, so he opened the freezer and grabbed a stainless-steel ice cream container and scooped out a tablespoon of a pale yellowish ice cream. I remember tasting something creamy and citrusy with a hint of maple and sweet potato.

Ramirez explained, "Peru has several distinctive cuisines based on regions. *Cocina Criolla*, which translates to Creole based on Spanish cuisine and Africans from the Senegambia region. *Cocina Andina*, traditional cuisine of Peru's Highlanders, and *Cocina Amazonica*, the cuisine of Peru's Amazonian indigenes. And then you have Chifa, which has its own cuisine as well, a fusion of Peruvian and Chinese food, brought to Peru by Chinese immigrants. And then you have something called Bachiche, which is the Italian Peruvian. Lastly, you also have what's known as Nikkei, which is Japanese and Peruvian. Now, in those specific cuisines there are dishes that represent those cultural combinations."

The various cultural influences have helped Ramirez understand Peruvian history. Like many second-generation American chefs, he rediscovered his cultural heritage at a later stage in life and started cooking learning the classic French techniques and working at French restaurants.

He had a newfound appreciation for the food after getting a little older and viewing it from a culinary career perspective. "I knew Peruvian food, but only from my childhood and certain dishes that I liked or that my mom would make.

"My parents emigrated from Peru and their Peruvian cuisine was all I really knew as a child. I would regularly visit Peru with my family and my grandparents, and we would spend the summer there. There was a big break as the last time I went there was maybe when I was sixteen or seventeen. I returned in my late twenties. I went on that trip with a different mindset. It was more career-driven, it was more to discover the culinary scene and what they were doing—it wasn't to visit family. When I saw what they were doing, I was blown away.

"There's a lot of great Peruvian restaurants in New York, and they're all delicious, but they kind of all do the same thing, that style of food that you find, it's all the same. I wanted to separate myself from that, to be able to reach more people, to push the cuisine forward and give it a name. Not that it didn't have one in New York City, but really kind of elevate it and bring it to another level. I wanted to make it one of the cuisines where that was always a topic of conversation."

Listening to Ramirez, I wondered where the culinary tradition begins, or if it is constantly evolving? His grandmother was of Nikkei heritage, but Nikkei was not a cuisine he was exposed to growing up. In 2019, Ramirez brought Nikkei cuisine to New York City by opening Llama San on 6th Avenue in Manhattan.

"I think in Peruvian cuisine, particularly, you need to know where it stems from. I think the history and the cuisine go hand in hand. Let's take ceviche for instance. When the Japanese arrived in Peru (early 1900), they taught us how to properly handle fish and how to properly cut fish."

In Peruvian style, the fish is cut in chunks with a lime marinade and onion. With the Japanese influence, the fish is cut sashimi style and the sauce is drizzled on top. These are called teradito.

"The people from Japan integrated Peruvian customs as well and it was like the second wave of what Nikkei cuisine was," Ramirez said. "History plays a very important part in Peruvian cuisine."

And today, chef Ramirez continues to tweak it, here in Manhattan.

"It's another perspective, right?" said Ramirez. "It's looking at it through a New York lens, you know; it's not Nikkei in the traditional sense. It's Nikkei how we see it here in New York, because we also want to utilize the seasons here. Our process would always start with a concept. We would think of a dish that we want to explore. Maybe a Nikkei dish or a Peruvian dish, or maybe a Japanese dish. We'll take that dish; we'll talk about it, and we'll try to dissect it. If it is a Japanese dish, how do we connect it to Peru and to New York? Same with a Peruvian dish, how do we connect it to Japan and to New York? That would be the process. It would start with an ingredient, a concept, a dish, or even a technique, right? And how do we bring it all together?"

I described to Wallace my food experience at Llama San restaurant sipping La Male Muerte cocktail—Singani (Bolivian brandy distilled from white Muscat), Bitter Bianco, Nori, Taru Sake, dry vermouth. Waiting on my first order of scallop ceviche, yuzu kosho (a type of Japanese seasoning), pitahaya (dragon fruit), and nori (a dried edible seaweed used in Japanese cuisine), I was thinking that chef Ramirez's story is a similar story to many cultural cuisines: one of evolution and the fusing of influences as inhabitants change in a particular place. I also heard a familiar element of someone loving family food and cooking it, but not realizing how much until getting older and viewing it through a chef career lens.

All these conversations with immigrants or second-generation Americans revealed how much early exposure to cooking influenced their interest in the kitchen, and how much their family influenced their way of cooking. Listening to chef Carlo Lamagna explaining the multiple adobo variations around the world made me realize how a dish can be an illustration of cultural understanding, awareness, and appreciation. And at the same time, thinking about my mother's opinion about the French Lorrain quiche recipe, made me wonder if sticking to cultural traditions and following recipes to a "T" was that important, or is the role of these chefs to find balance between tradition and creativity? All these chefs inspire a great respect for tradition as they want to understand everything about a dish before they start improvising.

In comparison, chef Levon Wallace's dish of smoked BBQ chicken with Chinese chili crisp and salsa macha, mixing Mexican, African, and southern cultures, is the perfect illustration of today's modern evolution of cuisine in the US. I fully echo chef Edward Lee's comment about the food evolution in this country: "The world is changing. The real world of food doesn't stop just because we want it to. It keeps evolving. And so, if we're going to be honest with ourselves, we must understand the nature of demographics and people and migration changes and how that food is being affected, and tourism is a huge part of it. Going to Montgomery, Alabama, and seeing that Korean food is very popular there because there was a Hyundai auto plant built in the middle of Montgomery, Alabama, that's creating a huge shift in the sort of cuisine of Montgomery, Alabama. And that's going to be there for generations to come. So, that's something that we must acknowledge. And just because maybe it doesn't fit in a traditional narrative, that doesn't mean it doesn't exist!"

There are many chefs all around the country, sons and daughters of immigrants, second-generation Americans, who are taking the inspiration from their parents' cuisines or their country of origin and putting their own creative twist on it.

At my next Skype call with my French family, I will remind them about the question they had for me twenty years ago: "How would you describe American cuisine?" I will tell them that it is a borderless cuisine that is always evolving as the result of waves of immigration and that reflects the mosaic of culture that America is today.

Chapter 5

CREATIVE DECISIONS

"Using the word 'creations' to describe dishes brings up
something that is a bit of a misnomer for a lot of chefs.
I don't view a dish as something that I created, or that
comes inherently from a creative place. I really feel that
cooking is an exercise in practicality."

—Chef Andrew McLeod

List of culinary individuals featured in this chapter:

Chef **Andrew McLeod** from
Avenue M in Asheville

Chef/Owner **Michael Gulotta** of
MoPho and MayPop in New Orleans

Pastry Chef **Antonio Bachour** from
Bachour Miami in Miami

Chef/Owner **Michael Fojtasek** of Olamaie and
Little Ola's Biscuits in Austin, Texas

Chef and restaurateur **Jamie Bissonnette** from
Toro, Copa, and Little Donkey in Boston

Chef **Hari Cameron** former chef/owner at
a(MUSE.) in Rehoboth, Delaware

Mixologist **Angel Teta** from Portland, Oregon

Mixologist **Bob Peters** in Charlotte

Mixologist **Jesse Vida** at Atlas Bar in
Singapore (was at BlackTail in New York)

Mixologist **Beau du Bois** at Puesto
in San Diego

Charlotte Voisey, global head of ambassadors
for William Grant & Sons based in Brooklyn

Consulting Chef **Elizabeth Falkner**
based in in Los Angeles

Chef, author, and restaurateur
Chris Cosentino in San Francisco

Chef **Kelly English** from Restaurant Iris,
The Second Line, Pantà in Memphis

Chef/Co-Owner **Fiore Tedesco** from
L'Oca d'Oro in Austin, Texas

Chef/consultant **Mark Welker**,
former executive pastry chef at Eleven
Madison Park and NoMad

Chef **Johnny Spero** from Reverie in
Washington, D.C.

Chef/Owner **Gabriel Kreuther** from two-
Michelin star Gabriel Kreuther restaurant
in New York City

Chef **Jeremy Umansky** from Larder
Delicatessen and Bakery in Ohio City, Ohio

Chef **Bryce Shuman** from former one-Michelin
star Betony restaurant in New York City

Pastry Chef and Entrepreneur **Sam Mason**
behind ice cream creations at Odd Fellows

Pastry Chef, Consultant, Recipe & Product
Development Specialist **Erin Kanegy-Loux**
from Brooklyn, New York

Retired Executive Chef **Andre Natera** from
Fairmont Hotel in Austin, Texas

I am always amazed when an artist, musician, painter, architect, or a chef comes with an idea, a painting, a piece of music, a building, a dish, or a drink out of the blue—from the ether to some extent. Only a few individuals can make something appear from nothing or nowhere. These people are called conjurers, geniuses, or conceptual innovators. However, creativity is multifaceted and can be demonstrated in various ways; everyone can become creative, it is something that can be cultivated and developed. Creativity engages several parts of our brain, our imagination, our conscious and unconscious cognitive systems, our emotions, and our self-motivation. Creative people are particularly good at activating and deactivating these brain networks, and everyone can work at developing their creativity, discover a deliberate approach to it, and make it a routine.

When taking over Avenue M in Asheville, North Carolina, chef Andrew McLeod faced the challenge of balancing his own new dishes on the new menu with elevated versions of loyal customers' favorites. When I questioned him about this, I used the word "creations" to describe his new dishes, and chef McLeod disagreed with the term.

I asked, "Why is the word 'creation' an issue for you?"

"Probably in the last twenty years or so," he replied, "ever since the food agricultural system has exploded, any chef in hotels or restaurants can sit down and write a menu by pulling out of the sky whatever ingredient they want. They sample any number of products from trucks, purveyors, or farmers, and bring those products in to execute dishes. Before this agricultural system took shape, our country was looking at what was around, the local food scene, what people were growing locally within reasonable distance, and that would be the driving force behind what you cooked. A lot more people took that approach and now there is a large period of novelty about 'the farm to table movement' and about responsible sourcing.

"It seems ad nauseam to me, because this is my understanding of what a chef is. This is what you do. We source the best produce that we can and that's our responsibility: to figure out how to translate that into something that somebody wants to eat. This process doesn't seem to me inherently creative or special."

I told McLeod that I was surprised by his answer, because from a food enthusiast's perspective there is an undeniable creative aspect to the process of coming up with new dishes, desserts, or drinks.

"You are celebrating and elevating the product, as everything starts with the produce," I told him. But I have noticed there are different schools of thoughts. Some chefs can over-complicate the process with sophisticated techniques while others will focus on a limited number of ingredients, remain simple on purpose, and let the produce shine on its own. The end result still gives the customer a unique experience.

"Wouldn't you agree that these dishes are created through your fingers or from the ones of your team members?" I asked.

McLeod didn't take "creations" as a slight; he was just not sure what the appropriate word was. It made him feel uncomfortable to think of what he does every day as something so special or creative. He looked at culinary creativity as activating technique, as a responsible act towards the people growing food, and as an exercise in mentorship with his staff.

"Absolutely," said McLeod. "You know, it is a story I am telling myself here, because cooking is a creative outlet for me, and a part of my life where I express myself creatively. It's just dangerous for me to think that way, because then I can get into this tragic artist syndrome, you know, 'I'm so terminally unique and whatever.' I really like to keep my feet firmly planted on the ground as much as I can. That's the way I can operate best by staying true and humble to what my purpose is, but I am an incredibly creative driven person in general."

After my conversation with McLeod, a series of questions popped in my head. Do chefs, pastry chefs, and mixologists follow some sort of process when it comes to creativity? Do they in fact have a process? Is the process similar when developing cocktails versus savory dishes or desserts? How does their creative process evolve as they gain more experience? Does it get more difficult with time? Do they address creativity in a unique way or does the process change if they must solve a problem versus being obsessed with a new ingredient? How do they challenge the imagination of their team members? How do they find the right balance between tradition and creativity? Where do they go for inspiration when what excited them in the past is not fulfilling them anymore?

I know that creative people typically fall into one of two categories: early birds or night owls. I am a morning person. As an early bird, I do my best work in the morning. It probably came from my mother's obsession to wake me up early every morning—even on my vacation! "Le future appartient á ceux qui se lève tôt," she used to repeat when, as a kid, I complained about her morning routine. This French idiom is the equivalent to "the early bird catches the worm." Therefore, I have since developed the following practice that usually involves a moment of solitude with meditation music playing in the background, and a notepad. Some people are great at being creative "on the fly," reacting to other people's ideas. I have learned through the years that my route to innovation requires solo time and writing my thoughts down on paper. The act of writing sharpens my attention. First, I dump my previously gathered observations and organize them in clusters, almost like a mind map or a story flow. Then, I must let go and step away. This is what I called the incubation period. That time could be short or long, from a couple of hours to several weeks, and I realized that I was able to shorten the incubation period by intermingling analytical or repetitive tasks between creative sessions. Eventually one day, a light bulb will switch on creating this "aha" moment when the elements from the mind map will come together and it will be time to share the story with other people, receive their feedback, and build the story further.

For me, the way to maximize creativity is to have a flow back and forth between solitude and working with a group. When I organize brainstorming sessions, I always ask participants to spend a few minutes to write down ideas individually and then share them with the group.

Listening back to my podcast episodes while working on this book, I was able to identify patterns among my guests when asked about their creative process in the kitchen or behind the bar, or when describing their innovative approach behind a dish or a drink that caught my attention during a tasting. Their creative approach usually followed one of these subsequent seven paths:

- Elevate
- Rotate
- Combine
- Substitute
- Surprise with intent
- Deconstruct, and
- Simplify

I realize that there are other ways for creating the future, but one or multiple combinations of these seven methods can quickly generate new ideas. As culinary individuals must constantly refresh their approach to innovation, alternating or combining some of these paths helps create new ideas.

Elevate

In recent years, bartenders have been elevating drink recipes to include unusual and rare ingredients such as Szechuan peppercorns or activated charcoal; claiming distinctive sourcing such as unique tea varieties or local gin brands; and using new processes such as milk-washing (adding whole milk to a spirit). Likewise, chefs heightened low cuts of meats by producing the origin story and provenance; they uplifted sauces with fermentation and adopted artisan processes such as cured and barrel-aged meat; focused on gourmet cheeses such as burrata and aged Manchego; and created in-house condiments and spreads.

Chef Michel Gulotta from New Orleans uses local protein sourcing to excite a customer's experience. "I have to be honest, at MoPho, a lot of our everyday dishes are based on commodities products. MoPho's guest check average is twenty-two dollars a head. We run with a twenty-two percent food cost. It cannot run at a higher food cost or else we'll go out of business. For all our specialty dishes, like our Louisiana seafood, we never compromise on them and then, if we're running a special, we always try to find local chicken."

Gulotta used the example of barbecue chicken thighs over a peach and tomato salad with roasted jalapeno and toasted dried shrimp cornbread.

"We got all the chickens from a local farm. The chicken thighs are much smaller, they're not as big and plump as the commodity chicken legs, so it's different for the guest. The guests were surprised how different the chicken was. They were true farm-raised chicken. They're not as big, they're not as plump because they run around all day. It's fun to do these specials where we really are showing the local produce and the local farm-raised animals. The week after, farmers had a really good price on Wagyu short ribs, so I got together with the team, and we came up with a dish for the following week. We usually come up with a dish for the following week on Saturday, and then we spend that whole week getting that dish ready and then we run it the following Friday."

Worldwide known pastry chef Antonio Bachour emphasizes the importance of revisiting classic desserts and continuing to celebrate them. In his new book, *Bachour Gastro*, several classic dessert recipes are elevated with new ingredients and techniques. I like his approach to modernize carrot cake.

"We use a simple carrot cake that my mom used to make at home thirty years ago, but I did a new interpretation with a nice aesthetic. I made a layer cake with pineapple jam and coconut whipped cream cheese ganache, and we decorate the top with mango. You know, like I said before, tropical fruit mango, pineapple coconut mango, pineapple cream cheese."

I have mentioned that quiches and croissants hold a special place in my heart. I could have used the following example in the Substitute or the Combine pattern sections, but to me, the ham and cheese quiche croissant, created during the pandemic by Antonio Bachour, fits the Elevate section best. Wait, *what*? Quiche and croissant together? I am in! Bachour used croissant dough as the crust for the quiche. "We were only open for takeout and delivery. I needed to create traffic to the shop in Miami. One day I said, 'Let's make a quiche croissant!' I posted on my Instagram that a quiche croissant would be available the next morning. We made only fifty-five and in five minutes we sold out. People were calling every day. We ended up making four hundred a day!"

Rotate

Rotating restaurant and bar menus with the seasons is common practice in the industry. Most chefs will set up their cards around "sets" that can evolve out of necessity or based on what is available in seasons and at the farms.

When I am in Austin, I love the pork chop dish that chef Michael Fojtasek has on the menu at Olamaie. I had it first in the summer with peaches, but Fojtasek explains that his dish evolves based on the season.

"Basically, it was a room temperature salad with sorrel and three components: peach, ham, and burnt squash. Over the course of the summer, as those peaches go out of season, we sub in pears, and at some point, apples will end up in it. We use salad as we run out of sorrel, but we will add a little bit more lemon juice to make up for the lack of acidity. The squashes, naturally, will rotate as well, based on the kind that are available. Sometimes you find yourself in a place where the dish, and the evolution caused by necessity, brings you to a place where you like the dish even more than the original. Sometimes you try something, and you don't like it, and you must start with something new. For me, it's a process that takes time and a lot of tinkering."

Fojtasek described his two-part menu. "One part is made of small plates that singularly stand on their own, and would be focused on one ingredient, and then the other part of our menu is more about the proteins. There's always fish, chicken, pork, beef, and a vegetarian dish. We consider them 'sets' and they would be about what is available at that moment at the market. Every dish on the menu can take a substitution here or there."

Beyond seasonal rotations, other cyclical elements could be introduced in menus. Some people follow trends from other industries, like fashion or colors. For instance, in 2021 the trend "Back to the '90s" was popping up everywhere, from looser jeans and vintage graphic t-shirts to platform shoes and corduroy, just to name a few examples. The "Back to the '90s" trend made its way to the bars also, with the return of the dessert cocktails such as chocolate or coffee martinis.

Consumers enjoy things from their childhood. Playing on consumers' memories and emotional connections to nostalgic aromas and flavors can bring success to new dishes, desserts, or drinks.

Combine

Combining ingredients, techniques, or influences are ways to create something new in food. This is often called "mash-ups." Fusion food and pastry hybrids are testimonies to mash-ups. Here are a few examples: taco pizza, sushi burrito, cronuts (hybrid between a donut and a croissant), townies (hybrid between a tart and a brownie), cruffins (hybrid between a croissant and a muffin), and duffins (hybrid between a donut and a muffin).

Many chefs leverage this path to create successful dishes and drinks. When I talked to chef Brother Luck, I asked him about the creative process behind this signature dish at Four by Luck.

"I never thought one of our signature dishes would be fried cheese, but it's such a simple dish. I had a traditional jalapeño popper: half a jalapeño stuffed with cream cheese and wrapped with bacon. I think it has such a great flavor profile because I like heat, salt, and fat. It really rounds the palette well. As I was eating that, I was like, 'Man, I'd love to re-create this.' I just got back from Japan, so I was all about the tempura at that time. 'How do I modify a tempura batter to actually encase cheese?' Because traditionally a tempura wouldn't hold it. The cheese would fizzle out. I figured out a batter that worked to encase the cheese. Then I started to blend Colorado goat cheese with cream cheese, toasted cumin, and coriander seeds, and then roasted jalapeños. One thing with jalapeño poppers is that the peppers are always too raw. The cheese is cooked, and the bacon is salty, but the actual pepper is never cooked all the way. We roasted and pureed it. We worked it into the cheese and made a spicy cheese. I wanted to eliminate the meat component. As I'm getting older, I'm becoming more aware of meat consumption in this country, so we eliminated the bacon element. That cheese is rolled into a sphere, dipped in a tempura batter, and cooked until the cheese is melted on the inside. Then we take the remaining scraps from the jalapeños, and we cook them down to make a jalapeño syrup. We serve that with just some simple pickle, onions, and a little bit of crème fraiche. It's such a clean dish. I mean, people lose their mind over those things. It's crazy!"

Fusion food has never been so popular, but chefs don't like to call it that. When it comes to fusion food, I like chef Jamie Bissonnette's view on the subject.

"I think there's a fine line between what people call fusion and a fusion mess, because all food is kind of fusion. Pizza was a fusion of a bunch of ingredients that were left over in the ovens and there was somebody saying, 'Hey, let's make pita, but instead of putting stuff inside of, let's put it on top and we'll call it pizza instead.' If we're going to do something based on something that needs to be traditionally thought of as authentic, we're going to figure out how to do it authentically. For instance, when we do anything with sticky rice in Bangkok, we do it the traditional way, in a bamboo basket over boiling water with a cloth on top. We always make the rice the proper way. What we do with it afterwards might not be traditional, might not be authentic to anything, but because the techniques were there, and the thought is there. We know what and how we're going to do something, but knowing why we're doing it is what makes it authentic.

"We [Bissonnette and chef Ken Oringer] were walking through the markets in Chinatown in Bangkok and we saw somebody making fresh yuba (tofu skin). We bought that tofu skin, we brought it back to the restaurant, and we decided to use that as our pasta to make a lasagna. I don't think there is any traditional tofu skin lasagna anywhere in the world, but we did it anyway. We did lasagna with ricotta and mozzarella and then we did like a spicy larb (a type of Lao meat salad) type beef that almost looks like Bolognese but added a lot more of the northern Thai spices to give some umami character. We baked it and it looked like lasagna. It had a sensory memory of lasagna, but if I put that in front of somebody who had never traveled outside of their own little neighborhood in the north end of Boston, somewhere in Jersey, or in Little Italy, who was not adventurous with other foods, they would eat that and go, 'What the heck is this?' The cool thing about being a chef is that you don't have to be traditional and authentic all the time. You can be innovative. You can use your own whimsy, but as long as you do it in a way that's educated, you're not just throwing things together."

"The cool thing about being a chef is that you don't have to be traditional and authentic all the time. You can be innovative. You can use your own whimsy, but as long as you do it in a way that's educated, you're not just throwing things together."
—CHEF JAMIE BISSONNETTE

Combining influences is something that chef Michael Gulotta did from day one when he opened MoPho in New Orleans. "It was a lot of give and take. It was a lot of screwing it up, because I had never been to Southeast Asia. I only knew what I cooked with my friends and what I grew up eating at the local Vietnamese restaurants. When we first opened, it wasn't very Vietnamese at all. We kept saying, 'We're not a Vietnamese restaurant. We are a New Orleans restaurant inspired by Vietnamese cuisine.' We are trying to find parallels between New Orleans and Vietnam. So that kind of gave us free rein. I started building a pantry with Vietnamese ingredients. I started making New Orleans dishes with Vietnamese ingredients, like the gumbo that we're known for. We do a pho on Wednesdays that is a pork pho. We took the approach that a Vietnamese person would take to making pho, but we add in smoked pork hocks, and we make the bones with pork bones, because that's very big in South Louisiana. For us, smoked pork is a big thing. I actually had discussions with Vietnamese friends of mine saying that 'well smoked pork pho is not a thing. In Vietnam. You would never put pork in pho.' I understand that completely. We're not here to do traditional Vietnamese cuisine. Just like if someone from France came to South Louisiana and we showed them a 'cubion' that is nothing like a French 'court bouillon.' They're very different things. One is an evolution of a traditional cuisine, which is what we're trying to do. We're trying to evolve the traditional Vietnamese cuisine here in New Orleans. Our whole idea is always like, 'What is a third genera-tion New Orleans Vietnamese person cooking for their wife or husband that is from Lafayette, Louisiana? What would they cook for them?' That's the idea of how we approach dishes at MoPho. Our Pi-Mi is a mixture of po' boy and banh mi, which is the traditional Vietnamese. We do a mix and we do traditional New Orleans po' boy staples—we do hot sausage, and we do fried shrimp, and we do fried oysters, but we put them on locally baked bread, and we do it with all the garnishes that would go on a banh mi. You have the pick-led vegetables, you have the jalapeños, you have the mint, the cilantro, the aioli. So, it's an exact split down the middle of Vietnam and New Orleans.

"Since the pandemic, every Friday is Pho-Que Fridays. So we made a barbecue dish, and we got local short ribs from Raines Farms, which is an all-Wagyu beef farm in North Louisiana, and we rub them down. One of our sous-chefs worked for chef Floyd Cardoz. She had this amazing rub that we put on them; we let them sit overnight, we then smoked them for six hours and put them in the oven, wrapped them up in plastic and foil, and slow-cooked them."

Another great example of adding a different cultural spin to a dish from Gulotta is their fermented black bean gumbo. "Whenever I go to eat at tra-ditional Vietnamese restaurants, I get the fermented black bean braised lob-ster, the fermented black bean braised shrimp, or the fermented black bean braised crabs. That flavor of fermented black beans always reminded me of gumbo. When we first opened MoPho, I made a good blue crab gumbo, and I added the fermented black beans because I had them in the pantry, and we ran it as a special and people just really loved the flavor. Over the years, I just kept adding more and more from that Vietnamese pantry. I started adding lime leaves, cassia bark, black cardamom pods, and now it's this dish that's always on the lunch menu at MayPop and it runs as a weekly special at MoPho. Every time we have it, it sells out."

Beside bringing distinct cultural features into a dish, another way of combining elements to create a new item on the menu without challenging customers is to add a twist to a classic recipe, or introduce a new flavor along with an anchor flavor that people can easily relate to.

One of my favorite executions of a twist on a classic is Toro's Uni Boca-dillo, his version of a grilled cheese sandwich. If I had to live only on one sandwich for the rest of my life, that would be this one! It made "The 50 Best Sandwiches in America" in *Men's Journal* back in 2015.

I traveled many times to Spain and always enjoyed the traditional boca-dillo (a sandwich made with baguette) at tapas bars. Chefs Jamie Bisson-nette and Ken Oringer made an awesome seafood grilled sandwich, replacing the cheese with butter. "Ken and I were talking years ago in Boston about another sea urchin preparation. A lot of people do sea urchin toasts, which we love. We came up with a crispy, pressed panino or bocadillo. Every culture that serves sea urchin, for the most part, has a dish where sea urchin is served with something that's buttery and rich, kind of acidic, and has some sort of spice added to it. It could be sea urchin on seasoned sushi rice like nigiri, or it could be on toast with butter and lemon. We decided to start with that, and we put things together and decided to make the butter a little bit more umami, so we added miso. Let's add something that makes it a little bit fresher; and we both love chives, but we realized that the chives didn't stand up to it, so we tried it with scallions. I can still picture the first time we made it on the line. All the ingredients for what we were going to put into it were already made for other dishes, and we just put them together on the piece of bread, then covered the outside of the bread with mayonnaise to make sure we'd get crispy and then grilled it. And when we took a bite, we were like, wow, it was amazing. We tried to put a little bit of mustard in it, but we felt the mustard was too strong, so we used pickled mustard seeds, and we finally found the right balance."

Another example of a twist on a classic was mentioned by chef Hari Cameron, who used a local delicacy, the whelk, on a chowder recipe. "The Delaware state shell is the channeled whelk. It looks like a conch. Nobody in Delaware eats whelk. They are all sent to China and to Europe, especially Italy. I was getting this beautiful whelk from my local fisherman and when I cook them, they have the texture of abalone or snails. They are super meaty and have an umami feel. We have Manhattan chowder and New England chowder. What would a Delaware chowder look like? We used a cream-based chowder and put some bacon in it. We used local seaweeds to flavor it with a more umami profile. We did a traditional thing where we deglazed it with sherry. It adds that kind of traditional chowder flavor profile, but using whelk. It's not something that people do in a chowder. It's not something that people commonly see or commonly serve. That was one way where the ingredient kind of dictated the recipe. It's serving something that's very familiar to people—the chowder, but with a twist, the whelk. A very common recipe done with an uncommon ingredient."

Substitute

Just because I don't have all the ingredients for a cocktail recipe I would like to make at home doesn't mean that I can't have a happy hour! Ingredient swap has always been part of a bartender's routine, and is a fun aspect of the job. In fact, this is how bartenders memorize seemingly thousands of cocktails: many recipes are similar, but with a few small tweaks.

Since my conversation with mixologist Angel Teta from Portland, Oregon, my favorite Old-Fashioned got a facelift.

"The Old-Fashioned is always going to be a whiskey cocktail, but it can be a lot more! Emmanuel, you should try a mescal Old-Fashioned. And what is good with mescal? Agave! You can put a little salt in it as well. Add mole bitters instead of regular Angostura bitters, a little orange bitter to pick it up on the acid side, and, finally, do a flamed orange peel. You can also buy smaller bottles of Amaro or Benedictine that bartenders call modifiers. You can just add a bar spoon of that and a bar spoon of whatever sugary ingredient you prefer. Personally, I like Amaro Nonino, as it really changes the flavors, and just a bar spoon influences the cocktail. Benedictine is a great one too. You could add Dry Curaçao and do a bourbon Old-Fashioned with a bar spoon of Dry Curaçao, a bar spoon of sugar, a little bit of orange bitters, and you've got a whole new taste profile!"

My favorite new "Old-Fashioned" at home is now: 1 ounce tequila, 1/2 ounce mescal, 1/2 ounce vermouth, agave syrup, mole bitter, orange bitter, a big ice cube, and an orange peel expressed on the glass rim. Simple. Thanks, Angel!

Another example of substitution is a twist on the classic Negroni by mixologist Bob Peters.

"When I know that they want sort of a boozy Manhattan-ish kind of a drink, I play just a little tiny trick on them, and I give them something related to a Negroni, but with bourbon instead of gin. As we all know, one of my favorite all-time cocktails is the Boulevardier, and I love the story of a bourbon Negroni and how that turns into a Boulevardier. Well, one of my favorite things to do is to substitute Cynar, which is a cousin of Campari, for the Campari. It's a little bit more bitter, less sweet, very herbal, and not quite as fruity as the Campari lends itself to be. Add two ounces of a good, strong bourbon. It doesn't necessarily have to be a hundred proof, but I love a good strong backbone bourbon with big shoulders that you can build flavors on top of and can still stand out, like Woodford Double Oak. Then I add three-quarters ounce of Cynar and a half-ounce of some nice vermouth, then stir it, and put an orange rind over it. It's simple, delicious, and so boozy, bitter, and lovely. That's one of my all-time cocktails for sure."

Surprise with intent

I generally start my dinner by ordering a cocktail, or if available, I do a cocktail pairing dinner. I am not a vodka person. My usual go-to spirits are bourbon, rye, tequila, mescal, or gin. When it comes to cocktail creation, I always want to understand how mixologists build up their drinks. Do they start with an overarching theme and then identify the ingredients and the ideal flavor combinations? Or do they begin with the spirit as the base and build each flavor one at a time?

Three elements are key in the cocktail bar business: knowing what loyal patrons like, mastering profitability numbers, and having recipes that can easily be executed and replicated by the staff. When it comes to putting together cocktail menus, do bartenders focus on seasonality, or do they come up with a theme menu to stay away from the routine of the seasons?

I loved what Jesse Vida did with the team at BlackTail in Manhattan. Vida was my first guest on "Flavors Unknown." I love The Nacional cocktail, which was created as part of their first menu at BlackTail.

"This is an iconic Cuban cocktail, named after and created at the Hotel Nacional in Havana Cuba," Vida explained, sliding the glass in my direction on the bar counter. "We do a modern adaptation on the classic, layering it with yuzu and gentian. This is originally a classic Cuban cocktail, but we use modern techniques and flavors. We added pineapple, layered in a yuzu syrup as well as gentian to give a floral bitterness on the finish, but it stays rich and tropical in the middle."

After a few sips, I told him I could taste every ingredient in it. Everything was present, but nothing was dominant. It just came off very balanced.

For Vida, the bartender's craft is part creativity, part performance, and part showmanship. "The creative part is obviously crafting the cocktail to order for the guests. The performance is the way in which you work. This goes back to your technique. Being technically sound isn't only executing on a level where things are coming out the way they're supposed to. There should be a little bit of blow and poetry—and the showmanship as you are entertaining guests, cracking jokes, and finding relatable topics."

I asked Vida if focusing on the Prohibition era in Cuba from 1910 to 1960 somehow limited her creativity at Blacktail.

"Well, definitely," said Vida with a smile. "The creative focus, to a certain extent, is based on a specific era in a time, and the styles of cocktails are based around the Caribbean influence of the 1910s and the 1950s. But I certainly wouldn't say that limits us in any way, because there is total freedom to bringing a lot of modern techniques or new and unique flavors—and kind of plugging them in—to what is generally a BlackTail cocktail."

Exploring new techniques and new ingredients provides chefs and mixologists options to innovate within their brand or positioning guidelines.

When Bob Peters creates a cocktail, he comes up with flavor combinations using local ingredients. When he worked on the Salted Maple Pear for the restaurant Grinning Mule in Charlotte, he had an idea to do something with a flavor association of maple, pear, and salt. I wondered what came first in the creative process, the spirit or the added flavors concept?

"I came up with the concept first," said Peters. "I thought it sounded beautiful. Said to myself 'Fall and winter, for the ingredients? No problem, I get some nice maple syrup and then some nice pear juice.' That part was OK. After that I had to figure out what spirit to work with that flavor combination. I always liked doing things that are a little bit unexpected, but very intentional. I went with a local gin. I love local products and I am very proud of what North Carolina has done with its craft distilleries. I love to feature them as much as possible. I used Cardinal gin small-batch gin, made by Southern Artisan Spirits in Kings Mountain, which is out of a small town. It has these beautiful notes of cloves and spearmint. And there's some frankincense as well and apricot seeds that give these delicate flavor notes."

He knew from experience that that gin would be insanely delicious with his salted maple pear concept. He mixed up a mild saline solution to put in it.

"It all came together quite elegantly. Of course, I had to play around with the ratios to make sure that it was not too sweet, too salty, or too gin forward."

Mixologist Beau du Bois explained that, for him, creating a cocktail starts with the base spirit, focusing on the overall flavor of the drink.

"Then it moves into the visual experience," said du Bois. "The impact the cocktail makes when it gets dropped down in front of the customers is critical to me. The visual presentation basically elevates the guest experience."

As an example, the passion fruit margarita du Bois created at Meadowood Napa Valley was a real taste-layering work in terms of cocktail making. "Put passion fruit in anything and people are going to order it. I really appreciate that about it, but I wanted to take it further so that the passion fruit wasn't very polarizing because that could also be a problem. Sometimes all you're going to taste is passion fruit and that's not always a bad thing, but in terms of making interesting cocktails, I think it can be. We were able to really go down the rabbit hole and make sure that we were basically helping the passion fruit calm down. That included using a big body tequila, a little bit of green tea to soften the passion fruit on the palate, and finally the glass was pre-seasoned with a ginger salt mist. That was very important because ginger also helped calm down the passion fruit and pull it in a different direction while keeping it balanced. I also made sure that every sip had that last little lick-on-the-lips-with-a-bit-of-salt characteristic. I don't tend arbitrarily to garnish the glass with something for it to look better. I want it to have an impact on the experience of the cocktail as well. If it's a garnish that provides an aromatic characteristic, that way it's elevating the drink. It should be considered as another component of the drink."

For Beau du Bois, every element elevates the customer experience.

Similarly, Charlotte Voisey, head of Ambassadors at William Grant & Sons USA (family-owned distiller), thinks about the overarching flavor idea first.

"It's an overarching flavor combination that I have in mind or am working towards," said Voisey. "Then I start to pull together ingredients that will help me get there. Within that, there's the theme of balancing. You need to make sure everything is balanced in terms of not just sweet and sour and strengths of the drink, but also the volume of different flavors, even texture, and how all of that comes together. Usually, I start with an overarching theme, unless I start with a very specific brief—for example, if we have a new spirit and need to create cocktails using it, we're starting with that spirit. The first thing I would do is to nose it and taste it properly to understand the nuance and the characters that the spirit has. Then I would work on adding flavors one-by-one to draw them out until I reached a cocktail that showcased that spirit specifically."

I asked her to give an example, maybe with the first scenario of the overarching theme or flavor idea that she mentioned: something she had done recently or something which is connected to one of her iconic brands.

"One of our brands is Monkey Shoulder. It's a blended scotch, but the whole premise around Monkey Shoulder is that it's made for mixing. It's not a traditional scotch that you sit down and sip neat, it is designed to be mixed in cocktails. For Monkey Shoulder, what we wanted to do was to push the idea of scotch in cocktails, as extreme as possible to get this message across. We came up with an overarching idea of making a Scotch Tiki cocktail with tropical flavors, something you wouldn't normally expect. It must be something that looks like a rum drink that probably could be served by the pool. It could be blended and served with crushed ice, a drink that you might find in a Tiki bar: that was the goal. Then we worked backwards to fit in the Monkey Shoulder. We came up with the different elements to feature some big tropical flavors. 'Does that come from fresh pineapple? Should we use simple syrup instead of just regular sugar? How does the temperature need to be? How does it need to look?' We worked backwards rather than looking at Monkey Shoulder like a scotch, and then thinking about scotch cocktails."

The most unexpected use of ingredient was given to me by chef Elizabeth Falkner. She is known for pushing boundaries when it comes to flavor associations and innovation in desserts.

"I made a black sesame, fermented black bean caramel sauce, a black sesame streusel, and then served them with just kettle creamy tofu. Why wouldn't you do that? Tofu feels like panna cotta to me. I like that combination so much! Also, the fermented Chinese black beans in a caramel sauce in dessert is so unusual, but it's salty and it has a umami character. And, of course, it goes together in a caramel sauce! That was fun to make because, both Western and Eastern culture can kind of go, 'Goodness me, I don't even know what this is, but it's really tasty!' I love that."

Deconstruct

For a non-native English person, "deconstruct" is one of the most difficult words to pronounce. Doing these interviews, I made a lot of people smile when attempting to use this word in a sentence.

Deconstructing is a classic approach in desserts when a pastry chef tears apart a classic dessert and plates each element on the plate. I like the new interpretation of what deconstruction means with what pastry chef Philip Speer does at Comodor in Austin. He introduces some Mexican cultural aspects of what a lava cake was originally.

"Our chocolate tamale is very popular. It really brings together flavors and ideas from places I grew up [a part of his family is from Mexico], with some places other chefs in the team grew up in as well. We are also coming from other restaurants we worked at. One of my favorite desserts of all time is from when I worked for Jean-Georges for a brief period. The Molten Lava Cake is a classic Jean-Georges. He's credited with that dessert. I wanted to mimic what the Molten Lava Cake was but in the sense of our restaurant Comodor. We made a chocolate tamale with nixtamalized masa (a traditional maize preparation process in which dried kernels are cooked and steeped in an alkaline solution), black cocoa, and we did it in the tradition of what you would do a savory tamale, but instead of the filling being meat or vegetable, we gave it a chocolate filling. We steamed it, we did it in a sphere, and then inside the sphere we had delicious chocolate. When the customer cuts into the sphere, they taste this kind of savory bitter and a little bit of sweetness on the exterior of the masa, then they get the stone ground corn masa flavor, and then it goes to this molten dark chocolate filling, like you would have in a chocolate lava cake. We paired it with a caramelized-milk ice cream and rolled it in candied sesame, candied amaranth, and rice crisp. That part is traditional to some candy that I used to eat in South Texas, which is an almost granola-like candy that was very traditional near the border with Mexico. It's crunchy with bits of caramel in it. I made a play on that and rolled it around the ice cream. You have all the textures, and some sweetness and contrasts. I want every bite to be its own experience. But I also want to be very cohesive."

The deconstruct could be applied to savory dishes as well. Chef Chris Cosentino did a play with asparagus and egg yolks. "We know that they work amazingly together with butter, and this opens up so many doors of what I can do with those three ingredients. It doesn't have to be a hollandaise sauce with grilled asparagus. I can take that to a whole other level. Now my creativity says I'm going to take the cream and I'm going to break it, I'm going to caramelize the milk solids, and add my butter element. The asparagus, I'm going to shape into a terrine. Then, I'm going to blanch them. I'm going to do white and green and show the color variations of the asparagus. For the egg yolks, I'm going to preserve them, and shave preserved egg yolks into a vinaigrette. Now, I've got a preserved egg yolk vinaigrette. You can change these three ingredients however you want, but it's understanding the approach, the simplicity, the technique that was already there because somebody worked through it. It's not reinventing the wheel. It's just making it your own."

Simplify

A culinary individual's creative process will evolve with experience and maturity. The opportunity, space, and challenge to solve will evolve over time. Early in their career, they start improving their skills by creating twists on classics, then it evolves into experimenting with sophisticated techniques, and finally, as time goes by, they hold back on their hyper creativity and focus on achieving simplicity.

Chef Kelly English from Memphis admits, "At the beginning of your career, you're trying to impress everyone at every single turn every time you do anything. I like to look at it as going out on a date. You can't constantly try to impress someone at every single second and at every single moment. I think it's the same way with food. There's got to be negative space to allow a time for things just to be fantastic. There's got to be a good time for things just to be surprising. And there's got to be times to sit back and ponder what you just had. Early in my career, it was all about impressing people all the time, no matter what. And now I really just want to cook whole-some food that means something and not food that is always here to impress. Sometimes, there's a buy to something that just warms your soul but doesn't impress, but it just hits you somehow. That's what I look for in every dish I make. We pay attention to different cultures that went into making up what Memphis is and what New Orleans is. We try to either pay homage to those cultures or we try to steer clear of them if it's an inappropriate thing for us to replicate, or if we are taking away someone's ability to earn a living down the street by doing something here, then we won't do it."

Chef Fiore Tedesco told me that he spent time in many fine dining kitchens and refined atmospheres learning sophisticated techniques, but it all led him back to the desire to really express all of that through "a very humble prism and format." He is always inspired by his grandmother's style of cooking, and the idea of a rustic, comforting family food experience..

"I am often taking these creative ideas and all these foods, and I am trying to strip away anything that's extra. Trying to simplify anything that has any pretense, or has anything that doesn't really ring true to the core and the comfort of the dish I am making. I want to display food and a brand of hospitality that is sincere, soulful, and honest."

Pastry chef Mark Welker explained his idea of minimalism: "We want things to look effortless on the plate, but once you eat it, you realize that the flavors and the textures and the technique are much deeper than what you thought. We want people to find the dish beautiful, but it should look effortless. It should look simple and minimal on the plate. Then when you go into it, you discover that it is not as simple as it seems. We don't want things to feel too fussy or to feel like there are so many components on the plate."

Chef Johnny Pero from Reverie says that his process has definitely changed. "When I was younger, I was definitely flipping through cookbooks, looking at dishes that people were doing, but it wasn't authentically me. We have all read these books, and you think you have these ideas, but really, it's just drawing from other people's ideas who have already created these dishes. Subconsciously, you're trying to think that it's your idea when it's not."

Similarly, when chef Johnny Spero is thinking about dishes today, he tries not to grab a cookbook and flip through the pages. Now, his creative process starts with a conversation with the farmers and purveyors. "Inspiration definitely starts with the ingredient now. Let's focus on highlighting the ingredients, not masking them, and let them stand out. Techniques should be used to elevate the dish, not to be a showpiece. There's a farmer that's right next to where my parents live in Baltimore County, and he reached out to me, and he brought a bunch of Sun Gold tomatoes, and all these other vegetables that he has. He gave me this box of vegetables, and we cooked them every which way, ate them raw, and that's where it starts. I focus on highlighting these ingredients, not masking them, and letting them stand out. Whereas when I was younger, it was more, 'Let's do the cool technique. What's going to be a showstopper? What's everyone going to stop and look at?' We don't necessarily have to tell a story about where it's from; it can just be delicious on a plate."

With all the experiences chef Spero gained while working in Denmark and in Spain and on his trip to South Asia, I wanted to understand what came to his mind after wanting to celebrate a great ingredient received from the farmer. Will he decide to bring a Nordic or Spanish influence to it, or would he create a dish with an Asian twist? How does it work?

He explained to me that the way he thinks about food now, and the way his flavors come together, is less about picking a particular country or flavor profile. "I am not thinking, this is going to be more Japanese style, or this is going to be French. Because they say America is a melting pot of culture, I think for most, as we travel, we've kind of melded these things together, and now we draw certain techniques and flavors from all the different places. My thinking process might just grab a technique that I learned somewhere. For instance, we started cooking a lot of our vegetables in liquid Shio Koji. They often get paired with other flavors that might be more associated with Scandinavia, like the scallop dish we have on the menu now. The scallops are dressed in Shio Koji and finger limes, and then it gets a mixture of this Époisses buttermilk emulsion. We make butter in the house and we culture that with Époisses (a pungent soft-paste cows-milk cheese from Burgundy, France), and then we use the buttermilk left over from the butter production to make the sauce. We have Japanese, Scandinavian, and then a French funky cheese. So, I think for me, it's hard to really kind of nail down the influence. Visually, most people would probably say that my food looks very Nordic, because they can associate with that. It's very inspired by nature. That's what our food is now, inspired by the ingredients; maybe it's an intentional thing; I try not to create stylistically so much from one place or another. I want the dish to be mine, and I think it draws just from who I am as a person.

"I've taken so much from other places and built a flavors and techniques database. Certain profiles work with different things, so I might use white soy miso for a sauce, but there's other ingredients that may not necessarily be associated with Japan. I think we just stopped thinking about compartmentalizing or putting these little ideas in boxes and have it fit perfectly inside. Let's just make it taste good. This means I will be using ingredients and techniques that I have learned from elsewhere, and as long as it's cohesive and it doesn't seem like it's trying to re-create some classic dish with a spin on it, that's what I want to do. We try to be authentic to who we are, and just try to use those influences to add to the dish."

I remember that chef McLeod mentioned that he was very much a proponent of simplicity as well. "I like for things to not have more than three or four ingredients in a dish. Once you get further past that, things start to get lost. It's something that I've also noticed in a lot of people that I've worked with, and worked for—as they mature, it's all about pulling things back, trying to highlight the key ingredients instead of covering up with techniques. I like to have things that appear simple, taste more complex, and surprising when you're able to hide the technique. I feel like that's much more special for the guests."

For chef Andrew McLeod, it starts with what you want to highlight or need to balance in the produce. "What do we need to add to it? What needs to be balanced out? Do we need to cut the acid or add more acid? How do we then take the idea that we have of making this real well-rounded thing and make it consistently executable fifty times a night, following that step-by-step process?"

"Inspiration definitely starts with the ingredient now. Let's focus on highlighting the ingredients, not masking them, and let them stand out. Techniques should be used to elevate the dish, not to be a showpiece."
—**CHEF JOHNNY SPERO**

On top of these seven paths to innovation, some of the chefs whom I interviewed mentioned techniques they have used to foster a creative mindset within their teams.

Chopped is the TV show where contestants are given a basket of ingredients and must create a dish based on them.

Beside playing *Chopped* (meaning literally cooking with a predefined basket of ingredients like in the TV cooking competition show *Chopped*), a leftover recycling contest, or holding a brainstorming session, four chefs shared some provocative scenarios that worked for them.

Innovation could come from a dare or a challenge. This is how chef Gabriel Kreuther's signature Caviar, Sturgeon, and Sauerkraut Tart came about. This tart is a must dish to order at the Michelin two-Star Gabriel Kreuther restaurant in Midtown Manhattan across from Bryant Park. Have the phones ready to capture posts on social media when the tapered glass cloche swirl of hazy applewood smoke is being lifted and twirled to release an aroma of wood smoked above a gorgeous little tart. The tart shell is filled with braised sauerkraut, topped with the sturgeon and a large dollop of the sabayon, finished with a quenelle of American sturgeon caviar, and a sprinkling of chives.

When I asked chef Kreuther about the creative process behind this dish, he explained, "My creative process can translate in many ways. It can be product-centric or seasonal. It can come from an obsession about something or the desire to take on a challenge." In fact, the sauerkraut sturgeon tart came to life because of a dare. "Somebody asked me why I didn't have sauerkraut on my menu although I am from Alsace. I always thought that sauerkraut didn't have its place in fine dining. This person said, 'I challenge you to figure something out with sauerkraut!' I love challenges. I came up with a tartlet with sauerkraut, but I wanted to bring it up. I love caviar—and we use caviar—but I decided to use sturgeon, which is rarely used. It's one of those things where you have the poorest product, which is sauerkraut, the most exotic one, which is the caviar, and then we have a fish that's not often used. We put everything together and it comes out beautifully.

"The next challenge was this is a very simple dish, so how can I elevate it in such a way that it's also fun on the table, it brings excitement, does something to people, and brings a little bit of drama? We decided to use a wine glass to pipe some smoke in it, and then take it off in front of the people.

It's something that is very pleasing. People love to eat it. It's now part of who we are. This tart with sauerkraut and sturgeon became one of our signature dishes now."

For chef Jeremy Umansky at Larder in Ohio City, Ohio, two elements are critical in the creative process. He said it must be collaborative and must follow a specific purchasing model.

"As much as one individual wants to take the helm, whether it's just instinctively or ego-driven, whatever it is, it always must be a collaborative process. Because when you're making food to serve a large amount of people, there are so many varying degrees of preferences for different things that working as a team is really important.

"The other big thing is that we decided at Larder that we would explore a different model of purchasing for the restaurant. This is what has driven so many of our decisions with food. We decided instead of ordering from an order guide and getting things for the menu in season from our farmers, we would buy almost everything from a maximum weekly budget. Let's say that we have $100 or $200 to spend with the farmer this week, and we ask him or her to bring us whatever they have. Sometimes we've gotten deliveries with ten cases of eggplants, and we've said, 'OK, there's going to be a lot of eggplant in a lot of dishes on next week's menu.' Other times, it's half a case of twenty different ingredients. As we just have a little bit of each one, how do we work each one of these into the menu? We rely intensively on seasonality and what's available at a specific given time to create dishes. That's why we decided that our menu would change every day."

During our conversation, Umansky explained at that time they had what they called a "squash salad" on the menu for at least a month, but every couple of days, it's a different version of the squash salad. "We're continually relying on the ingredients and the people producing them to give us inspiration for us."

This model works out wonderfully because there's only certain foods that they can offer at certain times of the year. This is how their now famous fried green tomato and fresh tomato sandwich was created.

"In the summer of 2019, we made a tomato sandwich. It was fried green tomatoes, fresh tomatoes, some beautiful lettuce, and a little bit of pickles. We can only offer it for maybe six weeks out of the whole year. People loved it so much last year that when we did it again this year, we were selling four times as many, because it had been a year since people had eaten this food and they loved it so much the first time. They were so ready for it to come back again. That's the driver, that's the inspiration: that intense seasonality, and enjoying something that is so special that you hold it in high regard."

They structure menus at Larder with recipes that are rotating based on what fresh produce is received from the farmers. "We usually have some sort of crispy pork belly sandwich on our menu. Sometimes it's a breakfast sandwich with some pimento cheese and a fried egg, other times, such as in the middle of summer, we just do it as a BLT. We'll pick a theme or a central ingredient and then just let the seasonality fall in around it. That happens quite often. A lot of times we try to make something, or a version of something, that we could run for two, maybe three days. Oftentimes, because people are drawn to what's rapidly changing at our restaurant, often when we make something that we think is going to last us a few days, it's often sold out the first day because people are so excited to try it."

Umansky's and his partners' purchasing model fosters creativity. Some chefs with a larger team have used the competition approach. Before the pandemic, Eleven Madison Park had the "cook battles," as remembered by pastry chef Mark Welker.

"Each cook had to turn in a document of an idea for a dish, a recipe. They had to draw a picture of all the elements, and then we picked the winners. It could have been, for instance, six winners out of the bunch, so then they got a certain number of hours that they were allowed to work on that dish. Then they presented the dish to a panel, and we graded the dish on four fundamentals that we followed when it came to working on food. The first was that it had to be delicious. I think that's a given—each dish that they presented had to be good. It had to be beautiful, and at Eleven Madison Park, beautiful meant minimal, it had to feel effortless on the plate and have a natural organic look to it. It had to have a story, so the third fundamental was to have an intent. Sometimes the intention of a dish might overlook the ingredient or the creativeness. Finally, the fourth one was creativity. We judged for delicious taste, beauty, intention, and creativity. The dish or dessert had to hit on all those four levels, but sometimes one would overplay the other one. At the beginning, anything was open because we didn't want to block creativity; the more guidelines and rules that you have, the more you just get stuck in your own head and then you're afraid to even say something. We wanted people not to be afraid to say anything."

Similarly, the now closed restaurant Betony in New York City organized team competitions. Chef Bryce Shuman evoked their special approach.

"Betony was a great creative hub of energy," says chef Bryce Shuman. "We were just constantly thinking about great ways of serving food and drink, and doing it in a comfortable yet fine-dining way. Everybody who worked there put so much time, energy, and heart in the work. We were constantly thinking about food and the creative process. The chef de parties would have to put up a dish based on a seasonal ingredient. One week it was apples, the next, broccoli, and then they would have to all come up with a dish centered around that ingredient. They'd have a week to think about it, plan on it, then they would refine their dish. They could get advice, and let somebody else taste it. Then we would talk about it, and the sous-chefs would come together to talk to the chef de parties. It was a discussion. Nobody was allowed to say whether they liked it or didn't like it; people were only allowed to describe the dish. From then, we would start to talk about choices. It always started out just discussing and describing the food. It was more about observing what was on the plate, rather than just taking their first impressions. Some interesting food came out of that. We might have selected a dish and kept on working on it and developed it into a final version that eventually made it on the menu."

After talking to chefs Kreuther, Umansky, Welker, and Schuman, I realized I had never imagined that setting up internal healthy competitions, or being confronted with a dare, could be productive ways to foster creativity in a professional kitchen or in a chef's mind. Nevertheless, creativity is not the main goal, and blending, substituting, or elevating ingredients isn't the answer, but allowing each flavor to contribute equally to achieving balanced synergy is the ambition.

I love the recent cookbook *Chasing Flavors* from chef Dan Kluger from Loring Place in Manhattan and Penny Bridge in Long Island City, New York. Kluger's main focus is the balance of flavors and textures.

"I want people to become more comfortable with flavor-building techniques, whether it's charring or roasting or smoking, as well as comfortable and confident in terms of building a pantry that they can use with all sorts of different products to create really flavorful meals.

"To me the peaks and valleys are how I like to eat and how I like to cook. One bite is one way and the next bite's another way. One bite is sweet, one bite is sour, and one bite is like an explosion in my mouth. The next bite is more mellow. One bite is crunchy and the next is soft. For me, balance is more than just sweet and sour. It's about sweet, sour, spicy, salty, crunchy, soft, and rich. I am always trying to balance those, again, creating the sort of peaks and valleys where one bite is more exciting than the next, but it doesn't mean that the next one is boring, it just means that it's setting you up for the next one. It goes up and up and down in these peaks and valleys. That's what I look for in my dining experiences as well as my cooking."

Ultimately, chefs, pastry chefs, mixologists, and home cooks want to achieve a balance of flavors and textures in a dish, a dessert, or a drink. There are five official basic tastes to play with:

- Sweet
- Salty
- Sour
- Bitter, and
- Umami

Some people would add smoke as well to the mix. They all matter in cooking and cocktail making. The objective is to play with ingredients that will balance these fundamental tastes. Sometimes, a recipe requires them all, but most of the time it only calls for two or three. This is why I have learned how to taste while I am cooking or making a drink. It is critical. This is my only way to be able to balance what I am making before I serve, eat, or drink it.

Many times, when following a recipe, I might get a deceptive outcome because the produce that I use are differently sourced from the ones the person was using while making the recipe, or the ingredients are not in season. When I am making a dish or a drink based on a recipe, understanding how to balance the basic tastes helps me make those dishes and drinks better.

Sweetness can round out and balance even savory dishes, without making the dish itself sweet. If I am cooking something savory, I may consider gradually adding a little bit of sweetness—not sugar, but ingredients that will add sweetness—and I notice how the flavor improves. It could be as simple as vanilla extract, which goes well with meat or a piece of carrot when sautéing onion and garlic. Obviously, sweet onion or sweet spices like cinnamon will come into play. Sweet potatoes, honey, applesauce, dates, banana, and shredded coconut are other ingredients that I have handy at home.

Never underestimate the power of salt in cooking. Salt brings out flavors in whatever it is added to, making it one of the most important components in cooking. Salty ingredients enhance sweetness and block bitterness. It is a general flavor amplifier. As in food, a pinch of salt can greatly enhance the overall flavor experience of a drink. Mixologists often use saline solutions in their drink recipes.

When I really want to brighten up a dish, a dessert, or a drink I will add something sour. The acidity will round out the other tastes of saltiness, sweetness, and bitterness. Obviously, all citrus juices play an important part. Beside the classic lemon, lime, and grapefruit, I love experimenting with yuzu, blood orange, calamansi (used in Filipino cuisine), and kumquats. Other sour ingredients I play with in drinks are vinegars, pickled fruit and vegetables, tomatoes, cultured dairy, and kombucha (a fermented, lightly effervescent, sweetened black or green tea drink). It can be as simple as adding a citrus vinaigrette in a taco.

Bitterness is an acquired taste. This is the last taste that we embrace as we grow up. Over time and repeated introduction, bitter taste becomes palatable, but some people never get to that state. There is a good explanation for this: our innate distaste for bitter foods is biologically programmed into our system, as many poisons and toxins have a bitter taste. Bitterness is critical to balance a sweet dish or drink. Bitterness brings complexity to recipes. When bitterness is required, I like to test citrus peels, cranberries, kale, radicchio, arugula, turmeric, thyme, and fenugreek (an herb similar to clover). For drinks, I love to have at home a selection of bitters and Amari.

Umami is a savory or meaty flavor, and often used as a flavor enhancer with other foods rather than being a stand-alone ingredient. Umami ingredients can bring a funky taste and "craveability" factor to modern desserts. It brings mouthfeel, or texture, to craft cocktails. Since my conversation with chefs Chris Shepherd, Trigg Brown, Carlo Lamagna, and Sheldon Simeon, I have a selection of soy sauce, oyster sauce, and fish sauces in my home cabinets. And Elizabeth Falkner gave me the idea to add some fish sauce in dessert and caramel!

I must add smoke to these five basic tastes. I know, smoking is a cooking method or preparation, and as salt, smoking certain foods had and has preservation properties. It does enhance the aroma and flavors of the food being smoked. Chef Edward Lee writes in his 2013 cookbook *Smoke & Pickles*, "Some say umami is the fifth [taste], in addition to salty, sweet, sour, and bitter. I say smoke is the sixth."

Chef Chris Cosentino talks about creating dishes that are round on the palate. If it's too much of one compared to the other, then it falls flat. "You have to encompass all of those things so it's round on your palate. It should be all those items. There is no one that's better than the other. You must really look at it from a bigger perspective and balance all those flavors intelligently for all those nuances to create something that sings on the palate. Figure out that balance and make it round on the palate, that's when it hums. And if it doesn't hum, it doesn't work."

When I talked to pastry chef Mark Welker and chef Elizabeth Falkner, I told them that I personally have a hard time with an overly sweet dessert at the end of a meal. I asked them how they balance all the components, obviously the sweetness but also bitterness, sourness, and even saltiness to give customers a great tasting dessert experience at the end of a meal.

Welker recognized that balance is the most difficult thing to reach. "I remember when in 2007 or 2006, I was staging at Le Bernardin. Chef Michael Laiskonis was there, and he always used to preach about using sugar like you would salt. That always really stuck with me, and that is something important. You should use sugar to season something, not to just make it sweet, not just for a result. I think the use of acid in desserts and just in food in general is important. Umami and saltiness can reduce too much sweetness."

It is most difficult in desserts, as sugar is part of the structure of the dessert or the ice cream. Welker mentioned that lemon and lemon desserts tend to be overly sweet, and that they have used miso in a lemon black sesame in ice cream, for example, to balance the taste. "The dessert was really sweet, and acid wasn't really fixing it, and what helped us was adding miso to the ice cream and just adding other layers of flavor, and it just works. Adding miso in ice cream is not new. I think pastry chef Sam Mason (see below) was known for doing desserts and ice creams like that. It's been around for a long time, and I think it's just becoming more confident and being able to take those risks and try things like that.

"We use a lot of vinegar for brightness and to lessen sweetness. A lot of our dishes at Eleven Madison do have some element of surprise, such as with an ice cream sandwich on a plate. Once you bite into it, there's going to be different layers of textures and maybe a liquid component that spills out onto the plate. That liquid component, if it's an ice cream, needs to be frozen. For that syrup to be able to be fluid, it needs to have a certain level of sugar to it. It's going to taste pretty sweet, so we'll use vinegar to brighten it up."

Chef Andrew McLeod mentioned that when the balance of flavors is achieved, then comes the time for execution. It seems to be always a trial-and-error step. "We want to play with the idea, sit with the guys, and make adjustments. Chef Sean Brock always had the "P.I.E. theory": product + idea + execution. There are often a lot of trials and errors before getting in a place we are pleased with."

When McLeod mentioned the trial and error process, I recalled a visit to Odd Fellows ice cream store in Brooklyn back in 2019 to talk with renowned pastry chef Sam Mason.

Behind the frozen bank, Mason was scooping a smooth, luscious, and flaxen cream with pinkish inclusions from his famous Miso Cherry ice cream. The swirling cream against the aluminum ice cream dipper brought me back to my yearly summer vacations as a kid on the French Riviera. Our family had inherited a summer vacation residence in Juan-Les-Pins from an old cousin, and every evening during the months of July, the family established the ritual of walking on the boardwalk along the Mediterranean Sea. One facet of this tradition I was fond of was the scoop of ice cream from the local ice cream parlor I would get every night. I made sure that each time I picked a different flavor. This is where my passions for ice cream parlors and flavor exploration crystalized.

While Mason was scooping the slick mixture, I was anticipating the frozen texture melting in my mouth with all kinds of flavors firing up my tastebuds, combined with the discovery of multiple textures coming from the fruit swirl and various inclusions.

I am a strong believer of getting my ice creams from ice cream parlors or ice cream shops instead of restaurants, unless it is a fine dining restaurant with a great pastry chef and a promise of an elaborate ice cream dessert. The two scoops of vanilla or chocolate ice cream served in a glass cup bored me to death during my childhood in France.

I named Sam Mason the Ice Cream Wizard to ask him about ice cream. His reputation for constant creativity started at WD-50 restaurant. WD-50 was a molecular gastronomy New American restaurant in Manhattan that was opened in 2003 by chef Wylie Dufresne, and closed in 2014. Mason was part of the team who opened the restaurant. In 2013, Mason opened his own ice cream business, Odd Fellows, in Brooklyn, and since then he never stopped creating exciting new flavors. He became an expert at juxtaposing sweet and savory ingredients, and some of his most popular flavor combos are:
- Miso + Cherry;
- Manchego + Pineapple;

- Thyme, Maple + Bacon + Pecan;
- Foie Gras + Peanut Butter + Cocoa + Caramel;
- Chorizo Caramel Swirl; and
- Caramel Ice Cream + Chocolate Covered Pretzels + Honey Roasted Peanuts + Crushed Homemade Butter Crunch Cookies

I liked the Odd Fellows shop at 175 Kent Avenue in Brooklyn. A high-ceilinged room with eclectic mirrors, and a portrait of Jesus holding a double-scoop cone, adorn the red and white candy-striped walls, and the brand mascot, a cymbal-banging monkey toy, was represented everywhere in the shop. Sam Mason has created more than three hundred ice cream and sorbet flavors since the launch of Odd Fellows. Our podcast episode that day involved a tasting session:

- Lemon Turmeric Ginger sorbet
- Rosemary Infused Goat Milk ice cream with Concord Grape and Walnut
- Peanut Butter S'mores ice cream
- Toasted Sesame Nutella, and
- Vegan Coconut Caramel Chips

As the door of the lab opened, the smell of sweet, caramelized mushroom filled the air of the ice cream shop. Intrigued, I asked Mason about this odd smell. "They are malted maitake mushrooms slowly cooked in sugar, water, burnt cinnamon, and vanilla," says Mason. "It's amazing where the mind and the thought process can go when you think of one simple ingredient, and then with the process of trials and errors, you can end up way off where you originally started. After the mushrooms are cooked, they are candied, and they taste like candy. Mushroom itself is a good medium to hold sugar and burn cinnamon. That ice cream went down a lot of paths before ending up what it is today. It started up as being a little more mushroom-centric. A lot of things don't feel right frozen, so you need to manipulate everything you put in ice cream to be palatable when it is zero degree Celsius. Water is obviously a major issue, and dried mushrooms obviously don't have a lot of water, but are still very tasty. If I could replace the water in the mushroom with sugar, they could be a nice texture to eat frozen. Manipulating water is pretty much everything I do in life!" It took Mason a great deal of screenings and tastings to achieve this wonderful ice cream with mistake mushrooms. Iterations are a key part of the creative process.

Another pastry chef, Mark Welker, shared that when he was working at NoMad, they conducted many tastings and a lot of local research. "We go out to eat in a lot of key places where we were located, but the most important is that we listened to the chefs that were on the ground working there. By the time we started to realize we needed to make changes to our menu in Los Angeles compared to the one in Manhattan, we had already listened to our local chefs and through the pre-opening and opening process, we had already been through the trial-and-error process."

For Welker the hardest step is that first time when you put all the components of the dish on the plate, "As we knew it was not going to be great and far from perfect. We did so many iterations. It could go on for weeks. We observed how these dishes evolved, and sometimes the dish didn't even get on the menu. You could work on a dish for three, four months, and day-to-day business gets in the way. Spring was around the corner, and then you needed to switch and create a spring dish to go on the menu. If that dish wasn't ready, and you knew your new idea was not going to be ready and the menu needed to change, then you had to pull a dish from a year before. That didn't mean you gave up on your new idea. You could shelve it and pick it up the year after and save your notes where you left off."

Most of the time, chefs do not have the luxury of a lab or a large team, and these iterations and tastings happen while the dish is already on the menu. For chef Michael Fojtasek in Austin, it requires him to ruminate on the dish, think about it, and write it down on his own. "Then," he explained, "I will execute the dish and taste it with my team. We will put it on the menu and then we will continue to work on it and the dish will evolve for however much time it takes until we're happy with it. The creative process for me is a rather long process. One of the things that I enjoy about our process at Olamaie is that dishes can go on and arrive at what we consider to be a place that we're happy with. It can still continue to evolve through."

When I asked about the creative process in the podcast, some chefs like Andre Natera, Kelly English, and pastry chef and consultant Erin Kanagy-Loux brought to my attention that innovation might not be the most important way to be impactful and relevant to the business.

Natera recalled the time when he closed his unsuccessful restaurant, and creativity was not the issue. "I was probably the best I could have been as a creative chef, but I recognized that maybe we weren't delivering the food consistently and maybe the service wasn't consistent. Sometimes the little things that matter are more important than the creativity we put on the plate. Recognizing the fact that delivering consistently good food, delivering consistently good service, and bringing a consistent experience to the guests might be more important in the restaurant world than creativity."

When I spoke to chef Kelly English about this, he agreed that creativity and productivity could be counteractive. "The hardest part of this past year (2020) when you talk about creativity is that creativity and productivity are not friends. It's very difficult to be creative and productive at the same time. It is like a guitarist trying to think about a new song that he or she is going to write while they're playing a different song. Your brain just goes fried. During the pandemic, all chefs and anyone that continued to work in restaurants had to be crazy productive. Also, when I'm going through my creative process, I like to keep in mind how we're going to accomplish something through service. It's easy to create a monstrosity of something that's very impressive, but that you can't really produce or get out of the kitchen. I always want to keep those things in mind."

Pastry chef Erin Kanagy-Loux describes a specific situation of the catering industry. "I was working for Danny Meyer (a New York City restaurateur and the CEO of the Union Square Hospitality Group). The attention to detail and the excellence that we always put in serving and performing was critical to the business. I had the creative freedom to figure out how to make something so amazing and beautiful, but I had to put it on a plate for four thousand people, or for Delta Airlines first class."

Innovation has to be relevant to the business whatever the context, and it has to connect with loyal and local customers. One of the limits of the creative process for culinary professionals is the way the customers receive new items on the menu. Changes must be made gradually or well communicated. It's the same deal at home—family and friends must welcome a new dish. It is important when creating something new to innovate without killing the excitement. Most brands anchor whatever they are developing with something people are familiar with.

"Sometimes you can get so creative and so overly think about the process that you forget about the customer and guests," confessed chef Chris Cosentino. "You're ultimately here to nourish someone and give them a wonderful experience and a taste memory. Sometimes learning restraint and holding back on creativity is more beneficial than anything, because too many people go hog wild and put too much stuff on the plate. They miss the point of what it's all about, which is you're there to make a guest happy. If your technique is sound and the product is great, then a guest has a good experience. Yet there are people who will say that's being lazy and there's not enough work being done. It's a catch-22."

Likewise, for mixologist Bob Peters, a lot of it is about developing a relationship with guests. "If I am starting a new program, a new restaurant, or a new bar, at first, I always like to start off sort of simply, and the next menu gets a little bit more complicated, and on the menu after I can get even more complicated. But during that time, I am building a relationship with my guests. They get to trust me more and allow me to do stuff more freely. And while they're getting to know me, I am also educating them."

Circling back to my conversation with chef Andrew McLeod at the beginning of this chapter, I asked him what his experience with challenges was with creating new dishes. When I spoke to him, he was a year in taking over an existing business at Avenue M. "Well, it's a practical decision. We don't want people that have supported this restaurant to feel excluded because we're changing, modernizing, and looking at what this restaurant is going to be for the next ten to fifteen years. We want them to still feel like this is their place. While at the same time, we have a lot of demographics shifting in the restaurant and different clientele being attracted, I may not want to present them with one of those existing dishes to think that chicken piccata or whatever is the best chicken dish that we could have on the menu for them. Don't get me wrong, we make a great one (chicken piccata), it's certainly tasty, they'll really enjoy it, but there are other things that I feel that we can do with those ingredients that are really going to put us in a better position as a restaurant and feel more cohesive in terms of a dinner menu. I've strong feelings that the restaurant has a one-page menu. It makes the most sense for us to be able to compartmentalize a little bit to free up some space and do some more interesting things with fish with other proteins, and to grow as a restaurant without excluding the folks that supported us before I came along."

I have the feeling that I only scratched the surface of what chefs have to say about the creative aspect of being culinary leaders and how to innovate with a team in the kitchen, or behind a bar. Most of them followed some sort of creative process; the humble ones confessed that they had none; others did it instinctively; and some adopted approaches that worked for their mentors or at places they worked or staged. I noticed that the seven paths to innovate—elevate, rotate, combine, substitute, surprise with intent, deconstruct, and simplify—could be similarly followed when developing cocktails, savory dishes, or desserts. Most people shared that their creative process evolved with experience and that it gets more difficult with time. Most of them reuse the same creative path that led them to creating previous successful drinks, dishes, desserts, or tasting menus. The creative process is something that chefs always have to renew. Obviously, no creative process would turn an idea into a successful item on a menu without a seamless execution, technical skills, and being able to deliver consistency.

Nowadays, not only achieving a balance of flavors is a must; bringing nutrition in the final product and connecting with tomorrow's consumer desires is also paramount. It's time to rethink what healthy eating can be, and bring a good-for-you, healthy, comforting experience to guests, both in a commercial setting and at home.

The pandemic accelerated changes that had already begun just before 2020. With the behavioral and attitude shifts towards food from the new consumer generations and the new future of work models, new opportunities for food and beverage innovation will emerge. More food options should be created with people having more at home breakfast and lunch occasions. Chefs are continuing to understand that the food delivery experience should be to enjoy food an hour or two hours later, after preparation, when it gets to someone's house. More creative packaging will come into play as convenience will continue to drive innovation.

What about increasing the awareness and need for more sustainability in the kitchen or at the bar with zero food waste? Here is another great challenge for innovation. Plant-based food is here to stay as more and more people are adopting the flexitarian diet. How can chefs make plant-based food more desirable?

As mentioned previously, salt is an amazing flavor booster. However, overall food consumed in this country contains too much salt. How can chefs reduce salt in their dishes while keeping the food appealing? Health and customization are the two main key drivers for tomorrow's food innovation. How can culinary professionals integrate holistic prevention and functionality in food and drinks? What does modern healthy comfort food look and taste like?

With the current challenges of staff recruitment and retention in the hospitality industry and the changes in consumers' expectations, are ghost kitchens the future of restaurants? And what does it mean for innovation in the food space?

Answering these questions will potentially lead to changes in the way we eat and drink, and subsequently generate new business models in the years to come.

"If I am starting a new program, a new restaurant, or a new bar, at first, I always like to start off sort of simply, and the next menu gets a little bit more complicated, and on the menu after I can get even more complicated. But during that time, I am building a relationship with my guests. They get to trust me more and allow me to do stuff more freely. And while they're getting to know me, I am also educating them."

—Mixologist Bob Peters

Chapter 6

BEYOND FRENCH TECHNIQUES

"The most important thing is to make people happy. The younger me would have said that creativity was the most important; now I would say technique, because you can't have one without the other."

—HARI CAMERON

List of culinary individuals featured in this chapter:

Executive Chef **Rikku O'Donnchü** at London House Private Club in Orlando (was at Amorette in Lancaster, Pennsylvania)

Retired Executive Chef **Andre Natera** from Fairmont Hotel in Austin, Texas

Chef/Co-Owner **Fiore Tedesco** from L'Oca d'Oro in Austin, Texas

Chef/partner **Kevin Fink** at E&R Hospitality in Austin, Texas

Chef/Owner **Michael Gulotta** of MoPho and MayPop in New Orleans

Masako Morishita from pop-up Otabe and Maxwell Park in Washington, D.C.

Chef **Erik Ramirez** from Llama Inn and Llama San in New York City

Chef **Carlo Lamagna** from Magna Kusina in Portland, Oregon

Chef **Fermin Núñez** at Suerte in Austin, Texas

Culinary director and restaurateur Chef **François Payard** based in New York

Chef/Owner **Dan Kluger** from Loring Place in Manhattan and Penny Ridge in Long Island City

Chef **Richard Landau** from Vedge in Philadelphia

Celebrity Chef and Restaurateur **David Burke** in New York, New Jersey, North Carolina, Colorado, and Riyadh

Chef/Owner **Kim Alter** of Nightbird and Linden Room in San Francisco

Pastry Chef **Emily Spurlin** formerly at Bad Hunter in Chicago

Pastry Chef **Antonio Bachour** from Bachour Miami in Miami

Chef, author, and restaurateur **Chris Cosentino** in San Francisco

The Culinary Ambassador at Amorette handed me the menu and said, "Our tasting menu this season is about the story of the regeneration of the forest after a fire."

Earlier that day, I drove to Lancaster, about 80 miles west of Philadelphia, to dine at Amorette. It was one of those beautiful crisp and sunny days, with waves of feathery cirrus clouds in the sky. Several weeks prior to this trip, I recorded an episode with chef Rikku O'Donnchü, who invited me to come to Lancaster and experience his food. He had taken the chef position at Amorette after working around the world, in the U.K, Denmark, New Zealand, and South Africa.

His cuisine promised immersive tasting experiences, and I learned his 2021 fall tasting menu celebrated mushrooms through a story narrating the regeneration of a forest after a fire. This theme came from O'Donnchü's time in Cape Town in South Africa, where yearly fires would regularly devastate parts of the city. Once, he and his wife had to evacuate their home, only to return to a house and garden full of ashes. While they were restoring the house, the impact of the fire on the soil—because of the quantity of minerals and nutrients—resulted in a great deal of new vegetation growing back in their garden. O'Donnchü was inspired by this life returning after the desolation of the fire. That experience inspired him to incorporate this positive message in his food.

This tasting experience with chef O'Donnchü was both nostalgic and whimsical. The delivery and the presentation of the dishes added a level of theatricality to the dining experience, in addition to tasting amazing ingredients and flavors. The creativity behind the dishes was undeniable.

The amuse-bouche rice crisps included bull ants entrapped in lemon sap and puffed crickets with cheddar, blue cheese, porcini, and jalapeño powders, served in a bonsai tree. The bread and butter were brought to the table as a wood log, accompanied by a mushroom-shaped rye bread with greenish compound mushroom and seaweed butter, suggesting the spores underneath it. Pickled shimeji mushrooms, and seaweed mushroom butter, represented the ashes on the log. In addition, the wood log was crowned with a French toast, made from the same bread, covered with white and black truffles and a purée Duxelles (a finely chopped mixture of mushrooms or mushroom stems, onions, herbs, and black pepper, sautéed in butter and reduced to a paste). Next to the toast was a mushroom cone with seaweeds, and layers of duck jelly and espuma (foam) sour cream topped with Kaluga caviar.

For the first course, chef O'Donnchü came to my table with a tray and presented its contents. "Here you have a can of worms, slightly smoked, with crispy mealworms; squids that have been marinated, prepped, sous-vide, water-bathed, sliced, and torched; harrisa emulsion; pickled baby enoki mushrooms placed on blood pudding soil made of dehydrated blood and quinoa, and cooked in rendered smoked bacon fat with a fermented chile emulsion. To go with that, we offer seaweed crackers, a caramelized foie gras tart with miso emulsion, a mushroom garden with chive emulsion, and, finally, a fried hen-of-the-wood mushroom with smoked caviar." On the tray were also two test tubes: one with a mushroom velouté (in French cuisine, this is a thick soup, similar concept to cream soup) and tea and the other one with clarified velouté, both offered as palate cleansers before my next course. That was definitely the most labor-intensive course on the menu.

The story of the menu continued with a mythological tale of the Greek goddess Aphrodite coming down to Earth to bless the forest and initiate its rebirth. The plating of that dish was reminiscent of the painting "The Birth of Venus" by Botticelli, with a scallop sashimi served inside a scallop shell, a coconut and yuzu fumé with cilantro oil, topped with compressed Granny Smith apple, apple gel, chili, and trout caviar.

The next course, titled "An Unlikely Friendship," could have been a great illustration of the "opposites-attract" food trend: a piece of seared tuna Toro belly, marinated in soy, mirin, and sake, served with a snails and Himeji mushroom risotto. The risotto was perfectly executed, and strangely enough the combination of earthy notes from the snails, coupled with the marinated profile of the fatty tuna, worked fine.

The final savory dish on the tasting menu was a hickory-smoked, semi-wild deer with fermented huckleberries, crispy sage, crispy Irish sea moss, smoked parsnip purée, huckleberry gel, and sage oil, served with an au jus made from the deer bones and infused with licorice, star anis, and fennel tops.

After the last spoonful of the savory section of the menu, I reflected on my overall experience. My personal favorite was the scallop course. First, I cannot resist any type of scallop option offered on a menu. Second, I loved the contrast of tastes and textures in that dish with the sweetness of the coconut and the sourness of the yuzu flavor lifted by the green profile of the Granny Smith apple.

The venison was cooked to my taste, but the dish was similar to other classic venison dishes I have tasted at other Michelin-star restaurants in the country. There was an undeniable French influence to that recipe.

I noted that the "After the Fire" menu was based on a robust series of techniques, and I ended that section of the menu (there were still two dessert courses!) with many questions. From my previous conversation with O'Donnchü, I knew he graduated from chemistry classes before focusing on becoming a chef; therefore, I knew I was expecting science-driven creativity for the dishes. But I was more interested in understanding what kind of culinary techniques he used.

Before the desserts, chef O'Donnchü invited me to follow him to the restaurant kitchen to see where the magic happened. It was the opportunity for me to learn more about some of the techniques he used in those dishes, even if I knew he would not divulge all the secrets.

"Let's start at the very beginning with the amuse bouche," said O'Donnchü. "I don't know if you are aware that we serve sushi at the lounge at Amorette? And before cooking the sushi rice, we wash it considerably to get it to a correct starch level. We don't just run cold water over the rice, we do it the traditional Japanese way. We put the rice in a container and leave it to soak, and we massage the starch out of the rice. By doing that, the water becomes cloudy and milky. After fifty minutes of the rice being in this waterfall, the liquid becomes extremely starchy. Instead of putting that starchy water down the drain, we transfer it in a pot and simmer it for about two and a half hours until it becomes a gross-looking rice sludge," said O'Donnchü, laughing. "It doesn't look appetizing at all, but we then add some curry spices, turmeric, ginger, and some aromates to give it a golden color. We wipe it very thin on a Silpad mat and then put it in the dehydrator. After about three hours, it becomes like rubber, and it is at that moment that we add the ants and the little leaves and other ingredients. We add another layer on top and dry it out overnight. We end up with a really hard, translucent, amber-looking substance, and we deep fry it to get it crispy. That's how we make these little rice amber crackers.

"Saving the waste material is not traditionally something people do, especially when it seems to be so useless, but I like to prove that actually everything can be of use."

"Are there any French culinary techniques that you have used in some of the dishes I tasted?" I asked.

"For sure. For instance, to go with the wild deer dish, there is a parsnip purée. We boil it in milk and cream, then remove all of the liquid and add the same weight in butter back to the vegetable. It is a classic French vegetable purée. This is delicious and some of these things shouldn't be changed. When it works—and it is not going to be any better if we do anything else—what's the point? We might as well keep it the way it was done for decades.

"Another example of French technique is in the foie gras tart shortcrust pastry that was one of the elements on the tray. The parfait was based on a foie gras torchon in a pastry case, and we brûléed the top. It doesn't get more French than that," declared O'Donnchü with a smile. "Tart, foie gras, brûlée, all in one! And we finish it with some apple confit on top."

I walked out of Amorette into the night and returned to my hotel, with more questions. Are culinary techniques, for chefs or mixologists, more important than creativity? Why are so many techniques used by American chefs still based on French culinary techniques and "mother" sauces (Hollandaise, Espagnole, Velouté, Béchamel, Tomato, Demi-Glace, and Mayonnaise)? Aren't these classic French techniques obsolete, considering the mosaic of cultures and the borderless cuisine that America is today?

While strolling in the chilly and dark streets of Lancaster, I couldn't help but think back to my childhood in France, where I learned how to make my first French mother sauce when I was about twelve years old. I had seen my mother preparing béchamel many times before, and, at that time, the thickening process of that white sauce looked mysterious to me. I wanted my mother to teach me to do it myself. One day, she finally decided I was old enough to let me cook on the gas stove. She showed me the right ratio of butter and flour to make the roux, the correct length of time to cook the roux to keep its white color and prevent it from turning brown, and to make sure to warm up the milk before adding it in several parts, to prevent the formation of lumps.

Making béchamel has always been for me a satisfying moment. I became quickly confident in the execution of the sauce, and my mother and I had many arguments, as I always wanted to take the sauce to another level and add stuff to the béchamel, like chopped parsley, grated cheese, white wine, or caramelized onions, and she always wanted to keep making it the traditional way. She was fine with adding gruyère cheese or cooked button mushrooms, though.

After making béchamel, I learned how to make mayonnaise by hand, from scratch. That one was a bit trickier. I did break my mayonnaises many times and learned how to troubleshoot the problems.

Thinking about it, I acquired many of the French techniques—*bouquet garni, chiffonade, julienne cut, fruit coulis, deglazing, en papillote, blanching, sautéing, braising, poaching, broiling, roasting, flambéing, and baking*—by cooking with Mother and my siblings.

I learned the fabrication of poultry, including rabbit and fish.

Every Saturday, I would go with my parents to Le Marché (the equivalent of the farmers' market) and watch them talk to the famers and select fresh produce, chickens, ducks, fish, and eggs.

When my father was still alive, he grew most of the vegetables for our household, and raised rabbits in a homemade hutch under our backyard porch. I remember witnessing my father slaughtering rabbits, hanging them by the back legs onto the back of our wooden garage door, then skinning, cleaning, and butchering them. I learned, by observing my father, how to disjoint rabbits and poultry. That was part of my childhood and I never thought too much about it.

Several years later, I learned how to scale, trim, and fillet round and flat fishes by observing my brother in his home kitchen in Provence. I always was impressed how his gestures and steps were meticulous and precise.

I was alone with my thoughts in the quiet and deserted streets of Lancaster late that night and, after reaching my hotel, I started scribbling some notes from my tasting at Amorette. While writing, I recalled a conversation I had about French techniques during a panel discussion in Austin a few years back with the three chefs Andre Natera from the Fairmont Hotel, Kevin Fink from Emmer & Rye, and Fore Tedesco from L'Oca d'Oro.

Chef Andre Natera shared that for many years in the US, if someone went to culinary schools (like The Culinary Institute of America, Le Cordon Bleu, or Johnson & Wales), he or she was usually taught by French chefs, at least in the early days.

Natera explained that it was only in the last fifteen years or so that we have seen the emergence of the American chefs taking over, but with a teaching still rooted in the fundamentals of French cooking.

"It almost feels like American cuisine was a kind of French cuisine, but done by Americans with slight changes," stated Natera with a smile.

When I asked these three chefs what was the typical formal training for a chef in the U.S., they all mentioned French techniques.

Natera answered first. "You still need to know how to braise, regardless if you're braising something that's Asian-influenced, or something that's French or Italian. Certain things don't change. There's a lot of value in learning the techniques; however, the modern chef needs to understand, be able to navigate through, and decide what might not be applicable and what definitely is. When I was in culinary school I focused more on the techniques and less on the different recipes, as I felt the techniques gave me a strong foundation. If you knew how to roast properly, it didn't matter if you were roasting or sautéeing a chicken, a duck, or a piece of meat. I could interchange that recipe based on the technique. What the French did well was to bring those techniques to the world," said Natera.

Fiore Tedesco added, "I agree that when people talk about what is formal training for a chef in US, or really anywhere in the world, that generally refers to French technique. But it relates, in fact, to the French brigade system, which is a collection of techniques and a style of running a kitchen.

"We all have to know it. It might be something that we fully embrace and run our kitchens following that model. Most American kitchens do still run according to the French brigade model. At L'Oca d'Oro, we have tweaked it. My kitchen is now a little far away from that system, as I would imagine I had my own imprint on the organization.

"But, Emmanuel, when you asked about French techniques and French kitchens, my mind first went to a disciplined, orderly space, where cleanliness and order are king. There is universal respect for that amongst chefs, and the cuisine that ties together those principles is amongst chefs always revered."

"What about you?" I asked Kevin Fink.

"We all have some form of relation with French food," he said. "It may be positive, it may be negative, or in between. But the expectation is there, and because of that it's less surprising, and that can be a really positive thing because we know what to expect; we can seek out comfort, we can anticipate it, we have this weighing of what it used to be.

"But it can also be a negative thing," he added. "If I'm looking to have a new and exciting experience, very rarely traditional French cuisine can't do that to me anymore. We're no longer having our first, second, or even third experience with it, and that's why I think the French created La Nouvelle Cuisine. But that movement was so enigmatic here."

"Why are American chefs not so often held to established recipes, compared to French chefs?" I asked.

"I would say the great French restaurants today have guidelines of recipes," answered Fink. "But they've all rewritten them to make them their own. This is ultimately what we are doing in America today. I believe that we are craftsmen more than artists, but that's just my belief. But in general, you don't want to replicate what somebody else has done well. You want to be inspired by it, but you want to make sure that you are not ripping it off."

Reflecting on these chefs' opinions as I later wrote in my hotel room in Lancaster, I realized that I was glad my mother and siblings showed me the ropes of French cooking techniques. I could not have grasped all the nuances by only studying cookbooks or, later, by watching YouTube videos.

I remembered a conversation about this topic with Chef Michael Gulotta, who is based in New Orleans. He commented that nowadays information is easy to access; young cooks want to skip steps and just throw ingredients together based on what they have seen online.

"I spent years as a line cook," said Gulotta. "I spent years working each station, watching others, and learning how to re-emulsify sauces, how to properly sear, roast, grill, and how to properly cook a risotto."

I told Gulotta that I watched my mother make risotto when I was a kid, but I doubt her Lorraine heritage (Northeast region of France) was the most relevant for making successfully traditional Italian risotto!

Gulotta commented that they have sticky rice dishes on the menu at Maypop, but they treat them like risottos.

"A risotto has many steps to it that a lot of people don't realize: the toasting of the rice takes time, the addition of the liquid should be made slowly, then making sure to stir the rice constantly, is key. And the pan needs to be pulled off the heat to work in all the fats, butter, and cheese. If you haven't worked with someone who knows how to do it, and has shown you the right way, it is difficult to pull it off."

It reminded Gulotta of his time working with pasta in Italy.

"It is similar to the chef I worked for in Italy, teaching me how to properly emulsify pasta and teaching me how it shouldn't have tons of sauce. He taught me that to make it properly, the sauce must cling to the pasta, and I had to sit there and repetitively toss the pasta while I emulsified olive oil into it, to make the sauce extra rich. These rules can't be learned in a book!"

Gulotta explained that now, a lot of his time is spent teaching and demonstrating techniques to his team.

"One time, one of my sous-chefs came up with a beautiful dish, but he let the cooks run with it. I had to explain to him that he needed to show them exactly the steps he did, because the dishes the cooks executed did not look like the original dish he created."

I made a mental note that, like any artisanal profession where craftsmanship is important, for someone to be great he or she has to absorb knowledge from a mentor. To remain successful in this business for a long time, people must surround themselves with greatness, whether those specific techniques are going to be part of someone's immediate future or not.

"I would say the great French restaurants today have guidelines of recipes. But they've all rewritten them to make them their own. This is ultimately what we are doing in America today. I believe that we are craftsmen more than artists, but that's just my belief. But in general, you don't want to replicate what somebody else has done well. You want to be inspired by it, but you want to make sure that you are not ripping it off."
—CHEF KEVIN FINK

Thinking back to my conversation with the three chefs in Austin, I remembered chef Fiore Tedesco saying, "I look at part of the French culinary training, including all the mother sauces, as learning trigonometry."

I was surprised by that comment and asked him to explain..

"Is it really going to be applicable to the cuisine I am going to create?" questioned Tedesco. "Well, if you're a mathematician, sure. But if you're not, then maybe in some esoteric way having that knowledge helps you be more creative and gives you more tools to feed your creativity. Whereas you may never make several of these mother sauces or you may never really directly use some of these French techniques in your cooking, fifteen years down the road you might need that knowledge for contextualizing an idea that you're working on, and that can make all the difference!

"I wouldn't say that learning it the French way is more prevalent or more important than learning the system of equally refined Italian or Japanese techniques. Having the discipline and the refinement of a technique ingrained in you is what's important."

Chef Tedesco's comment about other relevant international cooking techniques beside the French ways made me realized that similar techniques to making French mother sauces existed in other countries.

In Italy, for example, I believe that pesto sauces, Bolognese ragu, or Napolitan ragu could be considered the Italian versions of French mother sauces.

In Korea, cooking is based around three essential preparations, called janqs. I would say that Korean mother sauces are gochujang (spicy fermented pepper paste), doenjang (fermented bean paste), and ganjang (Korean soy sauce).

In Japan, Shoyu is considered the mother of all Japanese sauces. It adds flavor depth to Japanese dishes, as well as to Western dishes, such as stews, gratins, pastas, white sauces, vinaigrettes, or soups.

I had a similar conversation with Masako Morishita, originally from Kobe, Japan, but now based in Washington, D.C. After running a Japanese comfort food pop-up called Otabe over the past few years, this rising star is now introducing D.C customers to Japanese comfort food at Maxwell Park.

I told Masako that what I loved about Japan during my trip there was the appearance of simplicity in everything in life. I discovered that this also applied to their food, and I learned that when it comes to coking, Japanese cuisine could "simply" be explained with six basic tastes (salty, sweet, sour, bitter, hot spicy, and umami), five colors (white, black, yellow, red, and blue/green), and five cooking techniques (Kiru: cutting; Niru: cooking in liquid; Yaku: grilling; Musu: steaming; and Ageru: deep frying).

"The six flavorful artisanal raw materials that traditional Japanese dishes are built on," added Masako, "are Kombu (edible sea vegetable), Katsuobushi (dried bonito), Shoyu (soy sauce), miso (fermented paste based on soybeans, barley, or rice), mirin (sweet rice wine), and Sake. The complexity comes from combining these ingredients and using those Japanese techniques together. For example, Dashi is a broth that provides the fundamental seasoning of Japanese cuisine."

Kombu Dashi is for Masako the basic Dashi.

"It is the base for other Dashi. To make Bonito Dashi for instance, you have to make Kombu Dashi first. Then, you can add Kombu Dashi to almost everything, even if you're not making Japanese food. You can add the broth to any soup and stews and it gives a rich, deep, umami character to the final dish.

"Making Kombu Dashi is actually a technique," added Morishita. "You boil water and you add ten percent of the weight of the water in Kombu, after turning off the heat. You leave it for four minutes. Then the Dashi is done. It is important not to boil the Kombu, to avoid biter tastes to develop in the broth."

I learned from Masako that the umami character of the Dashi can be further developed by adding Katsuobushi flakes (bonito flakes). Other types of Dashi can be made by adding dried shiitake mushrooms to Kombu Dashi, or using chicken or duck bones and sake, or vegetables peels and scraps.

Dashi is a broth and not a mother sauce, but it has the principle. It is a base that contributes to other dishes.

After my conversation with Masako, I flipped through the Instagram stories of other chefs on my phone, looking for additional examples of international cuisines that could spark my memory of previous discussions about techniques and mother sauces.

A story I posted from the Nikke restaurant, Llama San, in Manhattan, evoked a conversation I had with chef Erik Ramirez about Peruvian cooking techniques.

Ramirez recalled the time he went to Peru to work with local chefs; one of the first things he noticed when he started to cook there was the way Peruvian chefs made their sauces.

Ramirez came from a traditional French cooking background and trained and worked in a French kitchen. One of the things he had learned is that when making a sauce, you should lightly simmer it.

"We treated a sauce delicately in French kitchens. Over there [Peru], they let it boil! They were creating another level of flavor. Everything was kind of emulsified into the sauce.

"At first I was like, 'Well, that's not how I learned,' but I understood the reason they're doing it and I saw the depth of flavor that it produced. There are certain things that apply to cuisines to make it what it is. In Peruvian cuisine, we boil the ingredients, we pureed them, and added them to what we call a sofrito."

"Sofrito is a close cousin to the French mirepoix," I commented.

"Sofrito is the closest thing that would come to a French mother sauce," said Ramirez. "We have a few different sofritos. We have one based on onion, garlic, and Aji (Peruvian chiles)—either Aji Amarillo, Aji Planca, or Aji Mirasol. That's our base. From there, you can throw in squash, seafood, or other ingredients. So, that's like a mother sauce. That base becomes many different types of dishes."

I asked him if he currently used French techniques at either Llama San or Llama Inn (the Peruvian restaurant from Ramirez located in Brooklyn).

"A French technique that we currently use at Llama Inn is something that I learned a while back that I still apply to certain stocks. I learned to start my fish stock with ice," he said with a hint of excitement in his voice.

"I let the ice completely melt, until it comes to a simmer. I have been told, at French restaurants where I worked, that it elongates the extraction process. From the point where the bones are sitting in the water, until it comes up to the simmer, it's where the flavor extraction takes place. Then, from the point where it starts simmering and cooking, this is where the flavors start to concentrate. This process gives also a cleaner stock."

Suddenly, Ramirez thought of something else interesting. He recalled that, when he worked in a fine dining French kitchen, he was told to pay attention when putting a piece of fish in the pan to avoid it catching on fire since the little moisture from the fish could connect with the oil and suddenly flame up. When this happened to him in French kitchens, he always was told to throw the piece of fish out. Now, with the food he and his team prepare at Llama Inn, they cook ingredients in a wok, and they want the sauces to purposely catch on fire because it gives that unique flavor that they are looking for.

"That's the flavor of the wok, that's like a slightly burned oil flavor!" explained Ramirez.

"Could salsa criolla be considered as a Peruvian mother sauce?" I asked.

"Not really," answered Ramirez. "It is true that we put salsa criolla on everything, but it is more a condiment. It's not a mother sauce because it's not a base to something that can become many other things."

Ramirez wanted to comment on two other Peruvian techniques, ceviche and pachamanka.

"I feel our base for our ceviches is a little quirky and you really don't see it everywhere, but I may be wrong. We put our fish stock with lime juice in a blender with a bunch of vegetables, and some pieces of fish. We then blend and strain the mixture. That's the first time I've ever seen something like that, and only for Peruvian cuisine.

"Pachamanka is the traditional Peruvian technique of cooking food in the ground. Basically, they create a hole in the ground, then line in river rocks that are heated. Then, they line up banana leaves, and put the food on top. They cover it and repeat the process, more rocks, more banana leaves, more rocks, and then finally they cover everything with dirt. They create a crude oven called *watiya*. This is originally from the Incan era, pre-Columbian period. The principle is based on showing respect to Mother Nature by cooking the food in the ground. You usually do that after the season with everything that you harvested, in order to give thanks to Mother Nature. Everyone is invited and you have a big feast."

Chef Rikku Ó'Donnchü mentioned similar techniques for cooking food in the ground when I was chatting with him in the kitchen of Amorette in Lancaster, and he was discussing his previous experiences working in New Zealand and South Africa.

"When I arrived in New Zealand, I saw the local Māori technique, which is a method of cooking food using heated rocks buried in a pit oven, called an *umu*. It's one of the best techniques for cooking whole animals in particular, because of all the fatty and tough parts of the meat that take a longer time to cook. It is cooking straight on hot coals, but the technique creates a vacuum and an oven in the ground, so you get this long, slow, beautifully-rendered crispy skin and fat retention in the meat, as opposed to all of the juices and liquids coming out when it is cooked on conventional barbecues."

Researching my Instagram stories about techniques, one post with chef Carlo Lamagna from Portland, Oregon, grabbed my attention. Lamagna and I talked about French techniques as a follow-up from our podcast.

Lamagna agreed that French technique has been taught as the standard in the kitchen, and that it was the French who created the first organized brigade system in a kitchen, and the formalized cooking techniques. "If you go back further, what the French did was in fact to bring in techniques that were considered more peasant-like, but formalized them, and created a proper grid work, giving them names and descriptions. That has been taught in culinary schools and in kitchens up till now. It became a standard.

"This is great, but at the same time, in recent years, we have started to see a surge in other cooking styles and other cooking methods," added Lamagna. "Do I still utilize French techniques in my restaurant? Absolutely. It's how I was trained, in twenty-two years of cooking. That system is the foundation I am rooted in. Do I still use these techniques and terminologies? Yes, I do. I tell my cooks every day to go ahead and sauté this, or boil that. Those terms are now ingrained in my vernacular.

"We can actually generalize and say that cooking techniques across the world have similarities. It's just a form of terminology; a braise is a braise; a stew is a stew; and to poach is to poach. But the differences that we see are in ingredient and execution."

Lamagna illustrated his point with the French technique called "en papillote."

"It is a classic French technique to wrap things in parchment paper and allow them to steam. Many other countries have done this forever. In the Philippines it's called *pinais*—they wrap the food in banana leaves and steam it. Filipinos wrap rices, proteins, meats, and all kind of different ingredients in a pouch, basically, and steam them. Other cuisines, like Singapore or Malaysia, do a version of it, or use a technique that's very similar."

"Do you have, in Filipino cuisine, something similar to the concept of the French mother sauces?" I inquired.

"In the Philippines, instead of mother sauces, we have techniques of cooking that become our base system. The most common is Adobo," answered Lamagna.

"Adobo doesn't describe a singular dish. It is a technique of cooking a particular ingredient. There are many different kinds of Adobos. Adobo *baboy* (pork), Adobo *manok* (chicken), or Adobo *baka* (beef). The second part of the name describes the three major proteins used. Adobo is the technique that is actually dictating the type of dish being made, and it becomes a kind of mother sauce, if you will. Depending on what you add to that adobo, that is what makes it that particular dish."

Lamagna continued his description with the dish Adobo baboy, where pork is added to a base of soy sauce, garlic, peppercorn, bay leaf, and vinegar.

"In other dishes, like *adobong puti*, there's no soy sauce, but other ingredients are included. Some people will add coconut sauce to turn the dish into something different. If you thicken the sauce with blood, that turns it into another dish called *binangonan*. If you had another particular ingredient, like say intestine and liver or other offals (also referred to as variety meats, it's the name for internal organs and entrails of a butchered animal), it becomes a completely different dish. But it's still that same base.

"At the restaurant Magna Kusina, we've been creating what we call an adobo mother," continued Lamagna. "It is an adobo base that carries over from the day before, that we add to the next day's adobo dishes. We take some of the adobo from yesterday and include that in the sauce of the day, and the rest goes into a second braise, a third braise, a fourth braise, a fifth stew, a sixth sauce, and so on."

I asked if there are any other mother-sauce-like examples in Filipino cuisine.

"*Sinigang*! Sinigang is a sour preparation. We use it for soups, or fish ceviche dishes called *Kilawin*, where the protein is cooked, and *Kinilaw*, where the ingredients remain raw. The sourness could be brought by using different types of ingredients. The most common are tamarind and any green fruits like green papaya, guava, and *calamansi*. I have even seen green apple and rhubarb being used by some Filipino chefs in the US," Lamagna explained.

"If we have leftover Sinigang, nothing is stopping us from adding it to the next day's recipe or using it as a base for another dish. Sinigang is less adaptable than adobo though," he added.

In our conversation, chef Lamagna said it was amazing to see how some of these traditional culinary techniques have evolved, stemming from survival in their country of origin to haute cuisine now.

"It is amusing to me to see a lot of Michelin-starred restaurants applying more rustic styles of cooking. Like live-fire cooking, for example. That's what I grew up on, cooking in the backyard at my grandmother's house. We would start a fire, we'd smoke, cook, and do all these different techniques. Now they're being adopted and elevated by Michelin-starred restaurants. On Instagram or social media, a lot of people are like, 'Here is a cool thing to do or to see.' And I'm thinking, 'Yeah! I've been doing this forever. I grew up with it!'"

Listening to Lamagna mentioning restaurants that use more rustic styles of cooking reminded me of another conversation I had with Chef Fermin Núñez in Austin. Núñez was talking about the beauty of Mexican cooking where you have to "go against the grain" with everything that he had learned with traditional French techniques. He gave me three examples using lobster, tomato, and salsa.

"They have the most delicious seafood in Ensanada, in Baja California. The way they cook lobster there is something I've never seen before. They don't do anything crazy about the lobster, but as a chef you learn to treat lobster in a very polite manner, by separating the legs and the tails and blanching them for five to seven minutes, and this is a very precious thing. When you go to the lobster town by Ensanada, they take the raw lobster, cut it in half over the charcoal grill, put some salsa on it, and that's it!"

Núñez's voice was full of excitement while he described the second example about tomatoes. "The Mexicans will tell you to burn it, turn it black, then smash it, and season it with a bunch of lime juice and salt and chilies. That, to me, is a Mexican cooking technique. In my restaurant, rather than focusing on using only true ingredients to Mexico, we use ingredients that are available locally, and apply Mexican cooking technique."

His third example was making salsa. Telling me that there are many ways to come up with a salsa, he illustrated that we could make three different sauces starting from the same ingredients. You can make it raw, by roughly chopping all the ingredients to get a quick salsa. You can take those same ingredients and fry them, and it becomes a completely different salsa. You can take, again, the same ingredients, char them, and smash them in a *molcajete* (Mexican version of a mortar). Same ingredients, three different techniques (raw, fried, and charred). Three different sauces.

In the spirit of Suerte, they add local ingredients. For example, they have a signature sauce at the restaurant called the tarragon avocado salsa. Tarragon grows locally, so they make a tomatillo, red onion, avocado, and tarragon salsa. "We don't call it fusion," said Núñez with an ironic smile, "We just call it our tarragon avocado salsa."

Naturally, mole came up in our conversation. Núñez was wondering who came up with the idea of taking thirty-plus ingredients, cooking them one-by-one, then mixing them all together (most of them being burnt), then adding tortilla, and grinding them using a machine that grinds corn. Then, cooking this blob of chilies, seeds, nuts, and spices for twelve hours, and finally deciding to add chocolate to it.

"That to me is very exciting," said Núñez. "More exciting than the five French mother sauces, and this is how we do it. If you're going to make a variation, there is a name for it. What is exciting for me is making something our own, because I feel that, unlike many other great cuisines of the world, Mexican cooking is mostly undocumented. There's been a few people that have been put in the work to teach us about what Mexican cooking is. But there's so much more out there that hasn't been documented. Probably because people are just cooking the way their grandmas used to, and just keeping that tradition alive. We don't know everything about Mexican food. That's the beauty of it!"

"It is amusing to me to see a lot of Michelin-starred restaurants applying more rustic styles of cooking. Like live-fire cooking, for example. That's what I grew up on, cooking in the backyard at my grandmother's house. We would start a fire, we'd smoke, cook, and do all these different techniques. Now they're being adopted and elevated by Michelin-starred restaurants."

—CHEF CARLO LAMAGNA

From my conversations with Morishita, Ramirez, Lamagna, and Núñez, and with worldwide information at our fingertips through travel and immigration, there is very little left of international cuisines and global tastes to which we haven't been exposed. Don't get me wrong, I still enjoy a traditional duck confit with cassoulet, a boeuf bourguignon, a quiche Lorraine, a Tart Tatin, a Paris-Brest—a classic French pastry, featuring a crisp, almond-studded baked ring of pâte à choux that's split in half horizontally, filled with a mixture of vanilla pastry cream, nutty praline paste, and whipped butter—and a French 75 cocktail—a cocktail made from gin, champagne, lemon juice, and sugar. Of course, I do! However, cuisines are maturing, expanding, and progressing beyond the French techniques.

Chef Kevin Fink, in our conversation in Austin, had a great comment about how some modern-day food, such as Scandinavian cuisine, have come the furthest from where they were.

"The reason why Scandinavian cuisine is having such a huge moment today," said Fink, "is because Scandinavians gave themselves permission to evolve their cuisine. For so long, it was not something that people were loyal to."

Fink explained that with what culinary individuals have learned from science, with the internet and through travel, chefs are now able to pick up cooking tools from other cultures and techniques from all around the world.

"Scandinavian chefs were able to indoctrinate this change into their cuisine the fastest because they did not have a ton of Francofiles saying, 'This is the way it has been forever, and it is the best way, because history has proven this!' Scandinavian chefs were able to say, 'Well, hold on a second, we know much more than our ancestors do. We're more technical, we now have different selections of products from around the world, and we can remake what is our cuisine modern.' That allowed them to push further."

What Fink said made me think about a comment from celebrity pastry chef François Payard. I was asking Payard about a comment that he made back in 2013 that some of the chefs he knew in France were a bit more narrow-minded compared to American chefs. Payard mentioned that French chefs have opened up a little since, but added the following comment:

"I still think that there is something about the French that make us little bit narrow-minded and conservative at times."

Payard explained that he doesn't see himself as conservative. People view him as conservative, though, because he makes the classic French desserts, but he always like to push the limit.

"I don't think I do the classics. What I do is just great tastes. If I do a Paris-Brest, I will do it my own way, but it will still be a Paris-Brest."

In the summer of 2021, Payard created two creative variations of the classic recipe and pate-à-choux technique of a Paris-Brest recipe: blueberry pâte à choux crumble, mascarpone blueberry cream, and lemon-thyme blueberry compote, and a salty-caramel cream one.

A few weeks after my trip to Lancaster, and my dining experience with chef Rikku Ó'Donnchü, I had dinner with friends at Loring Place on 8th Street in Greenwich Village. Loring Place is one of chef Dan Kluger's restaurants that celebrates seasonal, farm-to-table, and wood-fired dishes.

I love how chefs today cook and serve vegetables as the hero in the center of the plate, and I found so much to please my appetite for flavor-forward vegetable dishes on Loring Place's menu. As I have had dinner at Loring Place on multiple occasions, I suggested to start with a selection of my favorite dishes: the Baked Ricotta and Roasted Kabocha served inside a cast iron pan with grilled sourdough bread for dipping; the Wood Grilled Broccoli Salad with orange, pistachios, and mint; the Grandma Style Pan Pizza with tomatoes, mozzarella, and basil; and for more veggie action, the Crispy Spiced Cauliflower served that day with "creamed kale" and coriander, as the accompaniments of that dish change with the seasons.

Toward the end of the dinner chef Kluger came over to our table and I had the opportunity to asked him what was more important for him, technique or creativity.

He did not answer right away.

"Maybe creativity," he said, unconvincingly. "I feel like you can't have one without the other. You can be incredibly creative, but if you have no technique, you're never going to be able to follow through with it. You can come up with an amazing idea, but if you don't know how to facilitate it, what's the point?"

He added that creativity was incredibly important, but the understanding of basic technique was also critical to any cooking, whether it's at a home or restaurant level.

Kluger mentioned his time at Craft with chef Tom Colicchio in New York City. He explained that each station in that restaurant was set up per product type. "There was a station only for mushrooms and potatoes, and all the people did at that station was cook mushrooms and potatoes the whole day. Another station was for carrots and garde manger (someone who specializes in the preparation of cold foods), I believe.

"People became experts at these stations," said Kluger. "Experts on how to roast a mushroom or a carrot."

He commented that now young cooks would often come in and, if he asked them to roast carrots, they would believe they knew what they are doing because they went to culinary school.

"Most of the time, they will come back with a tray of undercooked carrots," continued Kluger with a disgruntled tone of voice.

"Many times, people don't appreciate the simplicity or the output of technique. Even a simple technique can have an incredible impact on a dish, by just roasting and caring properly. I don't go too in depth with forcing techniques on my staff, but I try to teach some of these methods in which you can achieve flavors through roasting, grilling, charring, and braising."

Driving back home to New Jersey that evening, I could not stop thinking about another great flavor-forward vegetable-tasting experience I had in Philadelphia at Vedge with Chef Richard Landau. Unlike Loring Place, Vedge was one hundred percent vegetarian, but the one thing that both places have in common is a chef cooking from the heart and demonstrating that, by using creativity and great techniques, vegetables can be incredible heroes on the plate. In fact, some of the techniques for bringing up flavors when cooking vegetables are very similar to the ones used for cooking meat.

Landau explained that he is a big fan of fleshy vegetables and meaty mushrooms because both types mimic meat, and he can use the techniques of braising, grilling, sautéing, and roasting to add flavors to these fleshy vegetables, greens, and root vegetables.

When I asked chef Landau how easy it was to apply these techniques to veggies, he admitted that it's definitely a labor of love.

"Vegetables don't have any fat in them, and that's the biggest problem. You have to get fat and seasonings into them, without covering them up, of course, as you don't want to just taste the sauce, you want to taste the vegetable."

Reviewing previous interviews, it was clear that no one can properly express themselves creatively in the kitchen without proper technique, but, more importantly, without having processed some key fundamentals.

In my discussion with celebrity chef David Burke, he reminded me that chef Jacques Pepin once said that cooking was all about fundamentals and how people learn the fundamentals correctly.

Burke thought that there were two kinds of fundamentals: the one related to having knife skills, how to stand straight at the station, and how to work clean in a kitchen; but he insisted that another fundamental was equally important—knowing how to mix and pair ingredients.

Burke highlighted how important it was for people to understand, for instance, how something could be digested, where an ingredient was coming from, or the history behind an association of ingredients.

"Why are we putting apples with the pork chops? Why are we putting oranges with duck? Or why pickle on a hamburger? Why is ketchup served with French fries?" asked Burke. "That question—why—should be in people's mind and asked a thousand times a week by a young culinary student!"

Burke believed that people needed to, geographically and historically, understand why certain things paired well together, before coming up with their own thoughts and recipes.

"The same as an architect needs to understand the fundamentals of how he can put a hundred stories on top of a piece of cement, culinary individuals need to ask themselves how it's going to work. How do I build this dish? Now, architects don't always worry about how somebody feels after they rent the offices in the building, but chefs have to think about how someone feels after they eat.

"Technique comes with fundamentals," added Burke. "Technique can be developed, but creativity is a blessing. There are some very good technical chefs out there that aren't that creative. But, for me, creativity is worth more than knowledge."

Burke commented that he is not the type of individual enjoying doing things a thousand times the same way.

"I just can't. I understand that about myself. I can teach something very creatively to someone and help them execute it, but personally I'd rather move on to the next creation. I don't want to be on the assembly line every day. I want to be doing something new. I want to master something and move on. That's part of my ADD-ish personality. It is part of my creative mindset."

In the chapter "The Flavor-Memory Database," I mentioned the olfactive memory, or sensual memory, that identifies smell, taste, sound, or color instantly, and brings images and experiences from the past to our imagination.

With the acquisition of the fundamentals, repetitions of gestures, and discipline, the body will remember the moves acquired during training. That is what is called the "muscle memory." It is a valuable form of memory that performers and dancers know well. It is amazing how the body retains information and can re-create each learned gesture automatically.

Muscle memory is critical in the acquisition of culinary skills. This is no different than a young artist sitting in a museum copying drawings and paintings from great painters. This is why many famous chefs and mixologists start by copying dishes and drinks from previously renowned chefs and mixologists.

When I had the panel discussion with the three chefs in Austin, I asked Chef Fiore Tedesco his opinion on the subject, as he was a musician in a band in a previous life, before becoming a chef.

"I am using the same discipline that I developed as a musician growing up. I spent thousands of hours of practice to make sure that I could articulate and express my thoughts and feelings with my hands, my feet, and my body. It took a lot of repetitions and a lot of discipline."

He said that he felt most connected to the world when he was creating. Not to say that anything he did was necessarily all that new, but it was new to him.

"Calling ideas from those places in the dark reaches of my brain and bringing them out into the world, to me it's the same process for a musician as for a chef. When I was a musician, I was playing the same song every night, then later on did a recording of the same song. I wanted to make sure it sounded the same. I tried to use that same discipline as a chef in the ways that I stay true to techniques and preparing different foods, while my focus is paying attention to what the ingredient is asking me to do."

In her book *The Creative Habit*, Twyla Tharp, American dancer, choreographer, and author, titled one of her chapters, "Before You Can Think out of the Box, You Have to Start with a Box."

She describes how she used real boxes for everything she'd ever done. She describes the box as "the raw index of your preparation." Over time, she fills the box with research material, background information, and little ideas and inspirations as she comes across them. It could be notebooks, news clippings, CDs, videotapes of her working, or of her dancers rehearsing, books, or photographs. The most important aspect for her is that nothing is forgotten; she doesn't have to worry about it, as everything is in one of her boxes.

Similarly, culinary individuals have their cookbook collections, journals, notebooks, classes taken, and recipes learned from their mentors. Like Tharp suggested, they have to start thinking within the box before they can cook outside of the box.

When I was in San Francisco at a dinner at Nightbird, chef Kim Alter said to me, "I still learn every day, but most of the time, when I apply a technique to a new idea, I'm already familiar with it, or with something that I've already practiced and mastered before. I then apply that technique to my idea, or the product that is available." Alter first works inside the box.

"When you work under a chef, you learn everything from him or her; and then when you become a chef on your own, you travel and work with other peers, and that's how you continue to evolve." In Tharp vocabulary, chef Alter is then starting another box.

When I asked pastry chef Emily Spurlin about creativity versus techniques, she said that, even in pastry, which is by definition technical in methods, she could see both sides. She explained that it is important for her to learn technique before being able to flex her creative muscles.

"We're all super eager to be able to try a bunch of stuff out. I might have this great idea but I might have no notion of how to execute it, and it can end up being a poor or final product. It's important to understand basic science in pastry and basic technique—which, of course, comes from French technique—but at the same time I do think that occasionally it helps to think outside of the box when you don't have that super-traditional training."

As it happens, Spurlin was a line cook first. She didn't go to pastry school and only had the baseline basic pastry training. If the training was helpful, Spurlin felt at the same time that it helped her to carry some of her savory cooking techniques into her pastry creations. She felt that maybe she would never have come to those ideas if she had a traditional pastry school education.

Similarly, world-renowned pastry chef Antonio Bachour saw the importance of both aspects in pastry. His first answer to my question of creativity versus technique was that the most important element was technique because, for him, millions of recipe ideas can be found online. Only pastry techniques will give someone the ability to make it happen. But like David Burke, creativity is, for Bachour, also critical, because otherwise he would make the same dessert over and over.

"I would get bored, you know? I believe in the wow factor in dessert, and I want to inspire people."

Antonio Bachour has several party shops in Miami, and Emily Spurlin works as a pastry chef in a restaurant in Chicago. They are both pastry chefs, but they operate in two different worlds, which has consequences when it comes to technique and creativity.

Celebrity pastry chef François Payard shared with me that most people have no understanding that being a pastry chef at a restaurant is very different than being a pastry chef at a pastry shop. In a restaurant, the pastry chef is only doing desserts "à la minute," something that is created to order. "That experience can never be reproduced in a pastry shop, because there is an excitement in a restaurant that is not possible to evoke with pastries that sit for hours inside a store showcase."

There are two kinds of pastry chefs: some who know how to make pastries in a restaurant and others who know how to make pastries in a bakery. The latter has to master the techniques required of a baker, making breakfast pastries, *viennoiserie*, chocolate, and bonbons.

To sum up, technique makes creation possible and creativity gives technique its purpose. Technique and creativity are two routines that feed off each other (pardon the pun). Culinary individuals need technical skills to put themselves out there creatively, and they put into practice their technical skills when they innovate.

Technique is the way to put an idea into action.

For chef Kevin Fink in Austin, ideas are a dime a dozen, and he feels that we all have several million unique ideas that happen in our brain over the course of a day. "How many do we put into action? Sometimes zero, sometimes less than five."

For Fink, the only thing that allows us to turn an idea into something actionable is the discipline of action. "Technique in the kitchen, that is your discipline!" added Fink. "There is nothing in food without techniques. You have no outlet. You could be the most creative genius; without technique, you have no way to play your idea out. I would venture to say that creativity is the easy part."

As a manager, I always like to look at it from a hiring perspective. What is more important for a culinary leader—technique or creativity?

Andre Natera was in charge of more than 150 people when he was the executive chef at the Fairmont Hotel in Austin. He shared that when he was hiring, he would rather hire someone with more strength and interest in technique than creativity.

"Sometimes, if I bring someone new into the kitchen, the first thing they want to know is when they can get their dish on the menu, or when they could start making their own food. My answer is, 'Well, I got the creativity part down. You don't have to worry about that. Just make sure you season it correctly!'"

Akin to what Kevin Fink mentioned earlier, when it comes to creativity, Natera added that if someone has the technique, then creativity is limitless. And if people don't have the creative part, they can always fall back on the technique, the fundamentals, and on consistently delivering good food.

Natera brought up another valid point: that creativity is sometimes short-lived, especially today with social media. When starting to cook, he sometimes found himself copying a dish without even knowing it. His subconscious brought back something he saw earlier on Instagram.

"From an employer standpoint," concluded Natera, "I would go for technique before I'd go for creativity. I recognize now that delivering consistently good food and good service and having a consistent experience is more important in the restaurant world than having creativity."

Going even further, celebrity chef Chris Cosentino stated that people need to be mindful as being too creative can have negative consequences.

"We are trades people," said Cosentino.

He was clear that ultimately, everything is based on technique. He used the example of making pasta. "You can't just wing pasta, for instance," he explained. "There's a technique to making the dough, to letting it rest, to rolling it out, and even in how to cook it."

He explained that there is a technique for whether it's making the base of a product or finishing a dish.

But sometimes creativity gets in the way.

"That's when some people end up with white chocolate and sardines, for instance. I don't believe it's always a relevant point when people are thinking too far off in left field. Sometimes, I feel people just want to be creative so that other people will pay attention to them."

At the end of the day, the most important thing is the customer experience and the balance of flavors. It simply has to taste good.

Once, chef Gabriel Kreuther said to me, "You cannot have only technique and no flavor. It's meaningless."

Back in the kitchen at Amorette, I asked chef O'Donnchü his view on technique versus creativity.

"I think equal parts of both is necessary. If you are technique-driven, great, you are going to produce some beautiful tasting food, but you're not going to give anyone anything that they haven't experienced before. If they're into the world of gastronomy, go to all these restaurants, and eat at these places all the time, there's going to be limits there.

"On the other end, you can have all the creativity of the world, but if you don't know any techniques, how are you going to roll it out? It's impossible. I think equal parts of both is critical. It is a good question, though. You may realize how important both are, and as equally important—without one there wouldn't be the other."

I ended my tasting menu experience with dessert in another room of the restaurant Amorette. The dessert was called Levitate and I was really curious about the name. I was the only guest in the room with chef O'Donnchü, his pastry chef, and a glass container that looked like an aquarium. In front of me was a dish already holding some sweet components that mimicked "soil," along with some "greenery," some "wood chips," and "porchini mushrooms."

"Before we continue the dessert in front of you, Emmanuel, we have a palate cleanser: an apple cider kombucha slushy infused with CBD oil."

The kombucha was served in a glass that looked like a pipe. While I was savoring my palate cleanser, chef O'Donnchü and his pastry chef were working on adding a rain cloud and some falling leaves onto the dessert dish.

The pastry chef dipped a white rose into a red-colored rose syrup, and I witnessed the changing of the color of the white rose as it was swirled in the syrup. He plunged the now pinkish rose into a bath of liquid nitrogen that instantly froze the petals, and then he crushed the petals in pieces atop my dish. It tinkled like broken glass as the fragments of rose petals fell like autumn leaves onto my dessert.

Then O'Donnchü took a huge cloud of foam made with elderflower and placed it into the glass tank. The foam cloud seemed to be levitating because of an elderflower-flavored gas swirling though the tank. O'Donnchü placed a piece of the cloud on top of my dish to finish the dessert.

It was a perfect combination of creativity and techniques which made for a memorable experience.

Chapter 7

THE KITCHEN AS A METAPHOR FOR LIFE

"Every time you think that you're on top of it or that you've got it figured out, there is something that comes around the corner that makes you really check yourself and think about whether or not you are really in control of your own destiny."

—CHEF MICHAEL FOJTASEK

List of culinary individuals featured in this chapter:

Retired Executive Chef **Andre Natera** from Fairmont Hotel in Austin, Texas

Celebrity Chef and Restaurateur **David Burke** in New York, New Jersey, North Carolina, Colorado, and Riyadh

Chef/consultant **Mark Welker**, former executive pastry chef at Eleven Madison Park and NoMad

Chef and Author **Chris Shepherd**, operating Underbelly Hospitality Group in Houston

Chef/Co-Owner **Fiore Tedesco** from L'Oca d'Oro in Austin, Texas

Chef/partner **Kevin Fink** at E&R Hospitality in Austin, Texas

Chef/Owner **Alison Trent** of Alison Trent Events in Los Angeles (was at Ysabel in Los Angeles)

Executive chef **Jean Marie Josselin** at JO2 on Kauai, Hawaii

Chef/Owner **Ehren Ryan** from Common Lot in Millburn, New Jersey

Chef/Co-Owner **Drew Adams** of Meloria in Sarasota (was at Bourbon Steak in Washington, D.C.)

Chef/Owner **Brian Ahern** of Boeufhaus in Chicago

Executive chef **Drake Leonards** at Eunice in Houston

Executive Chef **Alex Harrell** of Virgin Hotels in New Orleans (was at the Elysian Bar in New Orleans)

Chef/Owner **Gabriel Kreuther** from two-Michelin star Gabriel Kreuther restaurant in New York City

Chef **Sam Freund** from White Birch in Flanders, New Jersey

Chef **Leia Gaccione** from South + Pine in Morristown, New Jersey

Farmer Lee Jones from The Chef's Garden in Huron, Ohio

The first time I met executive chef André Natera was at the Garrison restaurant inside the Fairmont Hotel in Austin. He had listened to the episode with chef Philip Tessier and found the interview so intriguing that he reached out to me through Instagram. Andre and Philip have both been members of the organization Ment'or, a leading nonprofit devoted to inspiring culinary excellence in young professionals. One of Ment'or's missions is to select and train the most promising young chefs to represent the Bocuse d'Or Team USA at the world's most prestigious culinary competition in France. We agreed that whenever I was out traveling to Austin, we would get together.

I was a bit intimidated when I first arrived at the Fairmont. It is one of the largest luxury hotels in the entire state of Texas. To get from the bright, gorgeous hotel lobby to the restaurant area, I wandered through a vast atrium where the main bar of the hotel is located. I envisioned how packed the Fulton Bar would be during conventions, but in the middle of that afternoon, I only heard my shoes squeaking on the marble floor. The space was quiet and the blue and green beams of light from the sun playing with the glass lights hanging from a majestic oak tree reminded me of a scene from the science fiction-mystery movie *K-PAX*.

At the entrance of the restaurant area, a hostess welcomed me and guided me inside the first restaurant, Revue, and finally through the next door that led into what appeared to be a replica of a southern mansion, Garrison. Wow, I thought, a restaurant within another restaurant, just like in *Inception*.

Inside this fine-dining space, Natera interrupted his conversation with the chef de cuisine and sous-chef to welcome me. I was eager to have him on the show for two reasons. First, all my past guests worked at an independent restaurant or were restaurateurs; I had never interviewed an executive chef working at a hotel. Second, at that time he was overseeing about 150 people across different food and beverage concepts. If there was someone I could talk to about leadership in the kitchen, it was him.

To my surprise, one of the first things Natera shared was that, until this day, he wished he had been a professional fighter! Basically, he reached a certain point where he was at a life crossroad, and he chose the cooking career. In the mid-'90s, the hierarchy in the kitchen was close to the hierarchy of the gym, as he explained.

"There was a certain social hierarchy inside the locker room or in the training room that also applied in the kitchen. You have the chef at the top, the sous-chefs, then the chef de parties, and the commis after that. The same hierarchy exists at the gym: you have the head coach—everyone's very respectful and kind of walks on eggshells around him—and the professional fighters, the amateur fighters, and then the people that are just starting out. Like hierarchy, it also shares the same mentality: if you give crap, you only gave crap down, you were not allowed to speak negatively upward. There was a lot of that same mentality in kitchens early on when I first started out. It was really easy for me to fit in when I first got into kitchens because I respect that type of atmosphere and respect the hierarchy. Keep in mind, Emmanuel, that I went to culinary school in 1995. It was a little bit of a different era and there still was a lot of that locker room style mentality."

"I recall something similar that chef David Burke told me when I interviewed him," I said. "He called it coaching with vigor!" Burke also used the analogy of the sideline coach's game behavior: throwing paper on the ground, kicking the dirt, and yelling at the referees.

Burke said that the single goal is to win, and like them wanting to win the game, he always wants to win the service—to win the customer back!"

"Chef David Burke thought that if a chef was yelling too much," I continued, "he had the wrong team."

As Burke had explained it, "If you have the wrong team, you need to change the team, otherwise people won't necessarily operate with fear. When I was younger, my generation was raised with fear. Fear meant something. When parents yelled at their children, it meant something. Nowadays it's different."

"As a matter of fact, I saw physical abuse in the kitchen—yelling and verbal abuse," said Natera. "It was very common. Early on in my career, when that is all you know and that's all that is accepted, I was that way as well, and I probably could have been a better manager."

Natera shared an experience in which he was able to witness how this sort of conduct had passed down without him being aware of doing it.

"I had an epiphany moment one day with my sous-chef. She had a friend coming to the restaurant and she was cooking for her. I decided to back off and let her cook for her friend. I watched her run around the kitchen yelling at everyone, 'Oh, you're burning my sauce!' and 'Hey! You're not cooking my chicken correctly!'

"She was being very aggressive," continued Natera. "This was very uncomfortable for me to watch. What was surprising about the whole thing is that this chef was one of the sweetest individuals I knew. I was watching it as it went down and it was interesting for me to see how this sweet inno-cent chef turned into this tyrant. I said to myself at that point, *Ah! that's how I am!* A light bulb went off in my head. She usually wasn't that way. She became that person at that moment because that was probably how I acted. I was completely oblivious of my own behavior. I wasn't self-aware. That was the beginning of understanding who I was and what I needed to become to evolve as a chef in this industry."

There was definitely a duality going on. André was this very happy and friendly man who would help people when they were in a time of need. How-ever, André the chef was maybe a little bit more serious, a little bit sterner, a lot more disciplined, and definitely had zero tolerance for mistakes.

"People who knew me as a chef would say, 'Wow, he is a really hard chef.' And people that knew me as a person would say, 'What are you talking about? He is the nicest guy we know.'

"I realized that I had to find some sort of compromise between the two and to understand that André the chef and André the person could be one and the same. It took some time for me to really evolve into the person I am now and realize that for me to get better results I had to look back on my career and ask myself why was I more successful in certain places than other places? I understood that there was a direct correlation with my attitude, my view on things, and my leadership style, and the results that generated had nothing to do with my culinary ability!"

I related to Natera a similar experience Mark Welker shared with me when he was the executive pastry chef at Eleven Madison Park.

Mark reasoned, "Times have changed, and I will say I have grown up and changed a lot as well. When I first started, I was a little hotter tempered and fierier. They like to yell over there [France]. There was a lot of yelling back then.

"I look back and thought I maybe did not treat some people so nicely. Now, we try to manage a little bit more with kindness and positivity, especially with younger chefs. And I have learned that you get more out of them that way anyway. When I first started, I wanted to be in those intense environments because I knew that if I was getting yelled at that I'd messed something up and I knew that I would not do it again. I was like, 'OK, I've learned my lesson. Thank you for yelling.' But it just does not work that way anymore."

Natera asked me, "Have you ever seen the movie *Goodfellas*?

"Do you remember Paulie?" he added after I nodded. "There is a scene when they are talking, and Paulie is whispering in someone's ear and he is just kind of a messenger relaying a command. I would say that now my leadership style is probably like that. When I talk to my executive sous-chefs or my chef de cuisines, I whisper in their ears and then they will take it from there.

"When I see young cooks in the kitchen, I like to spend time with them, talk to them, explain things to them, and coach them through. However, the way that I work with someone new in the kitchen is sometimes different from how I would work with others who are very experienced. I hold them to a different standard. With a younger person, I want to make sure that they really understand the lesson, because I forget that they potentially do not know much about this business or this industry."

Every culinary leader I have interviewed had one or more chefs during their career who they considered their mentor. They surrounded themselves with people who served as a source of inspiration, a teacher, or a guide, and who, most importantly, pointed them in the right direction to help them reach their goals.

"Each of my mentors was somewhat unique," added Natera. "Some of them taught me how to think creatively, while others taught me how to be the exception to the rule. And some even trained me how to look at finances differently. All of them played a different role. I took a little bit from all of them. I could think of one mentor, and he always said, 'Just think differently and be the exception to the rule.' That's something that has done well for me in my career. I didn't want to look at the answer the same way everyone else did. I began to think abstractly, and see if I could come up with different thoughts. Thinking differently allows people to be successful."

"A mentor is someone who critiques but never criticizes," I said to Natera. "A mentor knows how to push his mentees out of their comfort zone. When I met chef Chris Shepherd in Houston, he said, 'If we're just going to sit on our laurels, we're never going to learn anything personally, so we work on new things and push the boundaries.'"

"In my mentorship program at the Fairmont Hotel," Natera went on, "everything was designed to push mentees out of their comfort zone. I wanted to help them overcome some of the obstacles that they were facing in their career. The reason I coach people how to ask for something—whether it'd be a discount or negotiating a price down—is because, if you can't ask for something in training, then when the time is tough you're not going to be able to ask for anything. When the time comes for a raise or for a new job, are you going to think you're worth it? A valuable lesson that I learned early on in my career is that people aren't going to give you something if you don't ask for it because people will assume you're not interested if you don't speak up. I know a lot of people that have been held back because they thought that someone will tap them on the shoulder and tell them, 'OK, you're ready for it.' Sometimes that happens, but it doesn't always. People who ask for the opportunities are surprised at how many doors open for them simply by asking."

I asked Natera what was his proudest achievement as a chef. When I had asked other culinary leaders about this, people never alluded to their business or the unique menus they had created. The response was always about young chefs they groomed, so Natera's answer didn't surprise me.

"What I'm most proud of as a chef," answered Natera, "are the people who work under me. I've seen them come up from a cook right out of culinary school, or maybe even with no culinary background, into a sous-chef position, or an executive chef position, or as a chef de cuisine. I am putting real investment in people, I am mentoring them, and seeing them grow is probably what I'm most proud of. There is no personal accomplishment that I would say is greater than the accomplishment in investing in people."

"A valuable lesson that I learned early on in my career is that people aren't going to give you something if you don't ask for it because people will assume you're not interested if you don't speak up."
—CHEF ANDRE NATERA

I came to the Fairmont Hotel in Austin again in 2019 for the recording of a panel discussion for the podcast. As I pushed open the door of the Garrison's private dining space, I saw a massive wooden table already set for guests to arrive; bottles of French wines from M. Chapoutier Crozes-Hermitage AOC were placed to the side on a credenza as a sommelier poured the red wine in a decanter ahead of the tasting. Chef André Natera was the host of this very special lunch. He and I had devised this idea several months before. I wanted to start the second season of my podcast with a unique episode, different from previous ones. We had discussed doing an episode including tasting and talking about the food.

I suggested inviting additional guests and Natera proposed he prepare a series of French dishes in my honor. "We can chat about French techniques and the state of the industry."

I asked chef Fiore Tedesco from L'Oca D'Oro to join the panel, and Natera asked chef Kevin Fink from Emmer & Rye to be part of the session.

We all gathered around the table in the fall of 2019 to enjoy delicious French food prepared by the team at the Garrison: shellfish plateau, toasty artichokes on a bed of labneh and smoked trout roe, pomme purée, fresh baked sourdough bread with kombu butter, Green Circle chicken stuffed with a farce (stuffing) based on the chicken thighs and aux jus, porterhouse steak with tallow, tarte Tatin, and almond tart to complete this memorable lunch.

During the lunch, chef Fink gave valuable advice for anyone who wanted to work in kitchens or in the industry.

"People need to figure out what they want to do in the industry. There are so many ways to be part of it. People can sell wine, make wine, or serve wine. People can raise beef at a ranch, roast meat at a restaurant, or farm vegetables. They should recognize what makes their heart full and how they feel at the end of the day. Do they feel overjoyed by what they are able to produce that day? Because if they don't, or if they feel tired, stressed, and they don't feel that sense of joy and gratitude for the work, then they are doing the wrong thing."

Chef Tedesco interjected with a smile, "I love you, Kevin, but that's a bit romanticized. You also must have the fortitude to recognize that nothing is just only stuff that you love to do. In our job—and let me specify that I would never choose another life—there are hard days, there are moments that are very trying. When I was a young cook, there were days I messed up. I didn't love every single day of it. That doesn't mean that I don't recognize, as an adult who's been there, that it was the best path for me.

"Now, I totally agree with you," continued Tedesco, "that if it isn't your calling, move on, because there are too many other people for whom it is, who will be better at it, and who care more. Recognize that life is hard and that you will be challenged. You will wake up some days questioning if you're doing the right thing."

"To refine what I was saying," reacted chef Fink, "it's more about making sure that this is something that people are in love with when they are getting into it. That is the entree to putting the work in, because if they don't feel full and gratified by the nature of the work, then the challenges ahead will beat them out of this business in five minutes. They won't belong. To be in this industry, to succeed and be able to think clearly and above the fray, they have to have a thick skin.

"Like most of us, I wasn't born with it," admitted Fink. "I had to learn how to toughen up, to think clearly, and do a really good job amidst all of it, but I knew that I loved the craft. I probably went a good year plus at a specific job without experiencing any joy, but I knew that this universe I lived in was the universe I loved. I was mad and frustrated at myself that I didn't know how to conquer it yet, but because I knew I loved it, because I knew that joy was on the other side of the rainbow for me, I was willing to put the work in."

Many conversations with other culinary leaders focused on the importance of mentors and mentorship. They emphasized that mentors know how to pass on to mentees the best way to become a great culinary leader on their own. Here are eight key pieces of advice most of them learned from their mentors and passed on to others.

Advice #1: Develop a thick skin

Line cooks in training learn that cuts and burns are just part of everyday routine. Literally and figuratively, mentors advise young individuals to build a thick skin if they choose to work in this industry.

Chef Alison Trent based in Los Angeles remembered hard times at the French Laundry: "This job gives you a lot of discipline and a thick skin. I witnessed people walking out of the French Laundry in the middle of service and I always wondered how someone could let their team down like that. I'm a loyalist and felt there was a big responsibility to succeed and do well, even if there were many challenges to overcome. I wanted to quit every day for the first year but just soldiered through. I was not going to be that person crying and running offline and not being able to do the job. It was really important for me to succeed."

Trent recalled that it felt like going to a battle at every service. "I was always very ambitious going through culinary school, and I wanted to surround myself with the best possible chefs to work for. When I moved to Los Angeles, I told a little white lie to chef Michael Cimarusti regarding how much experience I had, which was very limited at that time. He threw me on the fish station, and I got my ass kicked, but it really taught me the fundamentals of cooking, being in a professional restaurant with amazing ingredients, and feeling that culture of being part of a family with all the line cooks going into battle every service together—maybe you come out unscathed, or maybe you come out a few years older."

For decades now, the dining public has understood some restaurant kitchens to be difficult work environments, with exposure to yelling and/or to mental or physical abuse. This first advice doesn't suggest that anyone working in a kitchen should grow accustomed to bad behavior or take pride in a thick skin.

Advice #2: It is about hard work and passion

Mentors make young people realize that being a chef is a hard job, and to succeed in the long run, they must love it and be passionate about it.

Chef Jean Marie Josselin from the restaurant JO2 in Kauai, Hawaii has the best advice about hard work. "It's a passion. Forty years after I started cooking, I still enjoy it. The funny thing is, when I started cooking, I wasn't that great at it, but I wanted to try and improve. When I finally found a chef who gave his time to teach me and trusted me, I started to fly. That's something I always kept in mind, and now when I have young kids that come to my kitchen, I try to mentor them to become very good chefs and leaders. However, the new generation doesn't realize that it takes a long time to become a chef. They are very creative, but many can't fall back on what they know, what they have learned for years. That is one of the biggest differences that I have seen between now and then. The new generation is talented, though—I don't think there's a gap here. The gap is the way they consider the profession being very plush and easy, but that is far from being the truth. The truth is that you work twelve hours a day. You work when everybody's off and it is tough work.

A lot of people go into this job thinking, 'I am going to become this, and I am going to become that,' but they forget how hard it is to get to that point. At the end of the day, it is commitment, and it is love for the work, for the job. If you do not have that, then you cannot succeed in this business. This business is all about training and being there every day and being willing to always learn from different people and cuisines.'"

Advice #3: Stay focused

When chef Natera gave me a tour of the various kitchens at the Fairmont Hotel, each time we greeted someone, they always all answered him with the same phrase: "Awake and ready, chef!"

I was puzzled by their replies, and I asked Natera what that meant.

"The idea behind 'awake and ready' is that when we are in the middle of the action, or in the middle of service, we want to convey that we are present, focused, awake, and ready for whatever is coming at us that day. Whether that is a service, preparing to wash dishes, or serving guests, we know that it is a competent answer to be fully present regardless of outside distractions. That is not to say that what is going on outside of work is not important. We clearly care about our teams and our employees, but those conversations need to be held in a different location."

As role models, mentors teach young chefs to be detail-focused. I remembered chef Ehren Ryan, from Common Lot in Millburn, New Jersey, relating his experience of working for celebrity chef Pierre Gagnière in London at restaurant Sketch.

"It was all about the smallest details!" said Ryan. "I remember the way my copper pots were aligned. The handles had to all be in the same direction. It was about working clean and tidy. It was also about exploring, in depth, one specific ingredient and utilizing it entirely to your benefit, and how to take something as simple as a shrimp or a langoustine and create a meal that has three or four different ways of how to cook that shrimp or langoustine. Of course, we had all the bells and whistles at Sketch. We had foie gras and truffles that would roll in. I had never seen this number of truffles before. I had never experienced white truffles. I had never experienced blending foie gras into au jus to order, but that was the style it was. It was opulent."

Advice #4: Respect everyone, everything, and be accountable

Mentors teach young chefs about respect. Respect for the produce and their seasonality. Respect for the purveyors and how to create long-term relationships. Respect for their teammates. And, finally, the respect for the customer.

Chef Ryan still recalls, when he started working in Australia, his mentors teaching him to respect the produce all the way down to the smallest detail, such as taking out the wrapping tape around produce. "I was at a Michelin star restaurant, but it was a very small place; just the two head chefs and me. I got lucky and had a basically one-on-one training with Michelin star chefs. They taught me discipline, in terms of respect for the produce and respect for the details, even down to cutting the wrapping tape. We were not allowed to rip the tape, we had to cut it with scissors. And to this day, I still remember the reasoning behind it, that you are committed to the details. You are committed to being proud of being a chef and of respecting the produce."

Chef Drew Adams from Washington, D.C. said that his mentors taught him how to be accountable. "Hold yourself accountable and if you are not happy with what you are working on, then fix it! Do not just settle for anything less than perfect. I mean, we are never going to be perfect, but we always strive for perfection."

Chef Drake Leonard from restaurant Eunice in Houston took a different approach on accountability by teaching the three-foot rule. "Everything in a three-foot radius of you in the kitchen is yours. You can have a direct impact on that, and you can positively affect everything around you within three feet. Whether it is something on the ground, something that is not right, something that is dirty—pick it up, clean it up, take care of it, just try to own that space.

"We built the business, but everyone has to take care of it together. If we do not, we will lose it. That is the three-foot rule. If everybody takes care of everything within a three-foot radius, everything will be correct and as a chef, you will benefit from that and so will your staff."

Advice #5: Set goals early

Mentors help young chefs define their short- and long-term objectives.

Executive pastry chef Mark Welker is a strong believer in setting goals early on. "I think that setting goals is really important when you are young, when you are striving to start your career and trying to figure out where you exist in the world of cooking. Set your goals and figure out which place is going to help you reach those goals."

Chef Natera suggests that young cooks should imagine themselves in the future and figure out what they want to become. "I would ask young people to think bigger and project where they want to be in their career in ten, fifteen, or twenty years from now. Do they want to have a family and children? Are they looking for a balance in life? Are they looking to make more money? They should ask these questions. It is better off answering them early in one's career because, for example, if they spend most of their career in a restaurant and then one day they want to transition to a hotel because of health benefits or they want to make more money, that transition might be difficult. Maybe one day they want to own their own restaurant, but they are never going to learn about operating their own restaurant by working in a hotel. On the other hand, they will never learn about operating in a hotel if they have only worked in restaurants. I would say getting a good mix of experience and understanding the differences between the two is important.

"The most important thing is not to limit themselves and to understand there may be a day in the future when maybe a couple of restaurants have closed, or they have been shorted a couple of paychecks, or they need insurance or have kids, then the hotel job might be the right answer. It should not be frowned upon to work in a hotel when someone is trying to support a family, because, quite honestly, that is why we are all in this business, right? I mean we are in it for passion, but at the end of the day it is a means to how we live."

Advice #6: Lose the ego!

Several years back, hospitality reports stated that the biggest egos under their roofs tended to be the ones in the kitchen. And if reality TV has brought a spotlight on some amazing culinary talents, it also has created a few gigantic egos.

Chef Brian Ahern, from Boeufhaus in Chicago, tells young chefs to leave their egos out of the kitchen. "If you are a culinary student and you are going into your internship or extra, find the highest quality, most difficult kitchen you can find, and apply for a job. See if you can really do it. Do it day in and day out, and you will be fine. Just put your head down and work. No one knows anything when first going into a kitchen. I could go into a new kitchen tomorrow and even with my cooking skills, I still get that feeling that I am lost for a second. I do not know how 'Joey' runs his restaurant, so I need to take in as much knowledge as I can and take a step back.

"Young cooks must learn how to lose the ego and listen, just bow their head down, work, and the cream will rise to the top."

Ahern also mentions something that sounded funny to me at first but it, in fact, really makes sense: Cook with your ears!

"I tell my staff about this all the time; you will be learning some things that you don't like just as often as you do like them. Be conscious of that. Keep your eyes and your ears open. Cook with your ears. What I mean by that is that you should be listening to what is going on in the kitchen. You are listening to the piece of fish that you put in a pan, because the fish will tell you if the pan is too hot. If you are a young cook and you happen to be privy to a conversation between the general manager and the big-time chef you are working for, I do not say eavesdrop on them, but strap on them a little bit and on what they are saying. Maybe they are talking about how to market tables properly, or something else that you do not know. But if you were not cooking with your ears and paying attention to what is going on around you, you will miss it. There are opportunities to learn in every corner in the restaurant, and that is something wonderful about this business."

Coaches and mentors help up-and-coming chefs make quick decisions and to deal with the constant on-the-job pressures in a healthy way, by teaching techniques to strengthen their minds. If coaches and mentors give young chefs the ability to think, make mistakes, and be vulnerable, instead of favoring the development of their ego and pride, young chefs will benefit greatly.

Advice #7: Go on a culinary adventure

All culinary leaders I had on my podcast challenge the younger generations to travel to broaden their horizons. There are so many benefits of travel for younger cooks. It fosters shared cultures while encouraging conversations, and experiencing new food and drinks. It forms a bond between travelers and helps unite teams. As mentioned earlier, it helps build a chef's own taste memory database.

Chef Drake Leonard has shared on the show, "I would tell anybody to travel. Figure out where you want to go and go for it. There's never a good time nor enough money. You just have to do it and if the timing is right, and you have an opportunity—even if you do not always know if it is a good opportunity—you have to take it."

Leonard's words resonated with me and echoed my own sentiments. There is no better way to disconnect from your daily life; it makes people smarter and expands their social network. It exposes you to other cultures and gives so much opportunity to try new food!

Chef Alex Harrell told me that he really regretted not being able to travel earlier in his career.

"It was tough to challenge myself to continue to grow, to look at new experiences, and to get better. Now, I would tell my younger self to take more time to travel and to experience new things. That is so important. It is difficult when you are a line cook, and not making a lot of money, to try to take advantage of situations like that, but travel is one thing I really neglected throughout my career. It would have benefited me just to see other cultures, to experience it firsthand, and not just through photographs or books, but to feel it, taste it, and involve myself in it. That is one thing that I wish I had done."

Advice #8: Develop an understanding of the business

Lately, mentors help the younger generation becoming more business savvy.

"To be successful as a restaurateur you have to know the whole space, not just the food," said chef Sam Freund. And chef Burke emphasized how important it was to learn the business side from mentors. "You're learning their method of thinking and how to think like a chef, utilization management style, butchery, pastry—all that stuff—and then you start developing your own style. You start to learn about business and how to think like a businessperson. That's just as important."

If mentoring is rewarding, like chefs Natera and Shepherd described earlier, several chefs recognized that it can also be challenging at times. The most frustrating aspect is related to the new generation of chefs overly eager to move on from working alongside their mentor. Chef and restaurateur Chris Cosentino said, "Developing people is a key element, and you also have to have people who want to stay. As soon as some people get to a point where they feel their formation and development are controlled, that's when they leave because they want to be the chef somewhere else. It is really hard to mentor people that always want to be the boss."

Like in life, all good things must come to an end. It's hard for a mentee to say goodbye to someone they enjoy working with and have benefited from, as it is hard for the mentor to let someone go. Ending the relationship is a very important step to consider and to plan on when, why, and how to close it out. The mentee should focus on their next move, and the mentor on their succession planning.

The quintessential chef's hat is called a toque blanche. "Toque" refers to any brimless hat, and "blanche" is French for white. Traditionally, the chef's hat was meant to have a hundred pleats, symbolizing a hundred different ways to cook an egg. Today, if there might not actually be a hundred pleats in a chef's hat, the symbolism still stands; an additional pleat should be added. Depending on the structure of the establishment and the chef's rank, the chef might have to wear the Human Resources' hat more often than the chef's hat.

––––––––––

Later in the fall of 2019, I went, for the first time, to the two-Michelin star restaurant Gabriel Kreuther in Manhattan. His public relation agency reached out to inquire if I would be interested in having chef Gabriel Kreuther on the show.

I remember crossing Bryant Park and wondering how this first encounter would go. I never had the opportunity to taste chef Gabriel Kreuther's cuisine before and I wanted to experience it first before interviewing him.

My first course was a foie gras terrine and pistachio praline. As I was slowly savoring every bite of it, I suddenly noticed a man in a white uniform standing next to me on my right. I recognized chef Gabriel Kreuther, who seemingly appeared from nowhere.

Kreuther invited me to join him for a tour of the kitchen. It was intense. The service was on full speed, and everyone was focused on the task at hand. I was constantly asking questions and though chef Gabriel Kreuther was engaged in our conversation, his connection with the team was obvious. I learned later that several months after opening the restaurant, he and his entire team sat down and created the following mission statement: "Genuine passion and a relentless pursuit of excellence drive us to create an authentic and memorable experience."

Later on the podcast chef Kreuther explained, "It took us a while to put that together and we had long discussions about it. 'Genuine' because we must love what we do. If you do not have that genuine passion to bring the quality on the plate and to do what we do, then the work is too hard. 'Relentless' is something that is important because we are in the business where it takes a long time to get to a result. A lot of people are giving up right when they get to a crossroad and must make a choice between left or right, and they may make the wrong choice. That is what relentless is. Believe in yourself, believe in the team, believe in your mentors and who is driving the whole thing. And finally, 'memorable.' We are here to make people happy. We hope that this moment is going to stay engraved in their memory."

When I asked Kreuther about his management style, he answered, "I will say that I am coaching, mentoring, and inspiring. I wish for the whole team to work and move forward in the same direction. I do not like when somebody in a team thinks that she or he is the best—I do not like superstars! It's everybody together that makes it successful. It takes a village to do what we do. I want people to get better and better as they move forward with their career, and I want them to succeed. I give them all the tools, support, and advice necessary, if they want to listen to what's next for them."

The lengthy list of challenges might explain the tough training chefs go through to build their confidence: constantly being pushed out of their comfort zone, being held accountable, not being allowed to become complacent, and being pressured to make tough decisions.

Apart from external elements, the relentless pursuit for excellence is a challenge that these culinary leaders impose on themselves: the strive for perfection, the need for being unique, and for bringing something new all the time, the constant push, the requirement for perpetual learning, and endless search for new opportunities.

To continue the parallel with sports mentioned in previous chapters, Vince Lombardi, the football coach, once said, "We will never achieve perfection, but if we chase perfection, we will achieve excellence." This quote resonates perfectly with the world of chefs, and their decades of training programs.

"Don't just settle for anything less than perfect. We are never going to be perfect, but we always strive for perfection," said chef Drew Adams.

The pursuit for perfection starts at a young age. Young Brad Miller learned more than how to butcher at his father's butcher shop. "I learned how to push for everything. That's something I didn't realize I was going to use until I became a chef."

When chef Tim Hollingsworth was at the French Laundry, he learned two important lessons working with chef Thomas Keller. "Number one is the constant push and drive; nothing is ever perfect; and striving to be better and better would be a second lesson. He [Thomas Keller] has so much drive and so much passion."

Chefs agree that although that perfection is an illusion, it is the direction they are programmed to be constantly moving towards. This relentless chase for perfection puts a lot of pressure on them; their main objective, however, is to deliver consistency.

Discipline is a word that I have often heard during my conversations with chefs. It is important to explain that discipline is not used in the sense of punishment. At least, it should not be.

Chef Andre Natera shared what discipline meant to him. "I think first it's important that we understand the context in which we use the word 'discipline.' Sometimes the word 'discipline' can mean that you're in trouble. We're going to discipline this person because they're not doing something the way we want them to do it. But another way to use the word 'discipline' is to say, 'I have the discipline to do something every day that's going to yield a better result.' As an example, people choose to work out in the morning. That's not a punishment, but it does require discipline to wake up early every morning to go on a run, or whatever it is that they do to stay healthy. This is something good for you and it requires discipline. When we talk about discipline in the workplace, it's the discipline to do the right things that are good for you, for the customer, and for the rest of your team. That's the discipline we're looking for.

"As a leader, I needed to understand the difference between discipline as punishment and discipline as a means to deliver a result because it's the right thing to do. I had to understand that to have a disciplined kitchen, I had to expect consistency from everyone in most details. That's really where I understood the process of discipline, and the need to turn down the noise so the team could really focus on what's important, whether that was folding the towels a certain way, answering a question a certain way, putting the knife at a certain place, or cutting chives in a certain manner. There had to be a certain amount of discipline in the way we do things to achieve anything of value.

"We implement a lot of standards and consistency because people want structure and they want parameters. They want to understand the rules of the game to become better players, be able to let their creativity shine. If they understand the rules, they can work within them and find creative solutions. They don't have to think about all the variables. When we talk about consistency it's about defining those rules."

A few weeks after our first meeting, chef Gabriel Kreuther invited me to have the recording session for his podcast episode in one of the private dining rooms of his restaurant. In the series of questions I had prepared, one related to achieving two Michelin stars as the quest for any type of recognition, competition, or award. Michelin stars, especially, represent another type of internal pressure on the chef and the teams.

I recalled that the French chef Patrick Guilbaud, based in Ireland, once said, "Not everyone can be a three-star chef, but any chef who tells you they don't want three stars is lying. After the restaurant received their two Michelin stars, the team came to me and said, 'Chef, what's next now?' I answered, 'We're a team, let's pull everybody together and see what you guys think and what you all want to do together.'

"Everybody was excited and said, 'Chef, we have the second star. Now, we have to push for the third.' I replied, 'OK, if this is what you want to do, let's put our heads together, plan together, and let's walk towards that. There is no guarantee we're going to get that, but it's beautiful motivation.'

"The nice part is that everybody, from the dishwashers, the cooks, to the front of the house, the waiters, sommeliers, everybody really was part of that, and wanted to strive to try to get that third star. That's what's nice. It's nice to see that teamwork, that support, that one pushing the other for the next thing. That's the beauty of it."

The pressure of maintaining Michelin three-star status, and the possibility that a restaurant might lose it, could have terrible consequences. This is what apparently contributed to the suicide of the famous French chef Bernard Loiseau. Daniel Boulud, a good friend of Loiseau, said in a *Vanity Fair* article, "There was gossip that he [Loiseau] was going to lose his star, and I think he was devastated by the idea of that. He couldn't cope with the pressure."

An important challenge for chefs or mixologists is competition; the need to be different and make an impact. Today's technology transforms everyone into a food photographer. On Instagram in December 2021, there were over 470 million photographs with the hashtag *#food* and 280 million with the hashtag *#foodporn*. The urge to stand out has never been greater.

For some chefs, the pressure to be different is high.

"I need to be unique to stand out," says chef David Burke. "I've never been one to be as good as the restaurant down the street. I always wanted to be better. That's just my competitive spirit. More importantly, I wanted to be cooler and more unique. As a restaurateur and a chef, I'm a showoff. I think any chef, to a certain degree any craftsman, is a showoff.

"To explain, if you're a cabinet maker, you want to build the greatest cabinet; if you are a home builder, an architect, a painter, or a glass blower, you're going to want to show off and be proud of what you do. When I create menus and design concepts, it is the same. I need to be somewhat unique.

People expect me to come up with new things and are wondering what I am going to do next. I like to have a unique style and signature dishes."

I love to start my meal at any restaurants from restaurateur David Burke with his signature dish, Clothesline Bacon, which is featured on all his restaurants' menus. Grilled thick-cuts of bacon are hung on actual lines using clothespins and torched so that they heat up and begin to "sweat" and the fat drips onto pickles.

Other chefs put pressure on themselves and their teams with a higher menu rotation frequency than one dictated by the seasons. It comes from a place of passion, or boredom, or a craving to remain novel, and the fact that many chefs are driven by these challenges.

Chef Chris Shepherd believes that status quo is one of the worst things for people, and I personally love when he told me the story behind his restaurant One/Fifth in Houston.

"Sitting there and doing the same thing repeatedly was not what I built my company, Underbelly, for. Menus that don't change, and restaurants where the food is always the same—that's not me. Within the first two or three weeks after a new menu is running, I usually say, 'OK, what are we changing? Let's go. Let's do something else.' That's who I am, and I always want something different and always using a new flavor profile. If we're just going to sit on our laurels, we're not going to learn anything, so let's work on new things and let's push the boundaries of what we think can be done. That's the goal."

Shepherd's restaurant One/Fifth is one hundred percent based on this idea of constant change. The opportunity came up because of a five-year only lease, and Shepherd decided that he would change the concept every year. This is an unconventional approach in the restaurant business. I was curious to know how he came up with that idea.

"Literally, I was sitting in a business meeting," said Shepherd, "and people were talking to me about the property where the restaurant is located. 'It's a beautiful restaurant, but we're not really sure what we want to do with it long-term, so I just need someone to run this restaurant for a couple of years.'

"I said that I'll do it for five, but this is how I'm going to do it, and because I was trying to figure out what's next for me, I wanted to test different concepts and see what could stuck. Most of the time, you open a restaurant, you put a couple of million dollars into it, and then you hope it works. Do people like it? Am I cooking things, right? Are the costs in line? Is it a smart business plan—you think about all of that. I looked at this as a five-year thing. I'm still going to figure out where we could take it each year and think about what would be a restaurant that we really wanted to do. And then we could try it for a year."

I imagine that there were lots of logistical issues switching from one concept to another. Everything changed, from the menu to the wine, and even the décor. The first year the team did a steakhouse, the second year was Romance languages, focusing on French, Italian, and Spanish cuisines. The third year was Eastern Mediterranean, the fourth Gulf Coast, and the last year came during the pandemic, so they focused on more indulgent food with Southern comfort food.

Shepherd said, "If you're not passionate about it, then don't do it. That's the thing. I don't want to do something for eleven months and think *maybe* it will work out. No, I want to do it to see if it does work out, I want to do it to see if we really want to do this. If we want to have fun like this, if we're going to do this again in the future. That's what this concept is."

This seemed like a high-pressure plan, but an incredible way to test different concepts. Because of the success of the first-year steakhouse concept, Shepherd decided to take that concept, to keep the idea alive, and to launch Georgia James, a steakhouse restaurant.

Continuous learning is part of the culinary individual's routine. They constantly reach outside their comfort zone to grow—moving up the chain always requires mastering advanced skill sets. They are constantly learning, as chefs focus on improvements with each execution, and technology and social media accelerates the need for constant learning with global exposure to what everyone else is creating.

"This business is all about training and being willing to constantly learn from a different cuisine," said chef Jean Marie Josselin.

"Every five years or so the trend changes and here comes new ideas. We must stay open-minded and not be afraid to try different cuisines and establish a library of ideas where we can build up new dishes and keep our minds creative. Now, cuisine and cooking are becoming worldly. That's the beauty of our business. It's always changing."

The culinary world is sensitive to trends. Most of the culinary individuals I talked to said they do not really follow trends, but with their love for experimentation with new ingredients, preparations, flavor combinations, and techniques, chefs and mixologists are the ones creating the trends.

"Trends are important," continues chef David Burke, "I get asked every year about what the trends are and if they start to follow a certain pattern. I need to be able to edit a trend and take out that little nugget that's going to stick around. Then I figure out where it is going, which ones are going to get into the trend 'Hall of Fame' and live on!"

Burke told me that four things are important in this business: having an open mind, a good work ethic, a hunger for success, and enthusiasm. "You really have to like what you do to stay excited about things. I like challenges and it's very challenging to be in this business and to try to stay relevant. Opportunities are there if people want them. The must look for them. People need to figure out what they want to do and be creative. There are so many things that you can work with so it's hard not to be excited about it."

"Don't just settle for anything less than perfect. We are never going to be perfect, but we always strive for perfection."
—CHEF DREW ADAMS.

Beside intrinsic challenges due to their personality, the lengthy list of external challenges might explain the tough training chefs go through to build a strong mindset, from opening a business, to facing difficult food critics, or dealing with a pandemic. They are constantly being pushed out of their comfort zone, held accountable, not allowed to become complacent, and constantly pressured to make tough decisions.

Starting a business is an ambitious endeavor that comes with many hurdles. After developing a well thought-out concept, identifying the perfect location, and finding funding, these culinary leaders must get organized and stay on track, remain committed, hire the right people, create a successful menu, manage effective inventory, and, finally, engage with customers. It's not easy to maintain a work-life balance in that environment!

Chef Alex Harrell agrees. "Anyone who's ever owned their own business understands the ton of pressure, stress, and the amount of work that it takes and how much you have to commit of yourself in order to try to make it successful."

"And it doesn't get easier when the chef is a woman," shared Kim Alter, who spoke about dealing with the construction crew when working on a restaurant project. "They definitely bullied me. I got called the 'b' word and other names. I was there every morning because they didn't have project managers, and I was trying to manage the team, and it just got difficult. It would be a lie if I said that I didn't get treated differently because I was a woman. I started bringing my partner, who's a 6'4" man, to every meeting. That was the only way I felt things would get accomplished. I like to hope and think that women have the same opportunities.

"As of right now, with all the movements that are going on [#MeToo], with all the strong women that are in this business, like Dominique Crenn, Traci Des Jardins, Nancy Oakes, Melissa Perello, and Suzette Gresham—all these voices are moving the needle. There are many strong women chefs in San Francisco. They own their businesses, they run their businesses, and they're teaching the next generation. So, I'd like to think that people are looking at chefs now as a whole, not just as a woman chef and as a man chef, but as someone who is talented and smart and can operate a business whether they are a man or a woman."

Alter added, "But it is still difficult finding investment as a woman, and I have been quoted saying this before: I even was told that my food was amazing, my business plan was amazing, my location was awesome, but they didn't want to invest in me because they were afraid I would get too emotional because I was a woman!"

In 2020, only twenty-five percent of chefs were women, and the percentage is even lower for women chefs owning their restaurant.

If restaurants open, they also unfortunately close. That's part of life and the tough reality of the industry. Some restaurateurs choose to close on their own terms, at the height of success; others close because their investors ran out of money. Before the pandemic, around sixty percent of food businesses closed their doors in their first year of operation, and in December 2020, after ten months of the pandemic, more than 100,000 restaurants had closed permanently.

People think of grief as a response to the loss of a physical person, but it is the same with losing a significant place like a restaurant.

Chef Alex Harrell shared the difficult time he went through after the closure of his restaurant, Angela, in New Orleans.

"Angela was the culmination of twenty years of work. I always wanted to be able to have the opportunity and be fortunate enough to open my own place. That's what Angela represented. It was very difficult to go through all the ups and downs of that emotional process and see it close, and then hoping that you're able to continue in business for yourself with another project and having that kind of fall through as well. Somebody close to me reminds me all the time that it's just a chapter and it's not its own—it's just a step in the process. 'It's a part of the overall experience of living and you should not let it defeat you, but then you don't open yourself up to what the future holds and what your future opportunities could be.' I think ultimately you take those experiences, you learn from them, and you grow. It makes you smarter, wiser, and it helps you to toughen up a little bit and get you prepared for your next challenge."

Since then, chef Harrell worked at The Elysian Bar and more recently was named executive chef of Commons Club from the Virgin Hotel Group.

Chef Jose Garces went through a similar experience in 2018.

"It goes without saying that I was very humbled by the experience," shared Garces. "I am appreciative of the end result that happened, and with a lot of learned lessons that I'm taking with me as I move forward.

"I think during the time I won a James Beard award in 2009, I became an Iron Chef as well in 2009, and those events also catapulted my success and opportunities. I thought I was being very selective in terms of opportunities, but I was probably more opportunistic than strategic. As a young chef entrepreneur, I was perhaps more full of myself than I should have been. Looking back, I wish I had been a little more strategic about the brands that we were growing, the locations that we were getting into, and the brand partnerships as well."

What restaurant critics do is critique the restaurant, the food, service, drinks, and ambience. They do this on a regular basis, and they develop a palate. The role of food critics is important, and a necessary part of our culture. Their function is to deliver an unbiased opinion of the food quality and presentation. Restaurant reviews have helped to reshape the restaurant industry, but a bad review lasts forever. It can affect someone's business and the livelihood of hundreds of employees and others along the supply chain.

The following story, shared by chef André Natera, always comes to mind each time I leave a review about a food location on social media platforms—not that I consider myself as a food critic.

"In this business, when you get a little bit of accolades you start to believe what's being written about you," said Natera. "Then you associate your identity with the press that you're getting. This is what happened to me several years back, even though I never thought it would. I was involved in a restaurant, and one day we got a bad review that affected the restaurant and the people that worked there. We had to change concepts and little by little things just kept getting worse and worse with what was being written in the press. It started to affect all the other areas of my life. I couldn't disassociate myself from what was being written, and eventually the restaurant closed. It was a big blow to my ego, to my friends and my family, and I went through some dark times because of it. That's one of the reasons why I moved to Austin. I wanted to get away from Dallas and food critics and, for lack of a better term, stick my head in the sand and just get back to work without having to worry about the pressure of what the media was writing about me.

"It took me a minute," continued Natera, "to really understand that if I had a hundred different people write about me, I would have a hundred different perspectives on who I was. The fact of the matter is none of those perspectives is who I truly am. It's who they think I am. I had to take a step back and realize that what was being written—good, bad, or indifferent—was not me. It was their perception of me, or their perception of the product. It was very freeing to understand that I was more than just a chef, and that being a chef was just what I did. It wasn't who I was.

"After a few years of being upset about whether it was a food critic or a bad review, I was able to put that behind me and move forward. It was difficult. I thought it would be a lot easier. Thinking about it, I might have judged other people harshly when they went through a hard time, not understanding why they got so wrapped up in what was written. I was glad I went through it because I was able to understand who I really was, and I was able to reconcile those two different aspects of my personality.

"A restaurant costs a little bit over a million dollars to open. That's a big financial investment. When you think about all the people who are employed there and maybe the two or three other dependents they have, this is a big impact. Sometimes hundreds of people are impacted by a bad review, and sometimes those bad reviews have an agenda. Maybe they're just being written because they don't like a particular person, maybe it's just not the popular opinion, or maybe they're trying to spin a certain narrative a certain way to make something else trendier. There are a lot of different reasons, but the impact that this has on people's lives is something that's not discussed enough. When we talk about having a positive mental outlook—and chefs that have mental health issues, whether it's abusing substances or whatnot—a lot of this is based upon the pressures of supporting all these people that are tied to the restaurant, whether it's investors, whether it's their own money, whether it's the families of others who are their employees. This is a lot of pressure on a chef to perform. I'm not sure people recognize that. I think people just go in and say 'it was too salty. I'll never go back there' and not understand that we're dealing with people, and that there are going to be mistakes made in restaurants, and things aren't always going to come out perfectly."

Today, with the prevalence of social media, everyone has the power to be a food critic, and before writing a negative review on any apps like Yelp or TripAdvisor, I suggest you ask to talk directly to the chef or owner of the establishment, as several bad reviews can have dramatic consequences for a lot of people.

The restaurant industry was already in crisis before the pandemic hit in 2020. The huge wage gap between the front of the house and the back of the house, gender and race inequities, struggles to recruit a motivated workforce, and the challenge to retain them are just the main ones. The pandemic fundamentally changed the restaurant industry, but despite food business closures, bankruptcies, and uncertainty, the hospitality industry has proven to be more resilient than expected.

During the first months of the pandemic, I decided to learn more about the impact on the business directly from the chefs. In April 2020, I invited three chefs to participate in a panel discussion about COVID-19. They represented different regions of the U.S. and different restaurant styles: chef Naomi Pomeroy, based in Portland, Oregon, who helped define Portland as one of America's most culinarily creative cities with her restaurant, Beast; chef Ian Boden, with his restaurant The Shack in Staunton, Virginia, located at the foothills of the beautiful Appalachian Mountains, who has contributed to the revival of the Southern cuisine; and chef Gabriel Kreuther, who has proven, with his two-Michelin star restaurant in Manhattan, that the market for fine dining remains strong.

They shared that the pandemic contrived the following situations: many restaurants had to close their doors, chefs had to let their staff go, even faster decisions had to be taken to survive, and new ways to make money had to explored.

"In general, if a business-minded person looked at our restaurant business models, they would all say that we should shut down. This is not a good business," said Naomi Pomeroy.

"The restaurant business and the small businesses are the greatest employers in the US, though," says Gabriel Kreuther. "A restaurant is the DNA, it is the social fabric of a neighborhood, of a society."

"Before we were forced to close," says chef Pomeroy, "we decided it was the right thing for us to do just based on the virus and the drop-off of reservations."

Chef Ian Boden added, "The reality is that we were just spinning wheels. The restaurant was not paying its bills, the staff wasn't making any money, and the anxiety and the stress of the whole thing—the cosmic psyche—was bearing down on all of us."

"For me, it was a little bit the same," says chef Kreuther. "The hardest thing in that whole process was making those personal phone calls to people that worked with me for eight, ten, twelve, fifteen years and telling them that we were forced to close, and we had to temporarily lay them off. Those are very hard conversations that we had no control of."

"In general, if a business-minded person looked at our restaurant business models, they would all say that we should shut down. This is not a good business."
— CHEF NAOMI POMEROY.

Chefs are trained to be able to handle pressure and make quick decisions. The kitchen is a fast-paced environment, and a chef must make multiple decisions at once. They are used to encountering issues with menus, running low on ingredients, or employee problems. In these instances, chefs need to be able to find a solution very quickly so not to hold up service.

In June 2020, I recorded another episode about COVID-19, featuring two chefs from New Jersey who stayed open during the pandemic and quickly pivoted their business models: chef Lea Gaggione from South + Pine in Morristown and chef Sam Freund from White Birch in Flanders.

During the pandemic, food business owners and chefs had to make decisions on the fly.

Chef Gaccione recalled, "I put my whole life savings into my business and knew that it could be taken away from me so quickly. I have to be able to think on my feet, able to make quick decisions, and think on how I am going to make it through this. The milestone that made me pivot so quickly was the fear of losing everything. We just needed to figure it out. In this business, everything happens on the fly. We just figured it out on the fly. We wanted to make it work."

"I agree," added chef Freund, "you have to give yourself that opportunity to keep going. Managing my restaurant White Birch is hard enough when we were going full swing, and suddenly so many different things were thrown at us—different rules and regulations, and we had to adapt on the fly, and there's no time to think. The saddest thing was to let people go as you had built these relationships, and you can only keep so many people, and, at the end of the day, this is a business, and you must keep striving to perfect your business. I talked to my partner, and he wanted to close. And I said 'Absolutely not. We will be ready to go have a to-go menu.' You have to give yourself the opportunity to go on."

Many restaurants made permanent pivots to adapt to a new normal, and the industry continued to be creative by diversifying revenue streams and building deeper connections with local communities. Some businesses decided to join to survive. The pandemic led to the rise of ghost restaurants, simpler menus, more zero-waste kitchens, more local sourcing, and more consumers desiring foods they couldn't make at home.

When the pandemic hit, the entire food supply chain was impacted. Not only were the restaurant employees affected, but also the farmers who raised the animals, the farmers who grew the vegetables, and the purveyors, distributors, and truck drivers who brought the goods to the restaurant.

During the pandemic, I had the opportunity to interview Farmer Lee Jones from The Chef's Garden in Ohio and this is what he said: "All the restaurants were shut down. There were some that were trying to make things happen with takeout and delivery, but that's a small percentage. It affected us in a grand way. Within twenty-four hours, 100 percent of our customer base was gone. Our revenue stopped coming in, and you do not put a farm on furlough. It's kind of like a relationship. I'm going to refer to the farm in the female gender. She needs to be loved. She needs to be coddled and nurtured and tended to and cared for daily. You don't just flip the switch off and walk away, and come back when the pandemic is over and expect her to be receiving you with open arms! You just can't walk away. There's an intimacy with a farmer and their farm because you must love it and nurture it every day.

"This is in addition to the fact that we had to pivot to be able to generate income, because everything that we do is by hand. We have a hundred and fifty family team members. They're not all blood family, but they're family to us. We have a responsibility to those team members to keep them with income. Pivoting meant for us that we were able to go, we thought that it was an ethically responsible thing for our team members and for our farm, but also for people that needed healthy, nutritious, safe vegetables. In many cases, people don't have that availability. I was talking to a chef friend of mine, and he lives in a neighborhood in New York and there's a grocery store line of an hour and a half to two hours. They only let one or two people in the store at a time to get groceries, and you're having to possibly be exposed to the virus. This allows us to be able to harness fresh produce to ship it directly to anybody; it goes to their apartment, their front porch, and it goes directly from our farm to that individual. They get a box with something that they can eat from for four or five meals. It's our goal and I believe it's the most nutritious, best flavored vegetables that exist in America."

Twenty years ago, Farmer Lee Jones and The Chef's Garden created the Culinary Vegetable Institute. Chefs Thomas Keller, Daniel Boulud, Alain Ducasse, Charlie Trotter, Jean-Georges Vongerichten, Ed Brown, and other chefs were mentors to Lee Jones and were on the advisory board to build the Culinary Vegetable Institute.

"They've been like big brothers or fathers to me in mentoring and taking us under their wing," says Farmer Lee Jones. "Without them and other chefs throughout the country, we wouldn't have existed. At the beginning of the pandemic, I reached out to Thomas [Keller] and shared with him that we were in trouble. All the restaurants were closed, we needed help. He came up with an idea. I had just sent him a veggie box and asked him if he could do a shoutout on his social media. He did, but then he called me back a couple days later and said that Keith Martin from Elysian farms, who bred lamb, was in the same boat as I was.

"'How about if we put together five chefs?' asked Keller. "Each chef developed a recipe and a menu around a certain part of the lamb and our vegetables. It gave Keith and his team in Pennsylvania time to be able to process one part of the animal. Then Thomas put together a menu with different vegetables and created a dinner recipe with one part of the animal and our vegetables. He pushed that out on his social media. Then it was chefs Gavin Kaysen, Corey Chow, Tim Hollinsworth, and Daniel Boulud. You could go online to those chefs' social media channels, see their menu, and watch them cook that dish. Then you would go online at Chef's Garden and get the lamb and the veggies. We could get them delivered right to people's door. It was pretty amazing."

Farmer Lee Jones was convinced that their new business approach would not go away when the restaurants came back.

"We're developing a new marketing channel. We want a relationship with the end user who wants to know where the food's coming from. We hope that they will work with other small farms like us that are suffering and struggling out there, to reconnect and get to your farmer's markets. We encourage that. We know we're not the only answer, but we're part of the solution and we'd like to be a small part of every listener's future culinary life. I think that it does open doors. We've had conversations with people we never dreamed of having before the pandemic. Out of the ashes of this horrible pandemic, there will be things that will occur that will be good, and the new norm is going to look different from the norm in the past."

Before the pandemic, many restaurant owners and chefs were vocal on social media about the difficulty of finding young motivated and skilled people who wanted to work in kitchens or have a career in the hospitality industry. It seemed that there was a major disconnect and growing tension between the aging chef generation and the up-and-coming millennial generation.

A lot of people believe that there is a lack of motivation and skill with the young cooks.

Chef Michael Gulotta from New Orleans had a different opinion on this topic. "There're always gray areas, and you want to say, 'Oh yeah, these kids, they just don't want to pay attention.' There are some that really do want to learn all the techniques and really put in the time. But there's a lot of pressure put on young cooks to become the youngest best new chef. They must be the first to do everything. They must be the youngest chef to open a restaurant and, in my opinion, that's stupid. If they are not fully ready then they are just going to waste money, time, and energy. As an American culture, we put too much pressure on being the first to do everything and sometimes that's not the best approach. There was a big push in the early aughts to go to the culinary schools, to rush out and be the best youngest new chef. That was a fad. It was a bubble, and that bubble has burst. All the culinary schools folded long before the pandemic hit, because parents realized that their kid is not going to go to culinary school for two years for a ton of money and then get out to be an executive chef within a year. That's not how it works. It takes years of learning the craft, of spending hard times in hot kitchens and of learning how to be good at it."

The education system for this industry needs to change and adapt, as other chefs agree.

"When you're in culinary school." says chef Chris Cosentino, "you're promised a sous-chef job when you get out of school, and you're promised to make a certain amount of money. But now, they're teaching kids how to be on TV. When I went to culinary school, it was about cooking. There's something to be said for really wanting to love your craft. I learned something new every day. I'm forever learning, forever trying new things. The moment somebody says, I know everything, is the moment they should quit because they don't know %@$&*!. You'll never know everything. There are a million techniques out there. There are a million ways. Ultimately, we're just riding on the backs of thousands of grandmas before us. Let's just admit it and be OK with that. There are thousands of French grandmas who have cooked before me that will cook French food better than I ever will. There were thousands of Spanish grandmas who have done the same thing—and Italian grandmas, and American grandmas. We must remember that the basis of most kitchens was women, until restaurants. We must educate in a new way. We must train in a different way than I was trained. And we must excite the next generation to want to love this craft, the hard work, the tediousness, and the repetitive motions that they may find boring now."

Chef Kevin Fink from Emmer & Rye in Austin is also very vocal about this topic. "I believe that it's about stewardship and mentorship. Today, young cooks are stewarded and mentored from television early on, and their focus has shifted. Their expectations of the world are a bit different. Even the young ones come in with a different vision and quickly adjust to the reality of our kitchen and our service. Quite honestly, in some ways, we're dinosaurs. Shame on us for saying they are the problem.

"No, the world is changing, and we need to look at it in a different way. And if we expect it to be the same way that it was, we will be left behind."

Chef Brother Luck from Four by Luck in Colorado Springs reinforces this point of view by saying, "We've broken a lot of young cooks. We've created a mentality that this is the lifestyle of what it means to be a cook. When, it should be the exact opposite. We don't have a labor shortage right now. We have bad leaders. We have to change our industry culture."

The restaurant industry is evolving but there's still quite a lot of work to be done when it comes to inequalities in terms of workers' pay, gender, and race.

Less than eighteen percent of chefs are African Americans. Chef Lamar Moore (a celebrity chef who serves as an advocate and mentor, supporting youth transitioning into the culinary field) explained in an interview that "we have to work twice as hard just to keep up and three times as hard to earn the opportunity."

And in 2019, fewer than seven percent of head chefs and restaurant owners were women. Chef Edward Lee said, "We need to change the inequality in the restaurant business. We need a diverse leadership. The lowest rung on the ladder—busboys, dishwashers, waiters—is actually very diverse. There are plenty of men and women. There's plenty of people of color. There are all ethnicities and all backgrounds. As you get up the ladder and look at manager levels it becomes less diverse. We don't need more women as waitresses. We need more women in positions of power!

"We have a mentorship program [part of Lee's nonprofit, the LEE Initiative], where we take young female chefs who are in the early part of their career and give them training. We give them all the tools and mentorship. We show them what a path to success and leadership looks like. We found in our research that there are lots of women in entry-level positions. But somewhere along the line they all drop out for different reasons. One of them is the lack of a path to success. When you see a woman being passed up for promotions, not getting ahead, still doing the sh*tty jobs after two years, and not getting the same raises, it's very discouraging. So why wouldn't you quit and find another industry? What we're trying to do is combat that problem and help guide them.

"Any industry that is only run by men, or only white people, is just not healthy. It will not be the field that's going to lead going forward. I want to see restaurant businesses continue to thrive. I want to see it continue to succeed, and one of the ways in which it's going to do so is by having a fresh perspective on what we can do. In many ways, restaurants are stagnant. They've been doing the same thing for many years. We need a new perspective on things, and women leaders are going to offer that perspective. We're just trying to get them to a place of leadership so that they can carry the torch and create the best new restaurants for the next generation."

———————————————

I cannot make an exhaustive list of all the positive outcomes from having created the podcast *flavors unknown*. Here are my top three: it initially gave me a purpose. I was going through dark times, and I experienced numerous incredible tastings throughout the country, and finally, I met with wonderful people, a handful of whom became my friends.

Every podcaster has their top fifty dream guest list. If I had many from my original list, I still have individuals I would love to interview, such as

Thomas Keller, David Boulud, Tom Colicchio, Sean Brock, Stephanie Izard, Nancy Silverton, Jose Andres, Eric Ripert, David Chang, and Marcus Samuelson, to name a few.

As a result of my conversations with the professionals I have interviewed, I have absorbed a lot of their advice, about food, for me as an individual, and about leadership.

About food

- The quest for quality ingredients makes a winning recipe.
- Cook local, seasonal, and explore foraging.
- Support farmers' markets and local businesses.
- Favor vegetables issued from sustainable agriculture.
- Learn first by copying the classics and then add in your own twist.
- Recipes are only guiding lines.
- Make any food experience memorable.
- Be curious when traveling; taste everything; take pictures; write notes; bring ingredients back.

For me as an individual

- The future is collaboration.
- Always look for opportunities.
- Keep an open mind and adopt an attitude of constant learning.
- Network and stay connected.
- Anticipate and prepare for the unexpected.
- Develop a drive to explore, try, fail, and try again.
- Don't be afraid of failing. Resilience is the secret ingredient to success.
- Self-discipline is essential to create a plan, stick to the plan, and create habits.

About leadership

- Set the example.
- Be present.
- Great feedback is earned.

- Promote respect.
- Create a positive environment.
- Invest in people.
- Share accomplishment.
- Find amazing mentors who can guide and challenge.

All my life, I have been fascinated by the unknown. I love the process of learning and discovering new horizons. This applies both to professional activities and to my personal life. An existence without it would be wearisome. I guess it is inherited or learned from my parents, the place I was conceived, the way I was raised, and encounters I have made along the way.

Fifty years ago, my mother taught me how to bake a quiche. I can still today remember her docking the tart crust with a fork before baking (to allow the steam to escape so that the pie crust doesn't puff up in the oven). If her gesture seemed amusing to my kid's eyes, today I find it very important. She repeated something that she probably learned from her mother, and she passed it on to me. That simple gesture would be the foundation of my way of cooking, respect of the traditions with a desire for exploration derived from my longing for cognitive and sensorial curiosity.

Recently, taking a break from writing this book, I visited the Whitney Museum of American Art in Manhattan. On the eighth floor was an exhibition of the artist Jennifer Packer. I must confess that I didn't know the work of this painter prior to my visit, but I immediately connected with the pieces that were presented. I loved the way she put paint into the canvas, and her piece called "The Eye is Not Satisfied with Seeing" especially resonated with me. The title was a reference to Ecclesiastes 1:8, pointing to the idea of an insatiable human desire for knowledge through sensorial experience.

After four seasons of my podcast, *flavors unknown,* and after finishing this book, to "The eye is not satisfied with seeing, nor the ear filled with hearing," I would like to add "nor our taste buds with tasting."

Acknowledgments

I am, above all, extremely grateful to each of the guests on my podcast, *flavors unknown,* and to the culinary individuals I have selected whose stories are the essence of this book:

Drew Adams, Brian Ahern, Kim Alter, Antonio Bachour, Silvia Barban, Jaime Bissonnette, Matt Bolus, Trigg Brown, David Burke, Hari Cameron, Chris Cosentino, Beau du Bois, Kelly English, Elizabeth Falkner, Michael Fojtasek, Sam Freund, Jose Garces, Michael Gulotta, Tim Hollingsworth, Farmer Lee Jones, Jean Marie Josselin, Erin Kanegy-Loux, Dan Kluger, Gabriel Kreuther, Carlo Lamagna, Edward Lee, Drake Leonards, Brother Luck, Sam Mason, Andrew McLeod, Brad Miller, Bonnie Morales, Masako Morishita, Andre Natera, Fermin Núñez, Laura Özyilmaz, Sayat, Özyilmaz, Bob Peters, Erik Ramirez, Chris Shepherd, Bryce Shuman, Johnny Spero, Emily Spurlin, Fiore Tedesco, Angel Teta, Alison Trent, Jeremy Umansky, Shamil Velazquez, Jessie Vida, Charlotte Voisey, Mark Welker, Jonathan Zaragoza.

To the creative and driven chef Elizabeth Falkner, thank you for the wonderfully thoughtful Foreword. You hold a unique place in this industry, and I admire the several transitions you have successfully taken in your career. You are also a role model for the young generation of chefs and pastry chefs. It's a dream come true to have you in these pages.

I am thankful to the people who listened to the episodes of the *flavors unknown* podcast, especially to the those who took the time to DM me on Instagram @flavorsunknown and told me how much they liked an episode or the show. That's one of the things that keeps me motivated when doing my interviews with culinary leaders. Please, do not hesitate to continue to engage on social media.

I am endlessly grateful to my writing coach Debra Englander. Thank you for believing in my ability to become a writer, for giving me the confidence to write my first book, and for guiding me in the process.

Much like Madagascar vanilla and corn would not exist without human intervention, this book would not exist without my agent Janice Shay. Thank you for your valuable advice, editing this book, and getting me a publisher.

To Rachel Shuster, thank you for proofreading this book. Your suggestions make this book a better read.

To David Hancock, thank you for believing in this project and thanks to the whole team at Morgan James Publishing.

I could not have written this book without the initial support from my brother Dominique Laroche. Thank you for believing in it and for giving me hope at times when my mind was not into it. Thank you as well for going through half of the transcripts from the podcast episodes and bouncing ideas about potential structures for the book.

To Paul Delfino, thank you for being a supportive friend throughout all these years, and for the detailed and constructive feedback on the seven chapters. I am profoundly indebted to you for your generous help.

I was lucky enough to have had two Lauras as first readers. Thanks to my daughter Laura Laroche and to my friend Laura Steele who devoted substantial amounts of their personal time. Your feedback helped me tremendously to have better chapter flow and saved me from embarrassing myself.

To my son Alexandre Laroche, thank you for coming up with an improvised brainstorming session in the car one night driving back home from Manhattan to develop ideas for the book ending.

To Rebecca Federman, Managing Research Librarian at the New York Public Library, thank you for helping me with research about the impact of immigration on food, creativity processes, and cooking techniques.

To Shirin Terhune, thank you for your creative input on the book cover.

It is true that it takes a village to publish and promote a book. Thanks to Colleen McKenna and Liza Slavin for guiding me with organic engagement on LinkedIn and thanks to Jonathan El Kordi-Hubbard for helping me with creating communities and promotion on Instagram and Facebook.

I would like to express my special appreciation to Symrise. Thank you for supporting this project and giving me a job that I love for more than 25 years.

A special thank you to Nadia Piatachenko, who first planted the idea of this book in my head, and I am very glad she did.

Download The *flavors unknown* Digital Recipe Book. It is Free!

Many of the chefs quoted in *Conversations Behind the Kitchen Door* have allowed me to share a recipe from their vault! For some, this is a rare opportunity to see behind their kitchen door.

Discover twenty great recipes, specially selected by the chefs themselves.

Download the PDF to bring their expertise into your kitchen and explore their flavors.

QR Code

Or visit https://flavorsunknown.com/recipe-booklet

Scan the QR code above and enter your email to download the *flavors unknown* Digital Recipe Book with recipes from the following chefs

Brad Miller, Chef/Co-Owner of The Inn at the Seventh Ray
in Topanga Canyon, California

Kim Alter, Chef/Owner of Nightbird and Linden Room in San Francisco

Jose Garces, Iron Chef, author, entrepreneur, and food innovator from Philadelphia

Carlo Lamagna, chef from Magna Kusina in Portland, Oregon

Elizabeth Falkner, consulting chef based in Los Angeles

Alex Harrell, Executive Chef at Virgin Hotels in New Orleans

Andre Natera, former executive chef at Fairmont Hotel in Austin, Texas

Rikku O'Donnchü, Executive chef at London House Private Club in Orlando

Declan Horgan, celebrity chef on Heel's Kitchen – season 19

Michael Gulotta, Chef/Owner of MoPho and MayPop in New Orleans

And more…

Get the Full Digital Recipe Book Today!

Share what you make on social media by tagging @flavorsunknown and using #flavorsunknown

I can't wait to see what you cook up!

I've chosen to support

I hope you have enjoyed this book and the fascinating behind-the-scenes stories from American chefs, pastry chefs, and mixologists combined with my personal anecdotes. It's a privilege to live these culinary adventures around the world and be able to experience numerous tastings every year all over the country. I never take these for granted and realize that unforeseen circumstances plunge entire families into disarray, preventing them from enjoying simple meals each morning, afternoon, and evening. As a small token of assistance, and with your help, I'm giving back. With every purchase of this book made through website, flavorsunknown.com, I will donate $1 to World Central Kitchen (WCK) to help bring fresh meals to people in crisis.

Founded in 2010 by Chef José Andrés, WCK is first to the frontlines, providing meals in response to humanitarian, climate, and community crises while working to build resilient food systems with locally led solutions. WCK has served more than 60 million fresh meals to people impacted by natural disasters and other crises around the world. WCK's Resilience Programs strengthen food and nutrition security by training chefs and school cooks; advancing clean cooking practices; and awarding grants to farms, fisheries, and small food businesses while also providing educational and networking opportunities.

To learn more about World Central Kitchen, go to: wck.org.

Thank you for making a difference.

About the Author

Born in Versailles, France, close to the famous chateau of King Louis XIV, Emmanuel Laroche grew up savoring the best food and drink that France offers, eventually earning him the American nickname: "Champagne Charlie." His mother taught him to cook when he was six, starting with a simple yogurt cake, and moving on to Lorraine quiche, from the region his mother grew up. He married a woman who also loved to cook, and during the  first four years of their marriage, they never ate the same dish twice!

In 2002 he moved to the US for his role as VP of Marketing with Symrise North America—a global manufacturer of flavors for the food and beverage industry. He now has more than twenty years of experience in the food and beverage industry, both in Europe and in the U.S.

Through his job, Emmanuel has access to a variety of acclaimed people in the food industry. Since 2008, he has attended the yearly StarChefs Congress in New York City. In 2015, Emmanuel developed an exclusive partnership with StarChefs for Symrise and began moderating panel discussions with successful chefs, pastry chefs, and mixologists. In 2018, Emmanuel launched a personal podcast called *flavors unknown,* featuring a series of conversations with trending and award-winning chefs, pastry chefs, and mixologists from around the US.

Emmanuel currently resides in New Jersey, which acts as a home base for his travels around the country, conducting tastings, lectures, and presentations on food and consumer trends.

273

Social media links:

Instagram

Twitter

Facebook

LinkedIn

Bibliography

List of major sources that I relied on for facts and information or that influenced my thinking process.

Buttermilk Graffiti, Edward Lee, Artisan – 2018

Chef's Story, edited by Dorothy Hamilton and Patric Kuh, HarperCollins, 2007

Comfort Me with Apples, Ruth Reichl, Random House, 2001, 2010

Cooked, Michael Pollan, Penguin Books, 2013

The Creative Habit, Twyla Tharp, Simon & Schuster, 2003

Culinary fictions: Food in South Asian Diasporic Culture, Anita Mannur, Temple University Press, 2010

Eating Asian America: A Food Studies Reader, edited by Robert Ji- Song Ku, Martin F. Manalansan IV, and Anita Mannur, New York University Press, 2013

Eight Flavors, Sarah Lohman, Simon & Schuster, 2016

Ethnic American Food Today: A Cultural Encyclopedia v. 1, edited by Lucy M. Long, Rowman & Littlefield, 2105

Ethnic American Food Today: A Cultural Encyclopedia v. 2 , edited by Lucy M. Long, Rowman & Littlefield, 2105

The Ethnic Restaurateur, Krishnendu Ray, Bloomsbury, 2016

Fast Food Nation, Eric Schlosser, HarperCollins, 2001

Food Americana, David Page, Mango Publishing Group, 2021

Foodies: Democracy and Distinction in the Gourmet Foodscape, Josée Johnston and Shyon Baumann, Routledge, 2010

The Immigrant Kitchen: Food, Ethnicity, and Diaspora, Vivian Nun Halloran, The Ohio State University Press, 2016

The Kitchen Whisperers, Dorothy Kalins, HarperCollins, 2021

Letter to a Young Chef, Daniel Boulud, Hachette Book Group, 2003, 2017

On the Line, Eric Riper, Artisan, 2008

The Secret History of Food, Matt Siegel, Ecco and HarperCollins, 2021

The Soul of a Chef, Michael Ruhlman, Penguin Books, 2001

List of all podcast episodes (with QR codes)

Locations at the time of the episode recording

Episode 1: Mixologist Jesse Vida at Atlas Bar in Singapore (was at BlackTail in New York)

Episode 2: Chef Rebecca Wilcomb in New Orleans

Episode 3: Chef Jonathan Zaragoza from Birrieria Zaragoza in Chicago

\Episode 4: Mixologist Angel Teta from Portland, Oregon

Episode 5: Chef/Co-Owner Fiore Tedesco from L'Oca d'Oro in Austin, Texas

Episode 6: Chef/Owner Ehren Ryan from Common Lot in Millburn, New Jersey

Episode 7: Chef/Owner Michael Fojtasek of Olamaie and Little Ola's Biscuits in Austin, Texas

Episode 8: Chef/Owner Brett Sawyer of Good Company in Cleveland (was at the Plum Café in Cleveland)

Episode 9: Philip Tessier, When the U.S. Team won Bocuse d'Or

Episode 10: Philip Wolf, Cannabis Sommelier in Colorado

Episode 11: Chef Bonnie Morales from Kachka in Portland, Oregon

Episode 12: Pastry Chef and Entrepreneur Sam Mason behind ice cream creations at Odd Fellows

Episode 13: Chef/Co-Owner Drew Adams of Meloria in Sarasota (was at Bourbon Steak in Washington, D.C.)

Episode 14: Executive chef Jean Marie Josselin at JO2 on Kauai, Hawaii

Episode 15: Pastry Chef Emily Spurlin formerly at Bad Hunter in Chicago

Episode 16: Executive Chef Alex Harrell of Virgin Hotels in New Orleans (was at the Elysian Bar in New Orleans)

Episode 17: Chef Sam Freund from White Birch in Flanders, New Jersey

Episode 18: Chef Trigg Brown from Win Son in Brooklyn

Episode 19: Former Executive Chef Andre Natera from Fairmont Hotel in Austin, Texas

Episode 20: Celebrity Chef and Restaurateur David Burke in New York, New Jersey, North Carolina, Colorado, and Riyadh

Episode 21: Chef and Author Edward Lee, chef/owner of 610 Magnolia and Whiskey Dry in Louisville; culinary director of Succotash at National Harbor in Maryland, and Penn Quarter in Washington, D.C.

Episode 22: Chef/Owner Brian Ahern of
Boeufhaus in Chicago

Episode 23: Iron Chef, author, entrepreneur,
and food innovator Jose Garces from
Philadelphia

Episode 24: Chef/Owner Alison Trent of Alison
Trent Events in Los Angeles (was at Ysabel in
Los Angeles)

Episode 25: Chef Johnny Spero from Reverie in
Washington, D.C.

Episode 26: Chef/Owner Kim Alter of Nightbird
and Linden Room in San Francisco

Episode 27: About Show Host Emmanuel
Laroche

Episode 28: Technique or Creativity? Panel
Discussion with chefs Kevin Fink, Fiore
Tedesco, Andre Natera in Austin

Episode 29: 3 Chefs from Austin Question
Everything. Panel Discussion with chefs Kevin
Fink, Fiore Tedesco, Andre Natera in Austin

Episode 30: Sayat and Laura Ozyilmaz
formerly at Noosh in San Francisco

Episode 31: Flavien Desoblin, owner of the
Brady Library in New York City

Episode 32: Chef/Owner Gabriel Kreuther from
two-Michelin star Gabriel Kreuther restaurant
in New York City

Episode 33: Chef Hari Cameron former chef/
owner at a(MUSE.) in Rehoboth, Delaware

Episode 34: Chef/Owner Brother Luck from
Four by Luck at Colorado Springs, Colorado

Episode 35: Home cook and Author Ted Lee

Episode 36: Mixologist Beau du Bois at Puesto
in San Diego

Episode 37: Chef and Author Chris Shepherd,
operating Underbelly Hospitality Group in
Houston

Episode 38: Chef/consultant Mark Welker, former executive pastry chef at Eleven Madison Park and NoMad

Episode 39: Chef and restaurateur Jaime Bissonnette from Toro, Copa, and L ittle Donkey in Boston

Episode 40: Chef/Co-Owner Brad Miller of The Inn at the Seventh Ray in Topanga Canyon, California

Episode 41: Executive chef Drake Leonards at Eunice in Houston

Episode 42: COVID-19

Episode 43: Celebrity Chef Roy Yamaguchi in Hawaii

Episode 44: Farmer Lee Jones from The Chef's Garden in Huron, Ohio

Episode 45: Baker Mathieu Cabon at Magnol French Baking in Houston

Episode 46: Chef, author, and restaurateur Chris Cosentino in San Francisco

Episode 47: COVID-19 Prompt two NJ Chefs to Pivot business with Chef Leia Gaccione and Chef Sam Freund, New Jersey

Episode 48: Former Executive Chef Andre Natera from Fairmont Hotel in Austin, Texas talks about Leadership

Episode 49: Chef/Owner Michael Gulotta of MoPho and MayPop in New Orleans

Episode 50: Charlotte Voisey, global head of ambassadors for William Grant & Sons based in Brooklyn

Episode 51: Chef and restaurateur Tim Hollingsworth at Otium and C.J. Boyd's in Los Angeles

Episode 52: Chef Brian Duffy from Philadelphia

Episode 53: Executive chef Matt Bolus at 404 Kitchen in Nashville

Episode 54: Chef Jeremy Umansky from Larder Delicatessen and Bakery in Ohio City, Ohio

Episode 55: Nick DiGiovanni, a chef on YouTube, TikTok, and Instagram

Episode 56: Chef Lamar Moore from Chicago

Episode 57: Chef Carlo Lamagna from Magna Kusina in Portland, Oregon

Episode 58: Chef Bryce Shuman from former one-Michelin star Betony restaurant in New York City

Episode 59: Chef Andrew McLeod from Avenue M in Asheville

Episode 60: Chef Misti Norris at Petra and the Beast in Dallas

Episode 61: Cider Master Ryan Burk at Angry Orchard

Episode 62: Mixologist Bob Peters
in Charlotte, North Carolina

Episode 63: Consulting Chef Elizabeth Falkner
based in Los Angeles

Episode 64: Executive Chef and co-owner
of the Italian restaurant LaRina in Brooklyn,
New York

Episode 65: In-home personal chef and
culinary instructor chef Chris Spear of Perfect
Little Bites in Frederick

Episode 66: Author and Blogger Mely Martinez
– Mexico in my Kitchen

Episode 67: Chef Richard Landau at Vedge
in Philadelphia

Episode 68: Chef Shamil Velazquez
from Delaney Oyster House in Charleston,
South Carolina

Episode 69: Chef Levon Wallace at
FatBelly Pretzel in Nashville

Episode 70: Food Critic John Mariani

Episode 71: Pastry Chef Philip Speer from Comedor in Austin, Texas

Episode 72: Chef/Owner Dan Kluger from Loring Place in Manhattan and Penny Ridge in Long Island City

Episode 73: "Her name is chef", a documentary film by Peter Ferriero

Episode 74: Chef Kelly English from Restaurant Iris, The Second Line, Pantà in Memphis

Episode 75: Pastry Chef Antonio Bachour from Bachour Miami in Miami

Episode 76: Coffee Roaster Zayde Naquib at Bar Nine and Café Ten in Los Angeles

Episode 77: Pastry Chef, Consultant, Recipe & Product Development Specialist Erin Kanegy-Loux from Brooklyn, New York

Episode 78: Chef Erik Ramirez from Llama Inn and Llama San in New York City

Episode 79: Chef Alan Bergo

Episode 80: Panel Discussion with chefs André Natera from the Fairmont Hotel, Rick Lopez from La Condesa, and Edgar Rico from Nixta Taqueria in Austin

Episode 81: Celebrity Pastry Chef François Payard

Episode 82: Chef Junior Merino at M Cantina in Dearborn, Michigan

Episode 83: Chef Declan Horgan, Irish chef making moves in Washington, D.C.

Episode 84: Baker Kat Gordon at Muddy's Bake Shop in Memphis

Episode 85: Executive Chef Rikku O'Donnchü at London House Private Club in Orlando (was at Amorette in Lancaster, Pennsylvania)

Episode 86: Chef Tiffany Derry at Roots
Southern Table in Dallas

Episode 87: Food Critic Craig Laban from
The Philadelphia Inquirer

Episode 88: Chef Sheldon Simeon at Tin Roof
Maui in Hawaii

Episode 89: Chef Fermin Núñez at Suerte
in Austin, Texas

Episode 90: Chef Masako Morishia at Otabe
and MaxwellPark in Washington, D.C.

Episode 91: Chef Suzanne Goin at a.o.c.
in Los Angeles

Episode 92: Chef Matt Conroy at Lutèce
in Washington, D.C.

A free ebook edition is available with the purchase of this book.

To claim your free ebook edition:

1. Visit MorganJamesBOGO.com
2. Sign your name CLEARLY in the space
3. Complete the form and submit a photo of the entire copyright page
4. You or your friend can download the ebook to your preferred device

Print & Digital Together Forever.

Snap a photo

Free ebook

Read anywhere

CPSIA information can be obtained
at www.ICGtesting.com
Printed in the USA
BVHW070530240722
642211BV00004B/15